Pets and People:
The psychology of pet ownership

Pets and People:
The psychology of pet
ownership

Barrie Gunter

*Department of Journalism Studies,
University of Sheffield*

Consulting Editor in Psychology

Adrian Furnham

*Department of Psychology,
University College London*

Whurr Publishers Ltd
London

© 1999 Whurr Publishers Ltd
First published 1999 by
Whurr Publishers Ltd
19b Compton Terrace, London N1 2UN, England

British Library Cataloguing in Publication Data
A catalogue record for this book is available from the
British Library.

ISBN 1 86156 116 4

Printed and bound in the UK by Athenaeum Press Ltd,
Gateshead, Tyne & Wear

Contents

Chapter 10.

Chapter 11.

Chapter 1
Why do people own pets?

Humankind has enjoyed the company of animals since prehistoric times. Over many centuries, poets, writers and novelists have written about the relationship between people and their animal friends. Once seen only as a source of food or clothing, animals eventually emerged as members of the human social community as fellow hunters, gatherers, guardians, companions and confidants. Many centuries ago, acute observers had already noticed that the way we felt about ourselves and our place in the universe also reflected the way we treated our animals. Our behaviour towards animals parallels the way we behave towards one another. The significance of animals in this context might be that they remind us of our own animal origins. As such they bring us back in touch with nature, when in modern industrialized societies we so often lose touch with our biological roots. For many of us, living with a pet has a therapeutic value and may even contribute towards our understanding of ourselves.[1]

Folklore has highlighted the value of many animals as models of probity to which humans may wish to aspire. An old Talmudic passage states that 'if a man had not been taught the laws of propriety, he might have learned them from the animals; honesty from the ant, which does not steal from the stores of other ants; decency from the cat, which covers its excrement; manners from the cock, which courts the hen by promises and duly apologizes when he is not able to fulfil them; cheerfulness from the grasshopper, which sings although it knows it is fated to die; piety from the stork, which guards the purity of its family and is kind to its fellows; chastity from the dove'.[2]

In many cultures, myths and fairy tales express a basic world-view of their people, often through the behaviour ascribed to animals. Natural forces are made more comprehensible, closer to the human scale, when they are symbolized by animals. Ethical values, especially the struggle between good and evil forces, have often been depicted in terms of animals, as in stories such as *Moby Dick*.[3]

Humans have engaged in prolonged interaction with animals from antiquity.[4] The centuries-old bond between people and pets has satisfied

1

a variety of human needs. Animals first provided our basic resource needs for food, clothing and shelter.[5] Later the human–animal relationship evolved to meet higher-level psychological needs of humans for security and companionship.[6] Where once animals served primarily as food, co-hunters, herders and protectors, broad cultural changes in the way we live have contributed to the rise in importance of the role of the animal as a companion.

Keeping a pet brings more than simple pleasure by fulfilling some of the owner's basic psychological needs, however.[7] When asked, many of us consider our pets to be members of the family. Very often, we sense that our pet is attuned to our feelings.[8] They know when we are happy and when we are sad. They know when we are unwell and will try to offer some comfort. Pets can be so important in the family household that we spend more money on them than we do on our own offspring.[9]

Historically, pet ownership has been a worldwide phenomenon, prevalent throughout many different societies. It was common among the ruling classes of ancient Greece and Rome, as well as among rulers in Europe, China, Japan and Africa. It became more widely distributed across social classes during the 19th century, although it may have been common among poorer people before then. Other evidence indicates that pet keeping popularly occurred in tribal societies in North and South America, and in Australia. This evidence is not always systematic and has tended to comprise anecdotal accounts more than anything else. Nevertheless, consistent stories have emerged that domesticated animals were part of these early cultures.

Cats and Dogs

In order to understand why we have pets, it is helpful to trace what we know about the history of pet keeping. The two species of companion animal which stand out from the rest and feature most prominently throughout the history of pet keeping are dogs and cats.

The association between humans and dogs is an ancient one. There is fossil evidence for an association between *Homo erectus* and a wolf-like animal half a million years ago.[10] Evidence for the domestication of dogs goes back beyond 12 000 years ago.[11] Other writers have described archaeological evidence from among a tribe of hunter-gatherers in Israel 12 000 years ago, including a puppy buried with the remains of a human who was placed with his hand around the dog.[12] Such evidence indicates an affectionate relationship between the human and animal in this case. Such early fossil evidence has led several commentators to argue that the domestication of dogs may have begun with keeping them for pets rather than for other purposes, such as hunting or food.[13]

The domestication of cats and dogs occurred for a combination of reasons. Radical changes in human culture toward rather more settled ways of life in certain areas of the Near East created a social and economic environment appropriate to early experiments in the domestication of animals. Man had probably captured and raised wild animals as pets for a long time before this. But the relationship gradually evolved into a more durable bond of domestic partnership.

The dog is generally thought to be the oldest of domestic animal species.[14] The earliest fossil remains, dating from about 12 000 years ago, came from Iraq and Israel.[15] Later finds have come to light in the United States from about 10 000 years ago,[16] Denmark and the United Kingdom about 9000 years ago,[17] and from China about 7000 years ago.[18]

Evidence suggests that the earliest domestication of the dog took place in the Near East during the pre-agricultural Mesolithic period, following the last Ice Age. There was a shift at this time from semi-nomadic and specialized hunting economies of the Ice Age to the more mixed hunter-gatherer economies and relatively settled communities that arose after the retreat of the global ice caps.[19] The warmer and wetter climate resulted in a rich and diverse flora and fauna, particularly in the river basins and coastal plains. Complex agricultural civilizations arose in the Indus Valley, Sumer and Egypt.

Origins of the domestic cat are less easy to trace. One writer postulated a date of about 9000 years ago for the earliest domestication of the cat.[20] It is thought that there may be a connection between keeping cats and pest control. Therefore, pet cats may have emerged later, around 4000 BC, once large agrarian societies became established. Certainly cats are represented in drawings of the Egyptians dating back to 3000 BC.[21]

The domestication of animals may have occurred for various reasons. The most basic of needs satisfied by dogs, for example, was that of food. Although not widespread today, dogs were once eaten, although probably only in emergencies.[22] Young wild dogs captured for food during times of shortage might have escaped their fate, been tamed and remained as companion animals.[23] Another function served by dogs, given their inherent territoriality and ability to make a noise, was as guards and early warning devices against intruders. A further use for dogs was hunting, usually in packs. Their finely tuned tracking skills and stamina made them ideal for this purpose. This last use probably did not arise until much later.[24]

Pet keeping became and has remained widespread. The significant rise in our living standards, even in the early civilizations, created more leisure time for us to indulge in essentially non-productive activities such as art, religious ritual, and experimentation in the taming and cultivation of wild animals and plants. Such societies probably had long-term surpluses of food, which meant they could enjoy the luxury of keeping animals. The fundamental switch from simple pet keeping within the community to true domestication of animals in individuals' own homes was probably precipitated by relatively sudden and favourable changes in the environment in certain localized geographic regions.

Clearly, pets have served a variety of social functions down the years. The fully domesticated dogs, cats and other pets which we keep today, however, often service much more personal and idiosyncratic needs for their owners. As we will see in the next chapter, pet owners are known to differ from non-owners in terms of certain social, life stage and psychological characteristics. They may exhibit different social attitudes and personalities.

When companion animals live in close association with their owners, interaction with them can have at least three separate functions for their owners. First, there is the role they play in relation to our self-image whereby the selection of a pet is interpreted as making a statement about the owner. Second, there is a social function that concerns the extent to which having a pet acts as a social lubricant, and effects the quantity and quality of interaction with other humans. Third, pets can act as companions, providing a supplement to our interaction with other people or even, in some extreme cases, as an alternative to it.

Pets and Self-image

A person publicly identified with a companion animal makes a symbolic statement of his/her personality and self-image. Whether or not this process is intentional, the presence of a pet and the way it is treated can become factors that influence the image others form about us as well as affecting the way we see ourselves. The kind of pet we select, like the kind of car we drive or the style of clothes we wear, is a way of expressing our personality. Selecting a macho dog may be an attempt to project a macho image, whereas selecting a Persian kitten may be an attempt to project cute and defenseless feminine dependency.

One study of dog owners, based on a small and unrepresentative sample, found that a Great Dane served as a symbol of 'masculinity, power, strength, dominance, and virility', whereas a Chihuahua served as a symbol of femininity.[25] There are other examples of pets which seem to reflect the personalities of their owners. The hypochondriac may extend his concern with health to his pet's health. Hostile dogs may be selected as a means of acting out one's own aggression and hostility.[26]

Status-symbol Pets

Pets can say something about status. Some pets are expensive – to buy and to keep. The demography of pet ownership shows that pets, especially large pets, are associated with large incomes and large homes.[27] Kings and emperors collected elephants and lions as tribute; celebrities today keep ocelots or cheetahs. In 1974, 10 000 Americans owned big cats.[28] Unusual pets make a definite status point, being something that only someone of a certain status could own.[29] Status-conscious people are drawn to own exotic or bizarre pets.[30]

When a pet is viewed as a symbolic extension of the owner, then the pet not only lives with the owner, but does so at the same standard of living. Indulging one's pet becomes a way of indulging oneself.[31] Pets can be humanized to the point where virtually all of the services that are available to people are available to animals – for a price. One good example of this is stories about people with poodles who regularly take their pets to get their hair done at beauty parlours where they enjoy a shampoo, cut, blow-dry and manicure. Furthermore, they do not walk their dogs to the hairdresser but take them by special limousine, the dogs often wearing custom-made sweaters.[32] Other dogs not only go to school, but also to day care, to summer camp, or even to special restaurants.[33] Other examples of such excesses have been labelled 'petishism', which can be seen as a form of fetishism in our society.[34]

One American study found that of 224 pet owners, only 0.4% said they choose a pet for its status function.[35] Although pet owners may not be conscious of a status function, or may be unwilling to admit such motives, it is clear that having a pet, particularly an expensive, exotic, or difficult pet, proclaims the owner as a person of privilege. A companion animal, other than a guard dog, a seeing-eye dog or a hearing-ear dog, is an indulgence. Companion animals today, then, can be regarded as a luxury, part of our leisure lives; resources spent on them represent a discretionary use of our disposable income for those of us who have money to spare after taking care of life's essentials.

Pets as Social Facilitators

Being with pets can affect our social contact with other people. One function of pets is as a social lubricant, increasing the quantity and quality of social interactions. There are several different ways in which this can work.

First of all, pets attract attention. Having a pet can increase our social visibility, especially to other pet owners. Anyone who has been walking their dog in a park or in the open countryside will generally have experienced meeting someone else doing the same and striking up a conversation with them, often about their dogs. Large pets attract attention because of their size, but even small, especially unusual, animals may also be a focus of interest to other people.

There is a further spin-off from owning a pet which has social benefits. People with pets are generally perceived by others to be 'nicer' than average. A love of animals is highly thought of in our society. People have been found to describe scenes featuring animals as less threatening than ones without animals.[36] It seems likely therefore that people with pets are regarded as more approachable.

Making friends and being sociable often involves a considerable amount of small talk. Pets can be a source of such conversation. At the outset, pets may serve as ice-breakers. They can bring to an end those awkward first moments on meeting a stranger and not knowing what to say. Pets may, by their very actions, especially if they do something amusing, provide a source of mutual interest about which some kind of comment can be made. Pets can serve as a source of entertainment, giving us something to look at and be distracted by.

People with special interests in specific kinds of animals are recognized social types who are 'buffs' of one kind or another. For example, 'dogdom' refers to those people, collectively, who are interested in dogs,[37] and that interest provides many social contacts. The showing of dogs and cats accounts for a considerable amount of the social interaction of enthusiasts.

Pets as Social Barriers

If pets usually serve to facilitate social interaction, in some circumstances they can also be used to inhibit it. Some pets are deliberately chosen for their effectiveness in keeping others away. One writer has described a man who owned snakes commenting with satisfaction that relatives no longer came round.[38] Pets can be used as excuses to avoid dealing with other problems. For example, an elderly person may surround herself with dozens of cats or dogs, thereby becoming 'too busy' to attend to other matters. An excessive number of animals, which usually means an unhygienic and unappealing household, may also serve to disassociate the owner from unwanted and intrusive friends or family members.

Pets as Alternative Companions

Companionship is the principal reason that most people give for keeping pets. Although there have been suggestions that people with pets often do not like other people and prefer animals for companions, or are socially isolated and use pets as substitutes for people, pet ownership is not restricted to people who live on their own. The companionship need which animals can meet has certainly been found repeatedly for pet owners who live alone, but also exists for those who live with others, including in family households.[39] Another important variable, however, is childhood experience of pets. Those of us brought up in households with pets are more likely to have a pet ourselves as adults.[40]

The company that a pet can provide is often seen as something which has special value for the elderly and, as we will see in Chapter 8, pets can help to keep older people alive and feeling young. But even among young people, having pets around can stave off loneliness. Having a pet in the house has been found, for instance, to reduce feelings of loneliness among college students living away from home for the first time.[41]

The importance of pets to young people should not really surprise us. As we shall see in Chapter 7, children often enjoy special relationships with pets. The drive to own a pet is in fact closely bound up with experiences with animals early in life. As noted earlier, people who own pets as adults have generally been brought up with pets as children.

When interaction with animals too closely approximates interaction with humans, we say the animals have been 'anthropomorphized', that is, have been granted human attributes. If that interaction takes the place of human interaction, we consider the animals to have become substitutes for humans, and designate them as surrogates.

To some extent, almost all interaction with companion animals involves some anthropomorphism, and can in some way be construed as a surrogate for human relationships. Thus, one of the most significant factors in our relationships with our pets is in the degree to which they are treated as humans, and are used to replace them.

This conception of human-like characteristics within certain animals is of importance also in the context of deciding upon which animals can be deemed suitable to eat. Whilst a growing number of people are vegetarians, most remain meat eaters in modern western societies. Those of us who eat meat have no concerns about the idea of eating animals, though the ease with which this perception is held is probably helped by the fact that few of us have ever visited a slaughterhouse. The raising of animals for food and their subsequent slaughter, however, is acceptable only if the animals are not viewed in significant ways as being like humans. To eat fish, poultry, pigs, sheep or cattle is acceptable. The prospect of eating an animal which we are accustomed to thinking about in the role of a pet will generally be seen as repulsive. Horse meat, which is acceptable in parts of Europe, does not find a market in Britain or America. We view with extreme aversion the prospect of eating dogs, although dog meat is a delicacy in Hong Kong and in other parts of the Far East.[42] For us, dogs and cats have become anthropomorphized to such an extent that to eat either of them would be tantamount to cannibalism.

Human Names

The names people give to their pets may be tied up with the nature of their relationships with their animal companions. There is a view also that the names given to pets serve certain functions for their owners. Owning certain kinds of companion animal may carry a certain social status and serve to create an impression about ourselves which we wish to project to others. An interesting series of studies in the United States explored the reasons people gave for choosing particular names for their pets, asked people to describe the type of person they would normally associate with a certain type of pet, and examined veterinarians' records to get a better idea about the popularity of different pet names.[43] The findings suggested that people own pets for a variety of reasons, with companionship and affection for animals being the main reasons. Pets are also given a variety of names by different people for many different reasons. It was suggested that some names are chosen to reflect the 'human' qualities of the animal. The research also found, however, that the reasons given for the selection of a name did not always seem to correspond closely to the actual name chosen. Nor did pet names show any kind of relationship with identifiable characteristics of the owner or of the pet.

Talking with Animals

Owners have often been observed to talk to their pets in the same way they would talk to very young children. This form of talking to animals has been called 'doggeral', a kind of baby-talk intended to supplement non-verbal communication, such as patting and stroking the animal. Given the fact that animals cannot intelligently talk back, this animal talk in a sense represents little more than talking with oneself and of making observations and comments out loud without expecting a verbal response.[44] Talking to animals with the expectation that they do understand abstract thought, and can in effect talk back, is something else.

Talking with animals may go beyond simply having another creature to play the role of listener when human companionship is rarely available. According to some observers of human–pet behaviour, a pet may be a confidant of its human owner.[45] When a pet is the recipient of serious conversation and confidences, one must conclude that it is being given a human-like role.

In this regard research has reported that as many as one in three pet owners may confide in their pets.[46] In this way, pets can add meaning to their owners' lives. This is particularly true of elderly pet owners, though it is also a characteristic of pet owners of any age. Whilst dogs and cats can certainly fill a social vacuum, research has also shown that pet birds make particularly effective companions in this respect, especially those that talk back to their owners.[47]

Social Ceremonies

When pets are considered to be human-like, there may be celebrations of milestones in their lives. In a study by *Psychology Today* of over 13 000 American pet owners, half reported they kept pictures of pets in their wallet or on display in the home; one-quarter had had a drawing or portrait done of their pet, and one quarter celebrated the pet's birthday.[48] Elsewhere as many as 30% of pet owners reported celebrating their animal's birthday in some way.[49]

Surrogate Friends

Whether or not a dog is man's best friend, he is certainly one of them. Attitudes towards animals can range from aesthetic to utilitarian, but one important dimension is the humanistic one, in which pets are regarded with strong affection by their human owners.[50] The owner may do with the pet many of the activities also done with human friends: talking, eating, grooming, walking, relaxing and sleeping.

The role of friend is especially important for people who, for one reason or another, do not have many human friends. There are no data to indicate whether or not specific kinds of people have preferences for specific roles for animal companions. However, it seems likely that animals as friends would be most likely sought out by people who do not have many social contacts.

It is not only dogs that popularly fill the role of surrogate friend. Pet birds too have been found to satisfy similar social and psychological needs. Elderly people who live alone have been observed to form strong attachments to budgerigars that boost their owners' self-esteem and morale.[51] Bird owners frequently refer to being able to give their birds love and affection.[52] Owners are also likely to mention the friendship and companionship they get from their animal companions and the special value they place on being able to talk to, feed and groom their birds. Birds are fun and can make their owners laugh. They can provide particular enjoyment in the way they copy human speech.[53]

Pets provide social companionship for those individuals who are down on their luck. Observations in the streets and parks of cities such as San Francisco have shown that many homeless people own and maintain pets in spite of their dire circumstances. Homeless pet owners were found to be very attached to their pets and to have come from homes where, as children, they were accustomed to having pets around. Despite the fact that feeding their pets and veterinary care posed severe problems for these individuals who could barely afford to pay for their own survival, the companionship and affection obtained from pets outweighed everything else and made caring for a pet worth while.[54]

Surrogate Mates

Sometimes the role of pets goes beyond the simple role of friend to approximate more intimate and significant relationships. Pets can become as important as a husband or wife, and in some instances act as surrogate mates.[55] When pets are a source of conflict with a human partner, the preference for the animal companion over the marital one may become clear. A number of examples can be found in which someone, given a choice between dog or spouse, chose the dog. A pet acquired after the death of a spouse may be vested with much of the emotional attachment that was formerly invested in the late husband or

wife. Pets as surrogate mates may be of special value to the elderly,
where a spouse has died and no alternative human companion is likely
to be forthcoming.[56]
   The literature on pets tends to avoid mentioning the possibility of pet
animals as a focus of erotic attraction. In one exception, an animal
behaviour expert noted that although it undoubtedly takes place, scientific documentation is scanty.[57] The prospect of human–animal contacts
is real enough for it to be incorporated into religious and legal codes,
usually with severe penalties. When bestiality does occur, it apparently
involves atypical instances in the lives of a very few people. In their well-
known report on human sexual habits in the United States, Kinsey and
his colleagues estimated that in the USA some kind of erotic animal
contact had been experienced at some time by 8% of adult males and 3%
of adult women.[58]

Surrogate Children

One of the most prominent stereotypes about childless couples is that
they use pets as surrogates for the children they cannot have or do not
want. There are certainly cases of childless couples who invest in a pet
all the emotional value and maternal behaviour which might otherwise
go to a child. In general, though, there is limited evidence on this
subject.[59]
   Childless couples are not more likely than other couples to keep
pets. The reality is that most couples have both children and pets. The
probability of having a pet is greater, not less, if one has a child as well.[60]
   Although one exploratory study found that about two-thirds of childless couples had pets, of these, about half had fairly casual attitudes
towards their companion animals. The remaining half did tend, in
varying degrees, to place their pets in a child-like role.[61] Some actually
referred to a dog or cat as their 'baby', and were quite open about their
affection for the animal which was treated as a child. If pets are
sometimes substitutes for children who are wanted, they can also be part
of the process of deciding to remain childless. In some instances, experience with trying to raise a dog or other pet has increased awareness of the
tribulations of parenthood, and reinforced a disinclination towards it.[62]
   If pets act as children for the childless, they may also act as another
child for parents who already have children. One function of pets may be
to prolong the parenthood role for middle-aged or elderly parents.
According to one writer: 'The family pet *always* needs attention, and the
pleasure it brings its keepers derives partly from the sustained dominance
and importance of those who take care of it. The need to be needed is
powerful, and parents whose children have grown up are gratified by this
sustained dependence of their family pet over the years.' (p.288) [63]
   The interchangeability of pets and children may also operate in
reverse, in that sometimes children are treated as pets. In some families,

it has been observed that one child may be selected to fill the social role of pet. This child, the antithesis of a scapegoat, may be given special privileges, and seen as doing no wrong. He or she is fussed over, is used as a focus of attention, and is expected to perform an entertainment function by being ingratiating and eager to please.[64]

Surrogate Parents

Children in the family household may come to regard a pet as a surrogate parent. A large cuddly dog, with infinite tolerance for the tugging demands of a toddler, may extend to the child more patience and more contact comfort than the mother. Indeed, the parent who seeks out a pet for the child may recognize that though she is taking on the trouble of another 'child', the child is also getting the benefit of another 'parent'.

Is Pet Ownership Problematic?

One school of thought about pet ownership has suggested that people who own pets are in some way psychologically or socially inadequate. It may be a stereotype applied, for example, to women who live on their own with no children, or to childless couples. Even some comments made by psychiatrists about patients strongly attached to their pets reflect this notion.[65]

One prominent writer in the field, James Serpell, has argued strongly against the view that pet love betrays signs of emotional immaturity and weakness.[66] He suggested that this attitude to pet keeping has arisen as a consequence of the general way animals have been viewed in the Judeo-Christian tradition of Western Europe. This view holds that animals were created specifically to serve the interests of humans who have dominion over them. He also made the observation that pet ownership is too widespread a phenomenon throughout history and the world to be viewed as an abnormal response.

Why, then, do so many of us share our lives with animal companions? There is a growing opinion that the company of animals is an important aspect of human social structure.[67] Pets can help meet various psychological needs. Pets can provide emotional support. They are of special importance in this regard to the young and the elderly, and to those who feel socially or emotionally isolated. Pets can offer unconditional love and support. With children, pets represent friends who can be trusted and who, unlike parents or other adults, do not judge the child. For parents, a pet can provide a playmate and protector for their children.[68] The more important the companion animal is to a household, the more likely it is to supplement human needs for love, affection, friendship and companionship. Pets can be valued companions to people who have lost someone close to them, to those who are socially isolated and to those who have a healthy and complete family and social network.

Pet owners themselves are quick to recognize the many positive benefits of living with animal companions. Pets are especially likely to bring pleasure into the lives of their owners through their attentiveness, loyalty and affection. Pets welcome their owners when they return home, often with a great deal more enthusiasm than human companions.[69] In many ways, there are similarities between the relationships people have with their pets and the features we tend to most value in positive relationships we have with other people.[70] Pets are dependent on us in many ways, but also provide sources of fun, play and relaxation. Apart from being fed and, in some cases, needing exercise, pets make few demands on us.[71]

In the case of elderly people whose own children have grown up and flown the nest, pets give them something to care for. This adds meaning and purpose to an elderly person's life and may provide an incentive for them to look after themselves more too. After all, having a dependent animal means having 'someone' to be responsible for. This fact can have a number of spin-off benefits for old people including a longer life.

Some pets require exercise. For pet owners who opt to live with a dog, the need to keep the dog healthy also means keeping healthy themselves. Taking the dog out for a walk represents the sort of gentle exercise that can be of benefit to older people in particular. Throwing sticks for the dog to catch or playing ball with our canine friends can introduce even more vigorous forms of exercise into our lives. Chapter 5 looks in more detail at the importance pets can have for our physical well-being. In addition to the physical benefits, there are important psychological benefits which derive from walking the dog. Social contacts can be made with other dogs owners who are also exercising their dogs. Our pets give us a topic of common interest to talk about with other pet owners.

It has been claimed by some writers that pets are little more than parasites. In a strict Darwinian sense, there is nothing about pet keeping that adds to the fitness of the human species to survive.[72] Despite the fact that keeping pets can incur costs – the cost of purchase, feeding and veterinary care come top of the list – there is ample evidence that we are repaid in so many ways by loyal, entertaining and affectionate animal companions. Given that not everyone chooses to share their home or life with a pet, are those of us who do keep pets different in significant respects, psychologically or in terms of our personal or social circumstances, from those who do not? This is the question to which we turn in the next chapter.

References

1 Levinson, B. M. The value of pet ownership. *Proceedings of the 12th Annual Convention of the Pet Food Institute*, 1969, pp.12–18. Levinson, B. M. *Pets and Human Development*. Springfield, IL: Charles C. Thomas, 1972.

2 Cohen, S. Animals. *The Universal Jewish Encyclopedia*, Vol.1. New York: Universal Jewish Encyclopedia Co., pp. 321–328, 1939.

3 Melville, H. *Moby Dick*. New York: Hendricks House, 1952.

4 Reed, C.A. Animal domestication in the prehistoric Near East. *Science*, 130, 1629–1639, 1959.

5 Levinson, B., 1969, op.cit.

6 Mugford, R. A. The social significance of pet ownership. In S.A. Corson (Ed.), *Ethology and Non-verbal Communication in Mental Health*. Elmsford, New York: Pergamon, 1979.

7 Mann, P.G. Introduction. In R.S. Anderson (Ed.) *Pet Animals and Society*. London: Bailliere Tindall, pp. 1–7, 1975.

8 Cain, A. O. A study of pets in the family system. *Human Behaviour*, 8(2), 24, 1979.

9 Connolly, J. The great American pet: Costs and choices. *Money*, 10(10), 40–42, 1981.

10 Messent, P.R. and Serpell, J.A. An historical and biological view of the pet-owner bond. In B. Fogle (Ed.) *Interrelations between People and Pets*. Springfield, IL: Charles C. Thomas, pp. 5–22, 1981.

11 Clutton-Brock, J. Man-made dogs. *Science*, 1340–1342, 1977. Musil, R. Domestication of the dog already in the Magdelanian. *Anthropologie*, 8, 87–88, 1970.

12 Davis, S.T. and Valla, F.R. Evidence for the domestication of the dog 12 000 years ago in the Natufian of Israel. *Nature*, 276, 608–610, 1978.

13 Clutton-Brock, J., 1977, op.cit. Messent, P.R. and Serpell, J.A., 1981, op.cit.

14 Zeuner, F.E. *A History of Domesticated Animals*. New York: Harper & Row, 1963. Scott, J.P. Evolution and domestication of the dog. *Evolution and Biology*, 2, 243–275, 1968.

15 Turnbull, P.F. and Reed, C.A. The fauna from the terminal pleistocene of the Pelegewra Cave. *Fieldana Anthropology*, 63, 99, 1974. Davis, S.T. and Valla, F.R., 1978, op.cit.

16 Lawrence, B. Early domestic dogs. *Z Saugetierled*, 32, 44–59, 1967.

17 Degerbol, M. On a find of a preboreal dog (*Canis familiaris L*) from Star Cave, Yorkshire, with remarks on other mesolithic dogs. *Prehistoric Society for 1961 New Series*, 27, 35–55, 1961. Musil, R., 1970, op.cit.

18 Olsen, S.J. and Olsen, J.W. The Chinese wolf, ancestor of new world dogs. *Science*, 197, 533–535, 1977.

19 Harris, D.R. Agricultural systems, ecosystems and the origins of agriculture. In P.J. Ucko and G.W. Dimbleby (Eds) *The Domestication and Exploitation of Plants and Animals*. London: Duckworth, 1969.

20 Zeuner, F.E., 1963, op.cit.

21 Smith, H.S. Animal domestication and animal cult in dynastic Egypt. In P.J. Ucko and G. W. Dimbleby (Eds) *The Domestication and Exploitation of Plants and Animals*. London: Duckworth, 1969.

22 Zeuner, F.E., 1963, op.cit.

23 Fuller, J.L. and Fox, M.W. The behaviour of dogs. In E.S.E. Hafez (Ed.) *The Behaviour of Domestic Animals*, 3rd edn. London: Bailliere Tindall, 1969.

24 Sauer, C.O. *Agricultural Origins and Dispersals*. Cambridge, MA: MIT Press.

25 Hartley, E.L. and Shames, C. Man and dog: A psychological analysis. *Gaines Veterinary Symposium*, 9, 4–7, 1959.

26 Rosenbaum, J. I've got the meanest dog on the block. In *Is Your Volksvagen a Sex Symbol*. New York: Bantam, pp. 27–49, 1972.

27 Gee, E.M. and Veevers, J.E. Everyman and his dog: The demography of pet owner-

ship. Department of Sociology, University of Wisconsin, mimeo, 1984.
28 *Time*. The great American farm animal. *Time Magazine*, December 23, 42–46, 1974.
29 Muller, P. Preposterous pets have always been our status symbols. *Smithsonian*, 83–90, 1980.
30 *Newsweek*. The pet set: Chic unleashed. *Newsweek*, September 9, 74–78, 1974.
31 Veevers, J.E. The social meanings of pets: alternative roles for companion animals. In B. Sussman (Ed) *Pets and the Family*. New York: Haworth Press, pp.11–30, 1985.
32 *Time*, 1974, op.cit. p.44.
33 *Newsweek*, 1974, op.cit.
34 Szasz, K. *Petishism: Pets and Their People in the Western World*. New York: Holt, Rinehart & Winston.
35 Harris, M.B. Some factors influencing the selection and naming of pets. *Psychological Reports*, 53, 1163–1170, 1983.
36 Messent, P.R. Review of the international conference on human–animal companion band held in Philadelphia, PA on October 5th–7th, 1981. *Royal Society Health Journal*, 102, 105–107, 1981.
37 Stein, J. and Urdang, L. *The Random House Dictionary of the English Language*. New York: Random House.
38 Rosenbaum, J., 1972, op.cit.
39 Endenbury, N., 't Hart, H. and Bouw J. Motives for acquiring companion animals. *Journal of Economic Psychology*, 15, 191–206, 1994.
40 Endenbury, N. et al. 1994, op.cit.
41 Moros, K. Loneliness and attitudes toward pets. *Japanese Journal of Experimental Social Psychology*, 24(1), 93–103,1984.
42 *Time*, 1974, op.cit.
43 Harris, M.B., 1983, op.cit.
44 Hirsch-Pasek, K. and Treiman, R. Doggerel: Motherese in a new context. *Journal of Child Language*, 9, 229–237, 1982.
45 Slovenko, R. Commentaries of psychiatry and law shielding communications with a pet. *Journal of Psychiatry and Law*, 10, 405–413, 1982.
46 Beck, A.M. and Katcher, A.H. A new look at pet-facilitated therapy. *Journal of the American Veterinary Medical Association*, 184(4), 414–421, 1984.
47 Loughlin, C.A. and Dowrick, P.W. Psychological needs filled by avian companions. *Anthrozoos*, 6(3), 166–172, 1993.
48 Horn, J.G. and Meer, J. The pleasure of their company. *Psychology Today*, August, 52–57, 1984.
49 Beck, A.M. and Katcher, A.H., 1983, op.cit.
50 Kellert, S.R. Attitudes towards animals: Age-related development among children. Unpublished paper.
51 Mugford, R.A. and M'Comisky, J. Some recent work on the psychotherapeutic value of cage birds with old people. In R.S. Anderson (Ed.) *Pet Animals and Society*. London: Baillière Tindall, 1974.
52 Beck, A.M. and Katcher, A.H. Bird–human interaction. *Journal of the Association of Avian Veterinarians*, 3, 152–153, 1989. Hagebock, J.M. and Beran, G.W. Animals serving the handicapped. *Iowa State University Veterinarian*, 48, 20–27, 1986.
53 Loughlin, C.A. and Dowrick, P.W., 1994, op.cit.
54 Kidd, A.H. and Kidd, R.M. Benefits and liabilities of pets for the homeless. *Psychological Reports*, 74, 715–722, 1994.

55 Beck, A.M. and Katcher, A.H. 1984, op.cit.

56 Gee, E.M. and Veevers, J.E. The pet prescription: Assessing the therapeutic value of pets for the elderly. Department of Sociology, University of Victoria, mimeo, 1984b.

57 Schowalter, J.E. The use and abuse of pets. *Journal of the American Academy of Child Psychiatry*, 22, 68–72, 1983.

58 Kinsey, C.A., Pomeroy, W.B. and Martin, C.E. *Sexual Behaviour in the Human Female*. New York: Cardinal Pocket Books

59 Rosenbaum, J., 1972, op.cit.

60 Gee, E.M. and Veevers, J.E. 1984, op.cit.

61 Veevers, J.E. *Childless by Choice*. Toronto: Butterworths, 1980.

62 Veevers, J.E. 1980, ibid.

63 Koller, M.R. *Families: A Multigenerational Approach*. New York: McGraw-Hill, 1974.

64 Rollins, N., Lord, J.P., Walsh, E., and Weil, G.R. Some roles children play in their families: Scapegoat, baby, pet and peacemaker. *Journal of the American Academy of Child Psychiatry*, 12, 511–530, 1973.

65 Keddie, K.M. G. Pathological mourning for the death of a domestic pet. *British Journal of Psychiatry*, 131, 21–25, 1977. Rynearson, E.K. Humans and pets and attachment. *British Journal of Psychiatry*, 133, 550–555, 1978.

66 Serpell, J.A. *In the Company of Animals*. New York: Blackwells, 1986. Serpell, J.A. Pet keeping in non-western societies. *Anthrozoos*, 1, 166–174, 1987.

67 Horn, J.C. and Meer, J., 1984, op.cit. Katcher, A.H., Friedman, E., Beck, A. and Lynch, J. Looking, talking and blood pressure. The physiological consequences of interaction with the living environment. In A. Katcher and A. Beck (Eds) *New Perspectives on Our Lives with Companion Animals*. Philadelphia: University of Pennsylvania Press, pp. 351–362, 1983. Odendaal, J.S. and Weyers, A. Human–companion animal relationships in the veterinary consulting room. *South African Veterinary Journal*, 61, 14–23, 1990.

68 Salmon, P.W. and Salmon, I.M. Who owns who? Psychological research into the human–pet bond in Australia. In A. Katcher and A. Beck (Eds) *New Perspectives on Our Lives with Companion Animals*. Philadelphia: University of Pennsylvania Press, pp. 244–265, 1983.

69 Serpell, J.A. The personality of the dog and its influence on the pet–owner bond. In A. Katcher and A. Beck (Eds) *New Perspectives on Our Lives with Companion Animals*. Philadelphia: University of Pennsylvania Press, pp. 112–131, 1983.

70 Salmon, P.W. and Salmon, I.M., 1983, op.cit.

71 Berryman, J.C., Howells, K and Lloyd-Evans, M. Pet owner attitudes to pets and people: A psychological study. *Veterinary Record*, 117, 659–661, 1985.

72 Archer, J. Why do people love their pets? *Evolution and Human Behaviour*, 18, 237–259, 1996.

Chapter 2
Are pet owners different?

People have enjoyed a special relationship with animals from the earliest days of civilization. From hunting animals for food and clothing, we learned to cultivate them in captivity, which was much easier and less stressful. Some animals, however, were not seen as the next meal or a new fur coat, but rather as companions whose mere presence we found entertaining or comforting. Such animals were characterized by being domesticated, friendly towards humans, and might even show us greater loyalty and affection than other members of our own species.

Living with or in close proximity to animals has been a worldwide phenomenon. However, the nature of human–animal relationships has varied from one country to another. Cross-cultural differences in attitudes towards animals can still be seen today. Whilst a dog may be regarded as man's best friend in some cultures, there are certain parts of the world where dog eating has a long history. In China, for example, dog meat is believed to have medicinal properties that are considered to be especially potent in the heat of the summer. One belief is that because dogs are never seen to sweat, eating dog meat will protect against heat-induced suffering, and because dogs pant vigorously their meat is thought to be beneficial for respiratory diseases.

Dog eating is common in Korea, where cat eating also occurs. Although the Korean government has bowed to international pressure and officially prohibited the serving of dog meat, it remains a popular dish. Indeed, by usual Korean standards, dog meat is expensive when bought in restaurants. It can be obtained more cheaply from local markets. Although many households in Korea keep dogs as pets, these animals represent the lucky few selected from litters on the basis of their perceived energy, loyalty, strength and alertness. The unfortunate puppies that fail to capture their owners' favour tend to be sold to dog merchants and breeders who raise them to be sold as meat. Dog eating is not confined to the Far East. Some Native American cultures have dog-eating rituals and dog meats were even reported to be popular in parts of Europe at one time. However, in most modern industrialized societies today dogs have a favoured social status and eating dog meat is regarded as socially unacceptable.

Despite the long history of human associations with animal companions, there remains a view that pet ownership is not a natural or normal phenomenon entered into by anyone. Instead, it is contended that people who own pets are somehow different from those who do not. The distinctions that are made in this context have tended, more often than not, to be unflattering towards pet owners, who are regarded as suffering from gaps in their lives or inadequacies in their social abilities which they have chosen to fill by entering into emotional relationships with species other than their own.

It is true to say that some people seem to make a special point of having a pet, and do not like being without one. Others may try a pet out for size once and discover that it is too much trouble or does not give back as much as it costs. There is even evidence that animals can distinguish animal lovers from people who are indifferent to or dislike them. Research conducted with cats reportedly found that when feline pets are placed in a room with a person they do not know, who had earlier identified themselves as either liking or disliking cats, the animals were more likely to approach the cat lovers. This effect occurred even though both lovers and haters of cats were instructed to sit still and make no attempt to attract the cat's attention when it walked in the room. The researchers suggested that cats may be sensitive to subtle body movements of people and may distinguish people who like cats by smell.[1]

We have already seen in Chapter 1 that pets can fulfil a number of roles and satisfy various human needs. Are there any indications, however, that people who own pets differ from those who do not? Is there something special about the character of pet owners? Are pet owners distinguishable from non-owners in terms of their psychological make-up? Is there a pet-owning 'type'?

Psychologists have pondered on such questions for many years. Pets, as we shall see, are renowned for having certain beneficial effects for those who live with them. Pets can relieve stress, offer a respite from worldly troubles, and provide a loyal companion who will listen endlessly without passing judgement. But are certain types of people more likely to live with animal companions than others?

A number of distinctions can be made among people in the context of their relationships with animals. We can begin by examining the nature and extent of pet ownership to find out if living with companion animals is particularly prevalent among specified populations or population subgroups. Is pet keeping especially prominent among particular cultures or demographic groups? Should we expect different patterns of ownership among specific groups on the basis of what is known more generally about different groups' attitudes towards animals? Is pet ownership associated with particular lifestyles? Finally, are there distinctive psychological profiles which are significantly linked to pet ownership?

The Spread of Pet Ownership

Pet ownership is widespread. Figures from around the world testify to the global popularity and significance of sharing one's home and life with animal companions. By 1995, pet owners in Britain were keeping 7.2 million cats and 6.6 million dogs.[2] In the United States, the American Pet Products Manufacturing Association 'Pet Owners Survey' in 1994 reported that the number of pets in American households was rising.[3] The average pet owner was married, lived in a house, was under the age of 50 and did not have children living at home. The average number of pets per household was close to two. In all, 53 million American households (56%) were estimated to have pets. There were 54 million dogs and 59.4 million cats kept as pets. Around 29% of American households had cats compared with 36% that had dogs. In addition, there were 7.3 million reptiles in 3% of households. Of these households, 44% had turtles, 44% had newts, 33% had lizards, 24% had snakes, 8% had tortoises, 5% had frogs, and 4% had salamanders. In addition, 6% of American households housed 16 million birds, of which parakeets and cockateels were the most popular. There were also an estimated 12 million fish tanks in the USA in 1994. For dog, cat and bird owners, companionship and love were some of the most important benefits of owning a pet. For dog owners, security was also a significant benefit. The popularity of particular species can wax and wane over time. Between the early 1980s and early 1990s in the United States, for example, dog ownership fell, as did horse ownership (by 40%), whereas cats and birds became somewhat more widely owned.[4]

A survey at around the same time in Australia revealed that 60% of households had a pet. The survey found that 40% of households had dogs and 27% had cats. In all, there were 3.8 million pet dogs and 2.5 million pet cats in Australia. More than half of households (53%) had either a dog or a cat. Of those households that owned a pet, 68% had dogs, 45% had cats, and 25% had birds.[5] The research found that more families than single individuals owned dogs. However, cats were just as likely to be owned by a single individual as by a family.

A report in *Economie et Statistiques* reviewing pet ownership trends in France between 1968 and 1988, discovered that pet ownership increased – especially dog ownership – despite increases in pet care costs.[6] Over 20 years the number of dogs rose 66% from 4.2 million in 1968 to over 7 million in 1988. The number of cats also rose, but only by 15%, from 4.1 million to 4.7 million. In 1998, 33% of households in France owned a dog and 22% owned a cat.

Pets and Personal Circumstances

Pet ownership has been investigated in relation to family circumstances. Families are increasingly being regarded as ever-changing and adapting organizations rather than as fixed units. Within the family group, its different members occupy different roles. Pets may, in turn, be part of this group and may enjoy equal status with other family members. Understanding about the part that pets play in the family, however, requires a closer examination of the different stages through which family systems evolve. It could be that pet ownership is linked with life stage or personal circumstances which increase or diminish the feasibility or range of reasons for owning a pet.

A number of different frameworks for categorizing the stages of a family life cycle have been devised over the years. One scheme outlined several distinct stages: (1) establishment stage (newlyweds); (2) family with infants; (3) family with pre-school children; (4) family with school-age children; (5) family with teenage children; (6) family with young adults (launching); and (7) post-parental family (empty-nester).[7] Family life-cycle stage offers a useful framework for delineating reference points in the social development of different social roles and status in a person's life. In addition, the stages of the family life cycle are valid indicators of family structure, a concept that is essential to an understanding of the roles and functions of pets in families.

One examination of the social and emotional roles played by pets in an urban setting involved a telephone survey with 320 pet owners and 116 non-pet owners in Rhode Island in the USA.[8] They found that pet owners regarded their pets as important family members, especially those living in the city. Pet owners stressed the positive roles played by pets rather than any negative consequences. However, the nature of pet–owner relationships varied with the social and family circumstances of owners.

Marital status, number of children present in the home, stage in family life cycle, age and income were all related to pet ownership among city dwellers. Marital status seems to be a particularly important personal factor in connection with pet ownership. Its real significance, however, is to be found more in the context of attachment to pets than mere ownership of them. Pet attachment tends to be highest among single, divorced, widowed and remarried people, as well as among childless couples, newlyweds and empty-nesters.[9] Single, divorced and widowed people, as well as people in second or subsequent marriages, have been found to score higher on pet attachment than cohabiting couples and people in first marriages. The fact that people who are without a current spouse or romantic partner reportedly feel closer to their pets may indicate that pets can be an important source of emotional fulfilment. However, the observation that people in second or subsequent marriages are more attached to their pets than those in their first marriage is also interesting.

In the Rhode Island study, pet owners did not have more children than non-pet owners but did have more children still living with them at home.[10] Pet ownership was high among families with school-age children and teenagers. It was low among empty-nesters and families with infants. Families with very young children were less likely to have pets.

Stage in the individual's family life cycle was another important factor related to people's attitudes towards their pets. Pet attachment was high during the newlywed and the empty-nest stages of the life cycle, as well as among single and widowed people. It was particularly low among families with infants. Throughout the pre-school, school-age, teenage and launching stages of the family life cycle, people demonstrated a low degree of attachment to their pets.

Pet ownership has been found to be highest in households where the oldest member was between 30 and 49 years of age, again reflecting the greater likelihood of families in the middle years to be pet owners.[11] Pet owners also differ from non-pet owners in terms of income. Pet owners reportedly have higher incomes than people who do not have pets. Given the costs of owning a pet this finding is not surprising.

Although residential status does not appear to significantly affect the likelihood of owning a pet in the city, it may have more bearing on the type of pet owned. The Rhode Island study referred to earlier found that people who had dogs were significantly more likely to own their own homes than to rent, and to live in single-family homes than in apartments. Cat, bird and fish ownership, however, did not vary by residential location. Stage in family life cycle also affected pet ownership in the city and was related to the time when pets were acquired. Families were most likely to acquire pets during the newlywed phase, when they had children in elementary school, or when they had teenage children. By contrast, empty-nesters and widowed people were the least likely to acquire pets.

A nationwide survey by the American Veterinary Medical Association in 1992 reported that households headed by middle-aged (78.7%) or older parents (71.7%) were most likely to own pets. These were followed closely by young couples (70.4%), and young parents (67.4%). Single-person households (young – 48.7%; middle-aged – 43%; older singles – 29.2%) and older working (55.4%) and retired (41.1%) couples were much less likely to have pets of any kind.[12]

Research in The Netherlands found a number of differences between pet owners and non-owners, and also between owners of different types of pets in terms of type of household, location and family circumstances. Typically, owners and non-owners occupied different types of dwellings. Pet owners were more likely than non-owners to live in semi-detached or detached houses, whether in rural or urban locations. Pet owners were also more likely to be married and to have children still living in the family home.[13]

Personal Economic Circumstances

Family life stage may in part be related to pet ownership because it is also associated with varying degrees of affluence and financial stability. Pet owners around the world are spending more on feeding their pets and caring for their health, as pet food prices and veterinarian bills have increased. A study of French pet owners, for example, found that the cost of pet ownership increased by over 1300% between 1970 and 1988. Pet expenses represented approximately 1.1% of the family budget, which was similar to travel expenses.[14]

A link has been observed on repeated occasions between household affluence and pet ownership. Although socioeconomic class has been found to be a fairly weak discriminator of cat and dog ownership across Britain, ownership of birds, which are generally less costly to keep, is more commonplace in lower-income groups.[15] A survey conducted 10 years earlier in Britain, however, found a far greater proportion of high or middle-income households (73%) than of low-income households (44%) contained any pets.[16] Further evidence of a link between pet ownership and personal economic circumstances emerged from a survey conducted in The Netherlands which reported that pet ownership was more widespread among people in employment than among the unemployed.[17] A similar American survey, however, found no relationship between income and pet ownership.[18] Other American research which investigated pet ownership among adolescents, however, found that pets were more likely to be found among those families who were better off economically. There was a direct relationship between parents' income and the opportunity for adolescents to obtain the benefits of animal ownership.[19]

One measure of attachment to pets is how much money owners would be prepared to spend on medical care for their pets. One report on urban pet owners in the USA found that a great deal of money would be spent to keep their pets healthy and well.[20] Around one in six pet owners interviewed (17%) set an upper limit of $100, whilst almost half (48%) stated that they would be willing to spend any amount necessary if there was a chance it might help. One in 20 (5%) were willing to spend more than $500.

Despite the differences observed in regard to the attachment to pets as a function of marital status, number or presence of children in the household, or stage in the family life cycle, none of these factors differentiated between people in the amounts they said they would be prepared to spend on their pet's medical bills. Personal income was also unrelated to how much pet owners said they would be prepared to spend. There were some differences in what people would spend as a function of the type of pet, however. Of the dog owners, more than half (56%) were willing to spend any amount, whereas fewer than four in 10 cat owners (38%) would be prepared to do likewise. Whilst just over four in 10 (42%) people owning other pets stated that they would spend $50 or less for veterinary care (compared with 2.5% of dog owners and 4.7% of cat owners), surprisingly, a similar percentage (38%) said they would spend any amount. The overwhelming majority of pet owners in this American survey (80%), regardless of the type of pet they owned, said that their pet was very important to them.

Attitudes towards Animals

Pet ownership might be expected to reflect certain more general attitudes towards animals. People who do not like animals are also unlikely to own pets. An examination of attitudes towards animals might also reveal particular sub-groups within the population who are most likely to be favourably disposed towards pets.

Attitude surveys have consistently found that compared with men, women are less tolerant of abuses of animals and have less utilitarian views concerning other species. In one report, for example, female undergraduates showed more concern for pain and suffering of laboratory animals than did male students.[21] Another study found that more females than males claimed that they would refuse to shock an animal as part of a hypothetical experiment.[22]

Sex differences have been found on almost all dimensions of attitudes and knowledge about animals and it was concluded that sex differences were so large as to suggest that men and women have different emotional and cognitive orientations toward animals.[23] In this case, it was reported that women's attitudes toward animals were characterized by humanistic and moralistic orientations, whereas men's were more utilitarian and 'dominionistic'.

Gender differences in knowledge of and attitudes toward animals appear to develop during or before adolescence, depending on the dimension investigated. Sex differences in knowledge of animals, fear of animals and species preferences have been reported to emerge by the elementary school years.[24] It has also been reported that boys, but not girls, develop more detailed knowledge of animal young and animal care giving between pre-school and second grade.[25]

Males and females also behave differently toward animals. Kindergarten boys and girls have been found to exhibit different behaviours toward some species.[26] Male and female horse owners treat their animals differently.[27] Female children assume more responsibility for pets than do their male counterparts.[28] Not surprisingly, gender differences are also reflected in the relative involvement of men and women in the animal rights movement.

In addition to the study of differences between the way each sex behaves towards animals, research has examined the relationship among gender, sex-role orientation and attitudes towards the treatment of animals and views about animal welfare.[29] There were significant gender-related differences on nearly all of the animal-related measures. Men showed less concern for animal issues than did women. Generally, though, women were as likely as men to report that they were comfortable touching 'nice' animals such as kittens and butterflies, but were less comfortable than men with animals which had less savoury reputations such as spiders, snakes and toads. The only animals to which women felt closer than did men were horses and dogs. A feminine sex-role orientation (regardless of actual gender of respondent) was also linked to animal attitudes. Those individuals who had a more 'feminine' outlook on life exhibited greater concern for the well-being of other animal species but were less comfortable with the idea of touching some of them. Sociocultural theorists would explain these results in terms of the greater likelihood that women are socialized from birth to be more nurturant and caring, whereas men are conditioned to be less emotional. Women have been found to be more 'person-oriented' and better in their relationships with other people than are men. They also favour cute, cuddly animals more so than do men.[30]

A positive attitude towards animals in general might be expected to be an important or even essential antecedent of pet ownership. One of the most obvious characteristics of pet owners which you might expect to distinguish them from people who eschew pet ownership is love of animals. Surely pet owners must have a special affection for animals, regardless of what type of pet they own? This must be a fundamental requirement. Research into this question has in fact confirmed that people who live with pets do have a greater love of animals than people who do not own a pet.[31] People who do not currently have a pet, but who have owned one in the past, tend to show greater love of animals than people who have never owned a pet, though their feelings towards animals are less warm than those of people who currently live with a pet.

It is not necessarily the case, however, that pet owners differ from non-owners in their attitudes towards animals. It is not only the pet owners among us who like animals. Many people who do not own an animal and have never done so may still say they like them – and mean it. Pet owners, for some reason, are more willing to commit themselves to living with and caring for an animal. In other respects, though, people who own pets do hold different views of the world from non-owners.

People who do not own pets, for instance, have been found to be more independent and self-sufficient individuals, and they do not like taking on lasting obligations. These characteristics may go some way towards explaining why they do not own a pet. To begin with, they do not feel a strong need for the companionship to the extent that pet owners do. Moreover, they do not want the responsibility of caring for a pet. Non-pet owners have also been found to differ from pet owners in the importance they place on having a clean and tidy home. For non-owners it is very important to keep things tidy. They are not the kind of people who welcome dog and cat hairs on the furniture, dirty paw prints on the kitchen floor, or frayed carpets and upholstery.[32]

For pet owners, the idea that a pet could restrict their personal freedom does not occur to them. The owner derives social support from the pet, which is often seen as another person or member of the family. Such benefits far outweigh any concerns the pet owner has about the house being soiled. The pet owner feels alone without a pet. The animal provides companionship. It is an object of affection and 'someone' to talk to.

Despite their positive feelings about animals, pet owners are not totally free from social pressures which determine whether they should or should not keep a pet. A positive response from their circle of (human) friends is an important endorsement. The disapproval of friends may discourage a would-be pet owner from acquiring an animal companion.

Purchasing your own pet is also very important. People who have done this, as distinct from having had their pet bought for them by someone else, are much more likely to regard their pet as a partner. This means that the pet is valued all the more as an object of warmth and affection. This kind of relationship is also much less likely to be affected by the opinion of others.[33]

Is Pet Ownership Associated with Social Competence?

There is a view that people who show exceptional enthusiasm for owning a pet do so because they are hopeless with people. Clearly, a normal, well-adjusted person not only has friends but enjoys being with other people, at least some of the time. Withdrawing from all social contact with other people is usually regarded as a symptom of profound emotional problems. Being concerned about others, and wanting to enter into relationships in which we get to know other people, is a central aspect of normal healthy human development. As we have seen, owning a pet may be a source of companionship. But to what extent does it signal an inability to get on with others?

Evidence did emerge from the United States during the 1960s and 1970s that people who did not own a pet appeared to be more friendly and outgoing than pet owners. In contrast, people who owned pets liked other people less than did those who did not live with a pet.[34] Pet owners, meanwhile, claimed they attached less importance to relationships with other people. In this particular case, however, both pet owners and non-owners were alike in so many other ways. The evidence was based on what the individuals questioned were prepared to admit about themselves, which may not always have been totally accurate or truthful.[35]

A survey of young people at college in the United States revealed that those who owned pets were actually more socially aware and trusting of other people than those who did not.[36] Another study of American students found that pet owners reported spending more time socializing with others than did non-owners.[37] How sociable we are can often depend on our individual personalities. Some of us are naturally more outgoing, whilst others among us are more reserved or anxious in the company of others. So far, however, psychologists have failed to find any differences between pet owners and non-owners in terms of whether one group is more extroverted or nervous than the other.[38]

Other self-attributed concerns about the implications of pet owner-ship for social competence have indicated that young pet owners do sometimes regard themselves as less socially competent and as having less satisfactory friendships than non-owners.[39] Teenage pet owners have been found to report significantly greater loneliness than non-owners.[40] In contrast with these results, others have found that pet owners were most often selected by their classroom peers as confidants, companions and partners for leisure-time activities.[41] Other observations of the leisure activities of 12- to 14-year-olds found that pet ownership had a positive effect on social communication.[42] Owning a pet could make the owner the centre of attention with his/her peer group. Indeed, owning a pet in childhood has been found to correlate strongly with social skills, especially the ability to empathize with others, as an adult.[43]

Personality and Pet Ownership

The links between pet ownership *per se* and personality are far from clear-cut. Indeed, it has been suggested that differences in character between pet owners and non-owners are few and far between. Instead, a number of social stereotypes have attached to pet owners resulting in perceptions of them as being more lively, sociable, outgoing and confi-dent people, when in fact they differ little from non-owners. Pet owners may be thought of as being a distinct social group characterized by a common outlook on life. Though many non-pet owners may be just as extrovert and self-confident, they lack the distinctive group identity of pet owners and are therefore not distinguished by personal stereotypes in the same way.

Whilst pet owners as a group may exhibit few, if any, substantial differ-ences from non-owners on key personality dimensions, evidence of character differences can sometimes emerge on considering how attached owners are to their pets. Pet ownership in itself may be less a function of the personality of the owner than is the closeness of the bond that develops between pet and owner. One door-to-door survey of pet owners in Virginia and Washington DC in the United States found that whereas pet owners did not differ from non-owners in terms of their overall opinions about themselves, there were important differences in personality which seemed to depend on how much owners were devoted to their pets. Those owners who showed a very close relationship with their pets and who devoted a great deal of attention to them tended to be more introverted and had lower self-esteem.[44]

These results indicated that pet owners who worked especially hard at pleasing and pandering to their pets were shy and retiring folk, with perhaps limited social skills and a lack of confidence when placed in situations where they had to deal with other people. It is thought to be unlikely that pet ownership causes such characteristics to emerge, but it is possible that pets act as a substitute for human contact for people who have difficulty making and maintaining relationships with others.

Keeping a pet might be especially important to people with low self-esteem. The responsibility of looking after an animal companion that is dependent for its survival upon its human owner adds meaning to the owner's life. The unconditional affection which many pets bestow upon their owners may play an important part in boosting feelings of self-worth among individuals who do not think very highly of themselves. In the critical character-forming years of adolescence, how teenagers think about themselves can depend upon the kind of relationship they have built up with their parents. Evidence has emerged from a survey of American teenage pet owners that although pet owners and non-owners did not differ in the quality of their relationships with their parents, pet-owning adolescents did seem to have higher levels of self-esteem. If this finding is robust, it suggests that animal ownership seems to affect the individual more than the family. Young pet owners claimed that they gained responsibility and friendship and fun from their pets.[45]

The assumption that personality is linked more to degree of pet attachment than to pet ownership *per se* is reinforced by findings of personality differences associated with pet ownership among old people. Pet ownership has been found to have special significance for the elderly. Pets can provide companionship to old people who because of various circumstances associated with getting old have become socially isolated and less mobile. Not all old people own pets, however. Pet ownership in old age has again been linked to the personality of the owner. Elderly pet owners appear to differ from others of their age who do not own pets in a number of key respects, but especially in terms of having lower self-esteem, and a stronger need for help and support, and to feel cared about.[46] Pets may be able to make their elderly owners feel better about themselves by providing unconditional companionship and emotional support. This explanation of the value of pet ownership to elderly people is reinforced by the results of other research that found pet owners generally to be less independent and self-sufficient than non-owners. At the same time, people who avoided pet ownership were also more concerned about keeping their homes neat and tidy, whereas those who kept pets were much more concerned about avoiding loneliness.[47]

Differences between Owners of Different Types of Pet

Another important distinction is the type of pet people choose to own. For instance, are cat lovers different from dog lovers? Do bird fanciers differ from people who like peering into a fish tank? In other words, does the type of pet you own say something about the kind of person you are? Although agreement on this point is not universal, according to some psychologists, the pet we own does say something about our personality.[48]

We certainly know that people live with a wide variety of animal companions. Dogs and cats are the most popular pets, followed by birds and fish and other furry creatures such as rabbits, guinea pigs, gerbils and so on. Pet-owning households also vary in the number and mixture of pets they own. Some pet keepers have only dogs, whilst others have only cats. Some households, however, may contain a number of different species under the same roof. An American survey of a national probability sample of more than 400 pet owners and more than 800 non-owners spread across the United States reported that 47% of pet owners owned one dog, whilst 6% owned more than one dog. More than one in five pet-owning respondents owned just one cat, whilst 3% owned more than one cat. Under 1% of pet owners owned fish, and 5% owned other types of pets. Nearly one in five pet owners, however, owned combinations of varieties of pets other than dogs, cats and fish. Whereas households can be distinguished in terms of the types of pets they contain, are there any distinguishing features of the social circumstances or psychological characteristics of pet owners themselves that are linked to the types of pets they own?

There are certainly gender differences in pet preferences. Women have been found to be more likely to like and to own a cat, but less likely to have a dog, fish or bird as an animal companion than are men. Men tend to go for dogs most of all. Male dog ownership may also be linked to personality, with more extroverted personalities being most likely to own a dog.[49] Among adolescent pet owners, girls have been found to own cats more often than boys. For this age group, there are less clear-cut gender differences in ownership of dogs as such, but adolescent boys are more likely than girls to have large dogs.[50]

Some people claim to love all animals, whilst others exhibit a special liking for one particular kind of animal. One comparison of general pet lovers with no special animal preference, and of people who specifically liked dogs over all other pets and those who preferred cats most of all, found that there were differences in the personality characteristics of people in each group. It should be emphasized that the key criterion here was the type of pet most liked, rather than the type of pet actually owned. Ownership can be influenced by factors other than liking. Many of us may end up with a pet which we would not have chosen for ourselves out of preference either because we receive it as a surprise gift or we volunteer to pet-mind for an absent friend or relative. The type of pet preferred was found to differ between men and women as well as with the individual's personality.

Men who loved pets generally, and dogs especially, tended to be more dominant personalities. In contrast, female cat lovers were found to be more submissive, gentle people. All cat lovers, whether male or female, were more caring people. Male dog lovers specifically were often more aggressive types. Female dog lovers and cat lovers in general, however, tended to be low in aggressiveness.[51]

This research was extended to find out if personality type was associated with ownership of other types of pet, such as horses, turtles, snakes and birds. Two hundred American people aged between 14 and 74 years were interviewed by researchers. They were contacted with the help of vets, pet shops and general animal interest groups. All these interviewees invested a considerable portion of their money, time and energy in their pets, whatever type of animal they owned. Horse owners were found to be assertive and introspective, but not very warm. Male horse owners were aggressive and dominant, whilst female horse owners were easy-going and generally not very aggressive at all.

Turtle owners were hard-working, reliable and upwardly mobile individuals, whereas snake owners tended to be unconventional types who were always on the lookout for something new or different to do. Snake owners had a low tolerance for routines, and enjoyed changeable and unpredictable lifestyles. Animal owners with such personality characteristics might well be attracted to unusual pets because they enjoy doing things that are out of the ordinary. Furthermore, the evil reputation of snakes, though undeserved, could well be attractive to people who are somewhat unpredictable and unconventional themselves. This quirky, risk-taking nature of snake owners was underlined by the further finding that some of these individuals also owned creepy-crawly pets such as Black Widow spiders and tarantulas.

Bird owners were contented, polite, caring and unpretentious people. They were very sociable and sought to maintain a wide network of friends. In fact, their friends were very important to them. It was central to their lives that they should sustain good relations with their friends and they were very protective of them.

Like male horse owners, female bird owners could be dominant personalities, although bird owners in general were sociable and generous. Their open and caring personalities were attracted to birds who were expressive in both song and speech, as well as having attractive colours and showing affection by muzzling. Most bird owners had tame cage birds, comprising mostly parrots, mynah birds and budgies.

There were significant differences on some personality dimensions between pet owners. Horse owners were assertive, introspective and self-concerned, but they were not especially warm and caring, nor were they risk takers. Male horse owners were notably more aggressive and domineering than any other pet-owning group.

In general, turtle owners were hard-working and considerate types who wanted a better life not only for themselves, but also for the rest of the world. The explanation for this profile may be found in the cultural stereotype of the tortoise as a slow-moving creature, but one which seems to know where it is going and that reaches its goal before the swift but erratic and unsteady hare.

Sometimes it seems that the presence of a pet may induce changes in certain aspects of personality, or failing that, it may lift our mood. For old people and children, for example, being given a pet can increase feelings of self-worth. Even adult owners can benefit emotionally from having a pet. These differences can be found between pet owners and non-owners in terms of their sense of well-being. Dog owners and cat owners have been found to feel better about themselves as a direct result of having a pet.[52]

In this chapter we have seen that although pet ownership is widespread, it is often associated with people who can be distinguished by certain types of personality or by the owners' personal or social circumstances. Individual differences as such are not always sensitive discriminators of pet ownership *per se*, but may be more significant in relation to the level of attachment pet owners display towards their animal companions. Attachment to pets is a key aspect of the relationship owners and pets develop with each other and is central to understanding why some of us choose to share our lives with animal companions. The next chapter takes a closer look at the issue of pet bonding and attachment.

References

1 Derbyshire, D. Love him or loathe him, telepathic Tiddles can tell. *Daily Mail*, 1998, 3 September, p.17.

2 Johnson, P. Just what makes us such a nation of animal lovers? *Daily Mail*, 1998, 1 August, pp.12–13.

3 American Pet Products Manufacturing Association. *Pet Owners Survey*. Cited in *Anthrozoos*, 8 (2), 111, 1994.

4 AVMA. *Survey of the Veterinary Service Market for Companion Animals*. Centre for Information Management, American Veterinary Medical Association, 1992.

5 Urban Animal Management Coalition, 1994

6 INSEE, *Economique et Statistiques*, March, No.241, 1991.

7 Aldous, J. *Family Careers: Developmental Change in Families*. New York: Wiley, 1978.

8 Albert, A. and Bulcroft, K. Pets and urban life. *Anthrozoos*, 1(1), 9–25, 1987.

9 Albert, A. and Bulcroft, K., 1987, ibid.

10 Albert, A. and Bulcroft, K., 1987, ibid.

11 Purvis, M.J. and Otto, D.M. *Household Demand for Pet Food and the Ownership of Dogs and Cats: An Analysis of a Neglected Component of US Food Use*. Department of Agriculture and Applied Economics, University of Minnesota, St Paul/Minneapolis, 1976. Beck, A.M. Animals in the city. In A.H. Katcher and A.M. Beck (Eds) *New Perspectives on Our Lives with Companion Animals*. Philadelphia: University of Pennsylvania Press, 1983. Salmon, P.W. and Salmon, I.M. Who owns who? Psychological research into the human–pet bond in Australia. In A.H. Katcher and A.M. Beck (Eds) *New Perspectives on Our Lives with Companion Animals*. Philadelphia: University of Pennsylvania Press, pp. 244–265, 1983.

12 AVMA, 1992, op.cit.

13 Endenburg, N., Hart, H. and de Vries, H.W. Differences between owners and non-owners of companion animals. *Anthrozoos*, 4(2), 120–126, 1992.

14 INSEE, 1991, op.cit.

15 Messent, P.R. and Horsfield, S. Pet population and the pet–owner bond. In *The Human–Pet Relationship*. Institute for Interdisciplinary Research on the Human–Pet Relationship. Vienna: IEMT, Austrian Academy of Sciences, pp. 9–17, 1985.

16 Goodwin, R.D. Trends in the ownership of domestic pets in Great Britain. In R.S. Anderson (Ed.) *Pet Animals and Society*. London: Bailliere Tindall, pp. 96–102, 1975.

17 Endenberg, N. et al., 1992, op.cit.

18 Marx, M.B., Stallones, L. and Garrity, T.F. Demographics of pet ownership among US elderly. *Anthrozoos*, 1(1), 36–40, 1987.

19 Covert, A.M., Whiren, A.P., Keith, J. and Nelson, C. Pets, early adolescents and families. In M. Sussman (Ed.) *Pets and the Family*. New York: Haworth Press, pp.95–108, 1985.

20 Albert, A. and Bulcroft, K, 1987, op.cit.

21 Gallup, G.G. Jr. and Beckstead, J.W. Attitudes towards animal research. *American Psychologist*, 43, 474–476, 1988.

22 Tennov, D. Pain infliction in animal research. In H. McGiffin and N. Bromley (Eds) *Animals in Education*. Washington, DC: Institute for the Study of Animal Problems, pp. 35–40, 1986.

23 Kellert, S.R. and Berry, J.K. Attitudes, knowledge and behaviours toward wildlife as affected by gender. *Wildlife Society Bulletin*, 15, 363–371, 1987.

24 Bowd, A.D. Fears and understanding of animals in middle childhood. *Journal of Genetic Psychology*, 145, 143–144, 1984. Kidd, A.H. and Kidd, R.M. Factors in children's attitudes towards pets. *Psychological Reports*, 66, 775–786, 1990.

25 Melson, G.F. and Fogel, A. Children's ideas about animal young and their care: A reassessment of gender differences in the development of nurturance. *Anthrozoos*, 2, 265–277, 1989.

26 Melson, G.F. and Fogel, A, 1989, ibid.

27 Brown, D.S. Human gender, age, and personality effects on relationships with dogs and horses. Doctoral dissertation, Duke University, Durham, NC, 1984.

28 Kidd, A.H. and Kidd, R.M., 1990, op.cit.

29 Herzog, H.A., Betchart, N.S. and Pittman, R.B. Gender, sex role orientation and attitudes toward animals. *Anthrozoos*, 4(3), 184–191, 1991.

30 Hills, A.M. The relationship between thing–person orientation and the perception of animals. *Anthrozoos*, 3, 100–110, 1989.

31 St. Yves, A., Freeston, M.H., Jacques, C. and Robitaille, C. Love of animals and interpersonal affectionate behaviour. *Psychological Reports*, 67 (3, Pt2), 1067–1075, 1990.

32 Guttmann, G. The psychological determinants of keeping pets. In B. Fogle (Ed.) *Interrelations Between People and Pets*. Springfield,IL: Charles C. Thomas.

33 Guttmann, G., 1981, op.cit.

34 Cameron, P., Conrad, C., Kirkpatrick, D.D. and Bareen, R.J. pet ownership and sex as determinants of stated affect towards others and estimates of others' regard of self. *Psychological Reports*, 19, 884–886, 1966.

35 Cameron, P. and Mattson, M. Psychological correlates of pet ownership. *Psychological Reports*, 30, 286, 1972.

36 Hyde, K.R., Kurdek, L. and Larson, P. Relationship between pet ownership and self-esteem, social sensibility and interpersonal trust. *Psychological Reports*, 52, 110, 1983.

37 Joubert, C.E. Pet ownership, social interest and sociability. *Psychological Reports*, 61, 401–402, 1987.

38 Paden-Levy, D. relationship of extraversion, neuroticism, alienation and divorce incidence with pet ownership. *Psychological Reports*, 57, 868–870, 1985.

39 Serpell, J.A. *In the Company of Animals*. New York: Blackwells, 1988.

40 Bekker, B. Adolescent pet owners versus non–owners: friendship and loneliness. Unpublished doctoral dissertation, University of Pennsylvania, 1986.

41 Guttmann, G. et al, 1983, op.cit.

42 Siegmund, R. and Biermann, K. Common leisure activities of pets and children. *Anthrozoos*, 2, 53–57, 1988.

43 Paul, E.S. Pets in childhood: Individual variation in childhood pet ownership. *IZAL Newsletter*, 7, 6, 1994.

44 Johnson, S.B. and Rule, W.R. Personality characteristics and self-esteem in pet owners and non-owners. *International Journal of Psychology*, 26(2), 241–252, 1991.

45 Covert, A.M. et al, 1985, op.cit.

46 Kidd, A.H. and Feldman, R.M. Pet ownership and self-perceptions of older people. *Psychological Reports*, 48, 867–875, 1981.

47 Guttman, G, 1981, op.cit.

48 Johnson, S.B. and Rule, W.R. 1991, op.cit.

49 Edelson, J. and Lester, D. Personality and pet ownership: A preliminary study. *Psychological Reports*, 53 (3, Pt.1), 990, 1983

50 Covert, A.M. et al., 1985, op.cit.

51 Kidd, A.H. and Kidd, R.M. Personality characteristics and preferences in pet ownership. *Psychological Reports*, 46,939–949, 1980.

52 Martinez, R.L. and Kidd, A.H. Two personality characteristics in adult pet owners and non-owners. *Psychological Reports*, 47, 318, 1980.

Chapter 3
Why are we so attached to our pets?

Veterinarians have observed that people are often very attached to their pets.[1] Attachment is a term originally coined in literature on early child development, which initially referred to the bond that develops between a care-giver and his or her infant.[2] It has been defined in several ways. It can refer to an emotional state or feeling and also to specific behaviours that individuals use to keep another individual close to them.[3]

The formation of emotional attachments is central to normal human development. Ethologists have observed that humans exhibit many similarities to other animals in their basic needs and the kinds of behaviours displayed in relation to those needs. In addition to the drives of hunger, sex and aggression, humans and animals also display needs linked to territoriality, exploration and attachment. Attachment is of crucial importance to any species in which social relationships play a key part in its survival and development. Social bonds begin with mother and infant and then extend to include fathers, siblings, extended family, peers and usually opposite-sex partners. The initial mother–child bond derives from the child's needs for security and nurturance. Human children need to be cared for until mature enough to leave home and look after themselves.

Although the mother–child bond emerges as pre-eminent in psychological writings,[4] research with primates has found that the social environment beyond an offspring's immediate bond with its mother is also important. For example, infant rhesus monkeys raised with their peers but not their mother fare better as adults than monkeys raised with their mothers but isolated from peers.[5] This evidence does not mean that mother–child bonding is unimportant, but rather that other social bonds may be equally critical to a healthy psychological development.

Activities that build and maintain attachments between people may also occur between individuals and their pets.[6] Many of the interactions that take place between people and their pets resemble those that take place between individuals and their children, for example. This is because children and pets share many of the same attributes. Pets are similar to children in that they rely on someone to take care of them. Many pets can be picked up and carried, just like children.

As we have already seen, some writers on animal companionship have speculated as to whether people substitute animal attachments for human attachments. There is mixed evidence on this point. Certainly some pet owners appear to prefer the company of animals to that of other people.[7] At the same time, there is evidence that some pet owners profess to like people more than do non-pet owners.[8] Perhaps the most important point here is that companion animals provide an opportunity for humans to experience bonding. Furthermore, for those individuals who are shy with other people or lack social skills, having a pet can enable them to establish and get practice at maintaining personal and social relationships without the same anxieties that may be invoked when they are around other people.

It has been suggested by some writers that as pet owners we can use our pet to meet certain psychosocial needs which arise during childhood and before we reach our teens. At this stage of human development, it has been observed that pets can help the growing child in many different ways. It can reduce stress and anxiety in the child by providing a loyal companion that can be trusted as a protector or confidant. It can serve to instil a sense of personal responsibility in the child, in that the pet needs to be cared for and the child is often required to play an important part in this activity. Finally, the pet provides a companion who may serve as a substitute for absent friends.

There are two aspects of the human–animal bond that appear to contribute to why this relationship is generally experienced as positive. First, pets are non-judgemental in their affection. They love their owner regardless of whether he or she achieves conventional standards of success or attractiveness. Second, pets have many child-like qualities, even when full grown. They remain forever dependent upon their owner and have been characterized as simultaneously an animal, a child and our own infantile selves.[9]

Gratifications Met by Pets

Pets meet many fundamental human needs for their owners. As well as companionship, they can give us something to care about, help to keep us busy, make us feel safe, in some cases provide an impetus to take exercise, and give us something to touch or watch and be entertained by.[10] Pets can offer a sense of family and community to elderly and retired people. They can also serve as surrogate children to couples who are childless. The beauty of so many pets is that they accept us the way we are. Their attachment to us is unconditional. In so many ways, pets are beneficial for us, particularly for our emotional well-being.

The establishment of a lasting relationship with a companion animal will depend to some degree on whether it is a source of pleasure or irritation. A study of cat owners found that people like their cats to make a fuss of them, to approach and interact with them, to purr in their company and to display a distinctive personality. Whilst cats are renowned for being aloof, they are more likely to curry favour with their owners if they display some sense of emotional attachment that goes beyond ingratiating behaviour associated with feeding time. Cats will blot their copy book if they annoy their owners with destructive behaviour such as clawing the carpet, using the table leg as a scratching post, or repeatedly marking their territory indoors by urinating against household objects. Cat owners also get upset when their pets display a lack of sociability or affection, pick fights with other pets, or become fussy eaters.[11]

There are many illustrations of how bonds with pets can make people feel better about themselves and generally behave in a more positive way towards others. Providing elderly people in retirement homes with pets has been found to have a profound effect on feelings of depression.[12] We all need to be needed, to have someone to love or be close to. Pets, such as cats, dogs or birds, can fulfil this desire.

Pets show loyalty and devotion in ways which other people fail to match. This may be especially important for children. A child may lack confidence or often feel picked upon by parents, siblings and other people, who are always making demands and offer emotional support or friendship conditionally. Pets, in contrast, offer unconditional acceptance of the child without demands to perform in any special way. Furthermore, pets can foster feelings of responsibility in children and encourage selfless behaviour in caring for the pet.

The capacity of pets to provide a source of satisfaction for various needs is often the major reason why people have pets, especially dogs and cats. It is also a common underlying emotional mode in many relationships between people. The pet may be a companion, confidant and source of emotional support all rolled into one. Pets can also provide a source of therapy, boosting the confidence of the insecure, providing security to the afraid, and representing something to take responsibility for, when there is no one else.

Thus, relationships between owners and their pets can be many and varied. For some, the relationship represents a deep, personal and emotional bond. For others, a pet may be little more than a toy in the case of a child or another possession in the case of an adult. Like many other possessions, its appeal may fade with time. It is important to emphasize, however, that pets are neither toys nor should they be treated the same as inanimate possessions. Nevertheless, they are often, though cared for, regarded as little more than status symbols.

The Genesis of Pet Attachment

People's relationships with animals are often forged early in life. Those who have lived in homes with pets as children are generally more likely to have pets as adults. Furthermore, we will more likely than not own the same kind of animal as adults as we enjoyed sharing our home life with as children. Our ability to forge strong attachments with animals, however, does not seem to depend upon childhood experiences. Research has shown that we may be able to form a strong pet attachment whether or not we had a pet as a child.[13] There does appear to be evidence, nevertheless, that people may be able to form close bonds with certain animals and not others. Whilst we may acknowledge the comfort we enjoy from having an animal companion, this feeling may become more pronounced when we are asked specifically about our feelings regarding the particular kind of animal we happen to own.[14]

An antipathy towards certain types of animals can also be conditioned during childhood. A fear of dogs, for example, tends to operate in a classically conditioned sense, resulting from a bad experience in early life. Such fearfulness is much less likely to materialize if we have been brought up with a pet dog. But a frightening experience as a child is often likely to last through into adulthood.[15]

There are indications of greater attachment to pets among those with fewer close human ties, such as single and divorced people, when compared with families with children.[16] Women living alone were found to be significantly more lonely than those with pets or those living with other people.[17] A German study of single people with cats found that they played with their animals for longer than did cat owners with a close human relationship, and they were more strongly attached to their cats.[18] The distress following pet loss has been found to be greater for those living alone than for those sharing a household with other people[19] and to be inversely related to family size.[20]

Is pet ownership therefore influenced by the type of living circumstances? The living arrangements of modern Western societies contrast sharply with those in more traditional societies. For example, life in Indian cities where there are extended family networks living together with relatively little space and privacy offer quite different home environments from those typical of the West today. These differing cultures may also display quite distinct outlooks on life. The differences have been discussed in terms of Western society emphasizing individuality, rationality and control, free will and materialism, whereas Indian society emphasizes communal values, emotional expression, determinism and spiritualism.[21] These differences, in turn, can affect a wide range of people's activities and beliefs. They lead us to ask whether pet ownership may be accentuated in the affluent western world today because it is fulfilling emotional needs that in traditional societies are directed more at an extended family.

Cross-cultural evidence, however, has indicated that pet ownership is prevalent even when extended family networks are present. Differences in pet keeping among different cultures is more associated with different traditions and beliefs about animals than the extent of family networks.

Even so, within a particular cultural tradition, the existence of fewer social contacts would seem to accentuate attachment to pets. Even if actual pet ownership *per se* is likely to be found equally among people who live alone or live within an emotionally enriching and satisfying family system, attachment to a pet can be much more profound among individuals who have relatively few social contacts.[22]

Mechanisms of Bonding

A significant part of the relationship between pet and pet owner is the way they communicate with each other. Touch forms a centrally important aspect of this communication. Despite the stereotypes that women are more gentle and touching than men, research with pets and their owners has shown that men and women are equally likely to touch their pets. Men may stroke and caress their animals in much the same way, and to the same extent, as do women.[23] Dogs, in particular, appear to be a means through which men can both express and receive affection in public situations, without appearing to lose their masculinity. Another stereotype not supported by research evidence is that women tend to be most closely associated with small lap dogs as an outlet for their affection: women are likely to be just as comfortable and at ease with larger breeds.

Another mechanism linked to the relationship between humans and animals is the type of language owners use when talking to their pets. One obstacle to forming a human-like relationship with an animal is its limited intellect and lack of language. Nevertheless, many pet owners behave as if the pet can understand them and talk to them. Among a sample of 80 people from veterinary clinics, one American study found that 79% said that they talked to the animal as if it was a person and 80% believed that the pet was sensitive to the owner's feelings.[24]

We have already noted in passing that the way we talk to our pets often resembles the way we talk to very young children. Language directed towards babies and young children shows a number of specific characteristics that marks it out from the language used with other adults. It is referred to as motherese and consists of a number of features, such as short utterances, with many imperatives and questions, repetitions, simple sentences and tag questions ('aren't you?' at the end).

Recordings for such features of dog owners talking to their dogs have been taken to compare the type of language used with the dog with that used in conversations with adult humans.[25] This research has revealed that nearly all the characteristics of motherese were present in these one-sided conversations with the pet dogs. These findings suggest that a pattern of language presumably first used to aid interactions with young children has readily been co-opted for interacting with other social beings who are, like infants, presumed to be at a lower level of understanding than adult humans.

Another part of the relationship between humans and pets stems from the ability of humans to project thoughts and feelings onto animals. Most humans see others as having minds – embracing feelings, beliefs and intentions different from their own. One by-product of this ability, however, is that we tend to over-attribute such characteristics to others and when we do this in the case of animals it leads to anthropomorphism. Pets are treated as if they were 'people'. Relationships can then be formed which resemble those with other humans in certain respects.

Does the behaviour of the individual animal contribute towards pet attachment? To shed light on this question, James Serpell surveyed 37 dog owners and 47 cat owners who lived in Cambridge, England.[26] The results demonstrated a number of highly significant differences in owners' assessments of the behaviour of dogs and cats, particularly with regard to playfulness, confidence, affection, excitability, friendliness to strangers, intelligence and owner-directed aggression. The owners fell into two groups, those who were moderately attached to their pets and those who were strongly attached to them.

Dog owners rated their dogs as less confident in unfamiliar situations, much more excitable, more affectionate, less obedient, more active and less happy about being left on their own than ideal dogs. Cat owners rated their own cats as less confident in unfamiliar situations, less affectionate, more excitable, less obedient, less intelligent and more aggressive towards people they know than ideal cats. Moderately and strongly attached owners did not differ from each other in terms of their ideal ratings of either dogs or cats. In terms of the 'actual' ratings, very attached dog owners rated their pets as being significantly more intelligent than did moderately attached dog owners. Very attached cat owners regarded their pets as being more noisy than moderately attached cat owners.

The relationship, if any, between a companion animal's behaviour and its owner's attachment level is likely to depend on the person's prior behavioural expectations of particular species, breed or individual animal. In which case, 'actual' behaviour ratings may be less reliable predictors of attachment levels than average distances between owners' 'actual' and 'ideal' ratings for each behavioural attribute. Moderately attached dog owners have reported consistently large differences between the character of their own pet and their conception of what an ideal pet should be like. Cat owners tend to be less consistent in this regard, although moderately attached cat owners may see their own pet as much worse than the ideal than do very attached cat owners, especially with regard to how affectionate their animal is perceived to be.

Such findings also indicated that dog owners who reported weaker attachments to their pets were consistently less satisfied with most aspects of their dogs' behaviour compared with those who reported strong attachments. Weakly attached cat owners were significantly more dissatisfied with the levels of affection shown by their pets, but in other respects they were far less consistent than dog owners.

Differences in perceptions of 'actual' behaviour between dogs and cats were consistent with the generally accepted, popular depictions of these two species. Cats were widely considered to be more flighty, more stand-offish with strangers, and less demonstrative in their affections than were dogs, as well as being regarded as less excitable, active and playful.[27] The absence of any highly significant differences between owners' 'ideal' ratings of cats and dogs suggests a surprisingly high level of agreement between cat and dog owners regarding the behavioural attributes of the ideal pet. This might appear to contradict the widespread view that cat and dog owners are different types of people with differing expectations of their pets, although what is expected and what is considered ideal may be two different things from the owner's point of view.

With respect to their 'actual' behaviour, both dogs and cats differed significantly from owners' 'ideal' ratings. With dogs, the main discrepancies were associated with nervousness, fearfulness, excitability, lack of obedience and separation-related anxiety. The fact that 'ideal' dogs were rated as less affectionate than 'actual' dogs suggested that some owners were having problems with overly attached and dependent animals. People's 'ideal' conceptions of dog and cat behaviour in this study bore no relation to their level of attachment for the animal. It is therefore unlikely that the less strong attachments developed by some owners were a consequence of having exaggerated or unrealistic expectations of the pet.

Across most aspects of behaviour, owners' ratings of their own pet also showed little association with attachment levels, although more intelligent dogs and noisier cats tended to have more attached owners than their less intelligent and quieter counterparts. This finding indicated that, within reason, absolute levels of behaviour may be relatively unimportant to the relationship from the owner's point of view.

The average discrepancy between own pet ratings and 'ideal' pet ratings did affect owner-attachment levels, particularly in relation to dogs. Although the small sample sizes made it difficult to demonstrate many statistically significant effects, it was apparent that own pet–ideal pet differences were consistently greater among the less strongly attached group of dog owners. There was no consistent pattern among cat owners. Large differences in the way own pets and ideal pets were perceived were associated with nearer to ideal affection levels perceived by cat owners with strong attachments.

Social Meanings of Pets

According to some writers, pets can fulfil a number of functions for their owners that have distinct social meanings. As we saw in Chapter 1, one writer identified three functions of companion animals who enjoyed close relationships with their owners: the projection function, the sociability function, and the surrogate function.[28] The projection function entails the pet owner using the pet as a symbolic extension of the self. In other words, individuals make personal statements about themselves through the kind of pet they own and the way they relate to or treat the animal. The sociability function involves the role of pets in facilitating human interaction. Pets provide a subject of conversation. They can also serve as 'social catalysts' by bringing people into contact with other pet owners. For example, people who walk their dogs in the same park often strike up a conversation while their pets are sniffing around each other. Pets can also fulfil a role as surrogate friends. The surrogate function involves the extent to which interaction with pets substitutes for and supplements interaction with other people. In the extreme, owners may become so dependent on their pets that their relationship with their pet may not only supplement human companionship but actually replace it.

Sources of Evidence

The evidence for the close attachments that can form between people and their pets derives from a number of sources. Interviews with pet owners have frequently triggered disclosures about the deep bonds which they often develop with their pet. Pet owners often talk about their pets as if they are as much members of the family as is anyone else in the household. Not only that, people often talk to their pets as they would talk to another person. The deep emotional attachment is further reflected in the sense of loss and bereavement suffered by pet owners when a pet dies (see Chapter 9). One study among nearly 100 military households in the United States found that two-thirds of respondents (68%) thought of pets as being full family members, whilst three in 10 (30%) thought of pets as close friends. Nearly every respondent (96%) described their pet's role in the family as very important.[29]

A telephone survey of American pet owners living in urban locations found that pet owners stressed the positive benefits of living with companion animals and rarely mentioned any negative consequences. They generally reported having very happy relationships with their pets, although the precise nature of the relationship did vary with the social and emotional situation of the individual. Pet attachment was at its strongest among single, divorced and widowed people. But the companionship provided by pets is not restricted to people living on their own. Pets also provided special comfort to the so-called 'empty-nesters', that is, people whose children had left the family home to live their lives elsewhere. Attachment could also be strong among childless couples and newlyweds. Single and divorced people and childless couples were especially likely to treat their pets as if they were people. For the person living on their own, the pet represented a live-in companion to talk to, whilst for childless couples a pet was a substitute child.[30]

As well as evidence from what people say about their pets, research on human–animal attachments has also been conducted in a less obtrusive way by observing how people behave with animal companions. This sort of research has provided corroborative evidence for the closeness that can develop between pet owners and their pets.

The degree of intimacy of our relationship with another person is often signalled non-verbally. One indication of this is the physical distance we keep between ourselves and another person when having a conversation with them. The better we know someone, the closer to them we will stand. Observations of pet owners have shown that they keep the same distance between themselves and pet dogs as they keep with family members. Non-pet owners, on the other hand, will not tend to allow pet animals to get as close to them to the same extent.[31]

In one study of this phenomenon, the researcher spent more than 20 hours in each of 10 households observing family members interact with a pet dog.[32] This research showed that family members who reported less attachment to the dog interacted with it significantly less often than did individuals who, when interviewed, expressed a firm attachment to the animal. But this relationship worked both ways. Pet dogs apparently learned very well who they could get attention from. Thus, any member of the family who did not care too much for the dog and tended to ignore it rather than make a fuss of it would tend to be ostracized by the dog. The dog would initiate relatively little contact with that person compared with other members of the household who did recognize its presence. The dog knew who his friends were. Family members who reported a high level of attachment to their dog, but were absent from the animal for a period of time, would tend to make up for the lost time by making a bigger than usual fuss of the animal when reunited with it.

Further observations indicated that pets acquire the ability to elicit positive emotional responses from their owners. Positive responses are initially elicited from tactile contact or the good feelings that are generated when a pet shows enthusiasm for seeing its owner. The continued pairing of the pet with good feelings then leads the owner to view the animal as a source of comfort.

Issues Relating to the Measurement of Attachment

Many studies of human–animal relationships have focused on the degree of attachment people have to their pets. Several standardized measures for assessing pet attachment have been developed usually taking the form of questionnaires.[33] These kinds of instruments have the potential advantage of providing an objective, quantitative evaluation of the human–animal relationship from the pet owners' perspective.

One questionnaire called the Pet Attachment Survey (PAS) was designed to measure the degree to which individuals are attached to their pets.[34] This scale included items such as 'You feel sad when you are separated from your pet' and 'You don't like your pet to get too close to you'. The PAS was divided into two sub-scales: (a) a Relationship Maintenance scale that measured behaviours such as interaction, communication, and time or financial involvement with one's pet; and (b) an Intimacy scale that measured behaviours such as proximity and emotional importance of one's pet.

Because dogs and cats comprise the vast majority of animals kept as pets, questionnaires for assessing attachment primarily reflect the types of interactions possible with these species. Furthermore, the dog, through both observation and tradition as 'man's best friend', tends to serve as the ideal model of animal companionship in its ability to engage in a particularly wide range of behaviours similar to those exhibited in human companionship. For this reason, relationships with pets are often evaluated on the basis of behaviours that mainly pertain to human–dog interactions such as taking walks, travelling together, grooming, and training the animal. This is in contrast with assessing emotional aspects of the relationship such as the love, trust, loyalty and joyful mutual activity which can characterize relationships that humans enjoy with pets of all kinds. As a result, studies that have compared the attachment of dog owners and cat owners often have reported dog owners to be more highly attached to their pets than are people who have cats or other types of animal as pets.

The findings of a descriptive study showed that dog owners were more likely than cat owners to take their pets with them on errands and trips, and cat owners were more likely to allow their pets on the furniture. However, dog owners and cat owners were equally likely to view their pets as family members, talk to and share food with them, and to believe that their pets could understand their moods.[35]

Another study of pet attachment in the general population reported no differences between dog owners and cat owners based on six items common to interactions with both species, although dog owners and cat owners as a group scored significantly higher in degree of pet attachment than did owners of other pet species.[36]

More recently, a scale for measuring pet attachment has focused on the perceived comfort received from a pet. A sample of 87 cat owners and 58 dog owners completed the Comfort from Companion Animals Scale. Results showed that, when two items pertaining to dogs were included, dog owners showed a significantly higher degree of attachment. When only the 11 items pertaining to the emotional nature of the relationship were included, however, there were no differences between dog and cat owners. Although dogs generally may participate in a wider variety of interactions with humans than do cats and other pets by going for walks and playing outdoor games, cats can be an equally important source of unconditional love, affection and companionship.[37]

Cat owners have been reported to be as likely as dog owners to view the cat as a family member to talk to and to share food with, and to believe that their cats respond to their moods.[38] Australian adults reported liking cats and choosing them as pets primarily for their appearance and personalities.[39] In a British study, cat owners were found to take fewer and shorter recreational walks and initial improvements in health were not as long lasting as those of dog owners.[40]

A survey of 100 American adult cat owners to investigate various aspects of attachment to feline companions found that most of these respondents reported preferring cats to all other pets, citing ease of care, affection and companionship, and personality as the main reasons.[41] Comparisons of the benefits of having a cat as a pet showed that affection and unconditional love were the primary benefits of the human–cat relationship. The respondents in this survey reported that their feline companions fulfilled important needs for companionship and a feeling of being needed, in some cases even to a greater extent than their human companions.

Pets often demonstrate their affection by greeting us when we come home, staying close or sitting in our lap, sleeping with us, and seeking out our company in a variety of ways.[42] Although cats have a reputation for being independent, aloof, and less affectionate and interactive than dogs, the great majority of cat owners have been found to report some form of interactive behaviour as a reason for liking their cats.[43]

An important characteristic of animal companions is that they are unchanging in their interactions with us.[44] Unlike human relationships which often involve a variety of interpersonal conflicts, relationships with pets are relatively free of the pets' judgements and critical evaluations. Their affection for their owners seems independent of their owners' social or financial status, appearance, or day-to-day ups and downs and mood swings. Cat owners in this study regarded their cats as offering unconditional affection, undivided loyalty and devotion, and total acceptance.

Problem Attachments

The nature of attachments between people and companion animals can vary widely. Under circumstances in which pets and their owners have a number of interests and needs in common, fruitful human–animal interactions can be facilitated with both pets and their owners obtaining personal benefits from living together. Their common interests mean not only that they can tolerate living in close physical proximity, but also that there are some genuine psychological and social benefits that each can enjoy which promote an affiliation with each other. Pets enjoy the company of their owners and do not just hang around because they get fed. People, of course, enjoy the sense of companionship provided by their pets and very often pets and people behave together as if they were the same species. We have already seen that people talk to their pets in much the same way as they would to other people.

As with any other kind of close personal relationship, however, things do not always run smoothly. It is on such occasions that species differences suddenly rise to the surface. At this point the relationship may take on a new twist and lead to problems for one or both partners. Pets may behave in ways which their owners regard as problematic. Sometimes, however, the behaviour of the pet is in response to what the pet seems to interpret as undesirable behaviour on the part of the owner. Such behaviours might include, for example, leaving the pet alone and shut in a confined space for long periods of time, acquiring another pet, failing to recognize a change in food tastes, and so on. Neither people nor pets may be acting abnormally for their own species, but when each tends to relate to the other as the same species, conflicts can arise.

With pets such as cats and dogs, for instance, it is important to remember that they are usually raised by their owners from helpless infanthood and therefore generally become quite dependent upon the owner for their survival, not only as a youngster but also as an adult. Dogs, in particular, engage in all sorts of endearing behaviours such as acting happy when the owner returns, wanting to be touched by the owner, touching the owner, trying to be near the owner, entertaining the owner with their antics, or by being obedient, looking guilty when they misbehave and sad when the owner departs. Pets can generate a feeling of well-being in people, a feeling of being loved.

Pets can engage in greeting behaviours that can result in responses of affection similar to those that occur between people. The person may talk to the pet, often in the same way as to a friend or a child. The owners may ask questions of the pet, without expecting an answer – much as one might of a small child – and might stroke, hug or scoop up the pet in their arms.

Pets, particularly dogs, sometimes cats and even horses, greet a person in a way that is interpreted as being glad to see that person. Happy greetings tend to generate feelings of warmth in the recipient, and these feelings are of firm attachment. The greetings of pets are not the same as, but the context and responses are similar to, people–people involvement. Most pets have many positive attributes that encourage attachment. Unattractive characteristics have tended, in the past, to be selected against, whereas endearing traits are selectively chosen.

Can the Bond Become too Intense?

There are occasions when people become too attached to their pets. As with the bond between parent and child, an early attachment that satisfies a basic human drive must later be relaxed as the child becomes more independent with age. When an insatiable need to care or be cared for persists into adulthood, subsequent relationships with other people can be complicated or undermined. Parents who become pathologically fixated on their children even when they have grown up are doing neither themselves nor their offspring any favours in the longer term.[45]

When attachment is carried to an unhealthy extreme, it tends to be expressed in two ways. The first manifestation has been called 'anxious attachment' and derives from a constant feeling of apprehension about anticipated separation from a loved one. The result of this extreme emotional reaction is often the development of an over-dependent and clinging relationship between parent and child. The second form of expression of pathological attachment is compulsive care giving. Once again, there is an irrational fear of separation which becomes manifest in the form of obsessional care giving, which may often not be welcomed by the recipient. Whilst there is nothing inherently wrong about caring for others, when it develops into a compulsive behaviour it can be accompanied by a variety of maladaptive psychiatric reactions if and when the bond is eventually severed.[46]

Similar behavioural attachment can occur between pet owners and their animal companions. On these occasions a basic distrust of human relationships may contribute to a displaced and pathologically extreme attachment to the pet who represents a constantly available and willing recipient of the caregiver's need to feel that at least someone values his/her attention. The emotional bond that develops between owner and pet can be so deep that when it is threatened or actually broken enduring and complicated psychiatric reactions can arise in the pet owner.[47]

One psychiatrist reported a case of a 40-year-old woman who manifested a prolonged and intense grief reaction following the death of her pet dog. She had established a strong attachment to this pet during a period when she had suffered an exophthalmic goitre which had affected her facial appearance, leaving her self-conscious about her looks and unable to venture out very often. Despite support and reassurance from her husband and teenage son she continued to harbour self-doubts and a dread of rejection. She turned to the family dog which in time became the only relationship that mattered to her. She became obsessed with caring for the animal and never let it out of her sight. Another factor emerged during psychotherapy, however. For many years the woman had cared for her ailing mother. When she herself fell ill, her mother rejected her help, because of her own phobia about being around people who were ill. This rejection played a key part in the attachment the woman formed with her pet dog. The woman's compulsive caring for the pet compensated for her rejection by her mother.[48]

Problem Pets

Some of the most common problems people have with their pets are based on the attachment and type of relationship which exists between pet and owner. The most frequent complaints owners have concerning the behaviour of pets are aggression related to assertion of dominance, destruction of property when the pet is left alone, and spraying or urinating or defecating in inappropriate places. Dogs are often dominant towards owners and in maintaining this social position will exhibit aggression. Dogs that have rarely been separated from the owner will destroy household items, howl, cry or eliminate when left alone. Cats often spray, urinate or defecate in undesirable places in response to a change in the environment, unfriendly attitudes of people, or other animals being introduced into the home.

The strength of the human–companion animal relationship is often reflected by the person's response to separation from the pet, measures taken by people to ensure that the life of the pet is 'happy' and prolonged, and that the pet is not separated from the person. The cost of maintaining this relationship can be financial, estrangement from some human relationship (a friend who does not like the pet), or risk of physical injury to themselves or their children. Granted people can become very attached to pets, but why should the attachment occur in the face of physical injury to themselves or their offspring? Certainly there are immediate benefits to keeping a pet, but these hardly seem sufficient to warrant keeping a pet that is a menace or danger to others in the household.

Many owners who are very attached to a pet and faced with the dilemma of separation will say without coaxing, 'But I feel toward this animal as though s/he was my child'. The mechanisms of attachment have worked well to ensure parental responses and care. Women appear to be more attached to pets as they seem to be more easily attracted to and attached to children.

It may be possible, of course, that there are immediate benefits or probable immediate benefits that outweigh the costs and liabilities of keeping a dangerous pet.[49] These immediate benefits of pet ownership may be protection, a sense of security, health, well-being, or longevity of the owner or offspring.[50] If these benefits ultimately result in an increase of the owner's genetic representation in subsequent generations, it is worth putting up with some risks. The probability of an increase in genetic representation (benefit) must, however, outweigh the probability of a decrease in genetic representation (cost). Evolutionarily speaking, it makes sense to take risks if by doing so the probable benefits exceed probable loss. With problem pets, owners must weigh up for themselves whether the benefits of pet ownership really do exceed the costs of keeping a dangerous or nuisance animal.

Often pet behaviour problems can be successfully treated, but it is much easier to prevent their occurrence than to change them.[51] Because these are such common problems, it would be particularly wise to take some preventive measures when pets are placed as companions with lonely people or as therapeutic agents with individuals. These people may be more likely than the general population to have animals that develop these objectionable behaviours. These people are also likely to become very attached to the animal and suffer the consequences of the behaviour problem for a long time because they are afraid that the animal might be destroyed as a means of solving the behaviour problem. Such individuals may also, because of a disability, be less successful in treating a problem when it occurs.

In this chapter we have examined the bonds that can develop between pet owners and their pets. For some of us our pets are an important part of our lives. They are friends and confidants, sources of affection and targets of care giving. On some occasions, attachment to a pet can become so strong that neither the animal nor its owner can tolerate being apart for long. Anxiety over separation can lead to psychological problems in the owner and the onset of problem behaviour in the pet. Under such circumstances a battle for control ensues. Pets, in particular, may develop behaviour patterns that are designed to manipulate their owners. In the next chapter, we turn to the issue of control as a central facet of the human–pet bond.

References

1 Voith, V.L. Attachment of people to companion animals. *Veterinary Clinics of North America. Small Animal Practice*, 12, 655–663, 1985.
2 Ainsworth, M. and Bell, S. Mother–infant interaction and the development of competence. In K. Connolly and J. Bruner (Eds) *The Growth of Competence*. San Diego, Academic Press, pp. 97–118, 1974.
3 Voith, V.L., 1985, op.cit.
4 Bowlby, J. *Attachment and Loss*, Vol.1.: *Attachment*. London: Hogarth Press, 1969.
5 Suomi, S.J., Harlow, H.F. and Domek, C.J. Effect of repetitive infant–infant separation of young monkeys. *Journal of Abnormal Psychology*, 76, 161–172, 1970.
6 Voith, V.L., 1985, op.cit.
7 Cameron, P. and Mattson, M. Psychological correlates of pet ownership. *Psychological Reports*, 30, 286, 1972.
8 Mugford, R.A. The social significance of pet ownership. In S.A. Corson (Ed.) Ethology and Non-verbal Communication in Mental Health. Elmsford, NY: Pergamon, 1980.
9 Cain, A.O. A study of pets in the family system. In A.H. Katcher and A.M. Beck (Eds) *New Perspectives on Our Lives with Companion Animals*. Philadelphia: University of Pensylvania Press, 1983.
10 Beck, A.M. and Katcher, A.H. A new look at pet-facilitated therapy. *Journal of the American Veterinary Medical Association*, 184(4), 414–421, 1984.
11 Zasloff, R.L. and Kidd, A.H. Attachment to feline companions. *Psychological Reports*, 74, 747–752, 1992(a).

12 Mugford, R.A. and M'Comisky, J. Some recent work on the psychotherapeutic value of cage birds with old people. In R.S. Anderson (Ed.) *Pet Animals and Society*. London: Bailliere Tindall, pp. 54–65, 1974.

13 Endenberg, N. The attachment of people to companion animals. *Anthrozoos*, 8(2), 83–89, 1995.

14 Zasloff, R.L. Measuring attachment to companion animals: A dog is not a cat is not a bird. *Applied Animal Behaviour Science*, 47(1–2), 43–48, 1996.

15 Doogan, S. and Thomas, G.V. Origins of fear of dogs in adults and children: The role of conditioning processes and prior familiarity with dogs. *Behaviour Research and Therapy*, 30(4), 389–394, 1992.

16 Albert, A. and Bulcroft, K. Pets and urban life. *Anthrozoos*, 1(1), 9–25, 1987.

17 Zasloff, A.L. and Kidd, A.H., 1992a, op.cit.

18 Bergler, R. and Loewy, D. Singles and their cats. Paper presented at the 6th International Conference on Human–Animal Interactions, Animals & Us, Montreal, 1992.

19 Archer, J. and Winchester, J. Bereavement following death of a pet. *British Journal of Psychology*, 85, 259–271, 1994. Carmack, J. The effects on family members and functioning after death of a pet. *Marriage and Family Reviews*, 8, 149–161, 1985.

20 Gerwolls, M.K. and Labott, S.M. Adjustment to the death of companion animal. *Anthrozoos*, 7, 172–187, 1994.

21 Laungani, P. Patterns of bereavement in Indian and English society. Paper presented at the Fourth International Conference on Grief and Bereavement in Contemporary Society, Stockholm, Sweden, 12–16 June, 1994.

22 Stallones, L., Johnson, T.P., Garrity, T.F. and Marx, M.B. Quality of attachment to companion animals among US adults 21 to 64 years of age. *Anthrozoos*, 3, 171–176, 1990.

23 Katcher, A.H. Interactions between people and their pets: Form and function. In B. Fogle (Ed.) *Interrelations Between People and Their Pets*. Springfield, IL: Charles C. Thomas, 1981.

24 Katcher, A. H., Friedmann, E., Goodman, M. and Goodman, I. Men, women and dogs. *Californian Veterinarian*, 2, 14–16, 1983.

25 Hirsch-Pasek, K and Treiman, R. Doggerel: Motherese in a new context. *Journal of Child Language*, 9, 229–237, 1982.

26 Serpell, J.A. Evidence for an association between pet behaviour and owner attachment levels. *Applied Animal Behaviour Science*, 47, 49–60, 1996.

27 Serpell, J.A. 1996, op.cit.

28 Veevers, J.E. The social meaning of pet: Alternative roles for companion animals. In B. Sussman (Ed.) *Pets and the Family*. New York: Haworth Press, pp. 11–29, 1985.

29 Cain, A.O. A study of pets in the family system. In A.H. Katcher and A. M Beck (Eds) *New Perspectives on Our Lives with Companion Animals*. Philadelphia: University of Pensylvania Press, pp. 72–81, 1983.

30 Albert, A. and Bulcroft, K. 1987, op.cit.

31 Barker, S.B. and Barker, R.T. The human–canine bond; Closer than family tier. *Journal of Mental Health Counselling*, 10(1), 46–56, 1988.

32 Smith, S.L. Interactions between pet dogs and family members: An ethological study. In A.H. Katcher and A.M. Beck (Eds) *New Perspectives on Our Lives with Companion Animals*. Philadelphia: University of Pennsylvania Press, pp. 29–36, 1983.

33 Templer, D.F., Salter, D., Dickey, S. Baldwin, L. and Velebar, D. The construction of a pet attitude scale. *Psychological Record*, 31, 343–348, 1981. Katcher, A.H. et

al., 1983, op.cit. Holcomb, R., Williams, R.C and Richards, P.S. The elements of attachment: Relationship maintenance and intimacy. *Journal of the Delta Society*, 2, 28–34, 1985. Poresky, R.H., Hendrix, C., Mosier, J.E., and Samuelson, M.L. The companion animal bonding scale: Internal reliability and construct validity. *Psychological Reports*, 60, 743–746, 1987.

34 Holcomb, R. et al., 1985, op.cit.

35 Voith, V.L., 1985, op.cit.

36 Stallones, L., Marx, M.B., Barrity, T.F. and Johnson, T.P. Attachment to companion animals among older pet owners. *Anthrozoos*, 2, 118–124, 1988.

37 Zasloff, R.L. and Kidd, A.H. Loneliness and pet ownership among single women. *Psychological Reports*, 75, 747–752, 1994b.

38 Voith, V.L., 1985, op.cit.

39 Podberscek, A.L. and Blackshaw, J.K. Reasons for liking and choosing a cat as a pet. *Australian Veterinary Journal*, 65, 332–333, 1988.

40 Serpell, J.A. Beneficial effects of pet ownership on some aspects of human health and behaviour. *Journal of the Royal Society of Medicine*, 84, 717–720, 1991.

41 Zasloff, R.L. and Kidd, A. H. 1994b, op.cit.

42 Horn, J.C. and Meer, J. The pleasure of their company. *Psychology Today*, August, 52–57, 1984. Serpell, J.A. *In the Company of Animals*. New York: Blackwells, 1986.

43 Zasloff, R.L. and Kidd, A.H. 1994b, op.cit.

44 Beck, A.M. and Katcher, A.H. A new look at pet-facilitated therapy. *Journal of the American Veterinary Medical Association*, 184(4), 414–421, 1983

45 Bowlby, J., 1969, op.cit. Bowlby, J. *Attachment and Loss*, Vol.2.: *Separation Anxiety and Anger*. London: Hogarth Press.

46 Bowlby, J. The making and breaking of affectional bonds. *British Journal of Psychiatry*, 130, 270, 1977.

47 Rynearson, E.K. Humans and pets and attachment. *British Journal of Psychiatry*, 133, 550–555, 1978.

48 Rynearson, E.K., 1978, op.cit.

49 Smith, S.L.,1979, op.cit.

50 Mugford, R.A. and M'Comisky, J., 1974, op.cit. Friedmann, E., Katcher, A.H., Lynch, J.J., and Thomas, S.A. Animal companions and one-year survival of patients after discharge from a coronary care unit. *Public Health Reports*, 95, 307–312, 1980.

51 Tuber, D.S., Hothersall, D., and Voith, V.L. Animal clinical psychology: A modest proposal. *Annals of Psychology*, 22, 762–766, 1974. Voith, V.L., 1975, op.cit.

Chapter 4
Who is in control?

Owning a pet is a responsibility. To get the most out of the relationship, it is essential that owners understand their companion animals' needs, whether it be a dog, cat, bird or more exotic species. Whilst it is the owner's responsibility to care for the pet, he/she must not be too permissive and allow the animal to behave in any way it chooses. At the same time, owners should not be too severe. Some animals are more robust, psychologically, than are others. Too strict a disciplinary regime may turn an already neurotic pet into a nervous wreck.

It is important to realize that pets can both define and restrict your lifestyle. Having a dog, for example, means that you have got to be prepared to create opportunities for it to have the exercise it needs. Rural areas are better for dogs than urban areas because there are more wide-open spaces for them to run. For urban dwellers who choose to share their lives with a dog, it is probably better to live in a house with a garden or close to a park.

Pet owners have also got to be prepared to tolerate the consequences of keeping a pet. The inside of the home may be covered in dog hairs or cat fur. Bird cages and fish tanks need to be cleaned out periodically. Windows may be smeared with nose marks because both dogs and cats like to peer out of the window. When young and before they are properly house trained such pets may deposit faeces in unwelcome places. Puppies like to chew on soft furnishings and kittens are likely to claw curtains and seat covers. Nervous cats may spray urine against vertical objects to mark their territory in the home, and dogs that are kept locked up on their own for too long will cause all kinds of damage in a desperate attempt to seek attention.

The way people treat their pets is probably influenced by their perception of its position in their household. In most instances, pets are valued members of the household.[1] Very often, in fact, pets are regarded as a member of the family. This perception has been found to be almost universally present among dog and cat owners.[2] If pets are perceived to have lower status than family members, this may be reflected in the way they are treated. Equally, even with the status of a family member, their treatment will depend crucially on the style of disciplinary practice used by the homeowner or head of household with the rest of the family. This may be good news or bad news for the pet depending on whether, for example, the parent(s) in a particular household are rigid, authoritarian disciplinarians or adopt a more relaxed or democratic style of behavioural control.

A pet must be protected. Whilst obedience training can help it to mature to some extent, there is a limit. Some people believe that a pet should be allowed to live as natural a life as possible, to reproduce freely, and to roam and hunt as it pleases, be it a dog or a cat, or sometimes some other species. However, this 'ideal' may be in the best interests of neither the pet nor the owner, nor indeed the wider community.

When popular dog trainer, Barbara Woodhouse, once stated that there were 'no bad dogs, only bad owners', she gave voice to a commonly accepted stereotype: that of the permissive, over-indulgent owner with an unruly and badly behaved pet.[3] To some extent, such views were also tacitly endorsed by the dog-breeding community, because they helped to deflect attention from the behavioural problems inherent in some breeds.[4] No pet should be allowed to roam free today, for its own safety and for many other social and ecological reasons. How well particular animals can adapt to a restricted lifestyle can depend on a range of factors including the type of breed, owner's lifestyle, owner's attitude to animals and pet care, and the physical environment provided for the animal. Selective breeding to make animals more adaptable is one solution but is tinged with ethical reservations.

Much of the evidence linking dog behaviour problems with aspects of the owner's behaviour, attitudes or personality has tended to be anecdotal or inconclusive. Trainers and animal behaviour counsellors (or therapists) often assume, for example, that owners who 'spoil' their pets – i.e. allow them to get their own way – or who treat them like people, are more likely to cause, or contribute to, the development of behaviour problems than owners who are less acquiescent or anthropomorphic. It has also been proposed that particular types of dog–owner interaction, such as allowing the dog to 'win' in competitive games, feeding it before the owner's mealtimes, or allowing it to sleep in the bedroom or on the bed, may help to increase the likelihood of dominance-related problems.[5] One research study, for example, detected a statistical relationship between the occurrence of dominance aggression and the owner's degree of emotional attachment to the dog, as measured by his or her tendency to allow the animal to sleep in the bedroom, or to feed it tit-bits or specially prepared food.[6] Elsewhere, a large survey of American pet owners failed to find any significant association between dog owners' anthropomorphic attitudes or 'spoiling' activities and the prevalence of behaviour problems.[7]

It is possible, however, that dog owners vary not only in the way they treat their pets, but also in terms of what they perceive as problematic behaviour. Owners who spoil their dogs may also be more likely to let them get away with behaviour that less tolerant owners would frown upon. Although being very strict with a pet to the point where violent means are used to control behaviour is unlikely to engender a positive relationship between animal and owner, an overly loose style of behaviour control may be just as bad. If the animal interprets a *laissez-faire* disciplinary style as weakness on the part of its owner, it may attain the upper hand in all kinds of situations. The poor owner will be rendered unable to control the animal at home or anywhere else. Training in obedience may cultivate a respect for the owner that will encourage the pet to behave properly without having to be constantly shouted at. Treating a pet like a member of the family is all very well but, as with other family members, the animal must learn to follow the rules of the household.

Owners' lack of knowledge or experience of dogs is also commonly considered to be a contributory factor in the aetiology of behaviour problems,[8] although one survey found no statistically significant associations between the prevalence of problems and the amount of dog-owning experience of owners.[9] The value of formal obedience training as a means of controlling behaviour problems has also been questioned. But scientific evidence has emerged on more than one occasion to indicate a reduced prevalence of behaviour problems in dogs which received formal obedience training.[10]

Despite the popular idea that dog owners are often responsible in some way for their animals' behaviour problems, the scientific evidence is scarce and contradictory. Some studies have failed to detect any links between the quality of the owner–dog relationship and the occurrence of behaviour problems, whereas others suggest that some behaviour problems may be associated with certain aspects of owner personality, attitudes and or behaviour.

A retrospective analysis of findings from a sample of 737 dogs to investigate the association between the prevalence of different behaviour problems and various aspects of either owner behaviour or owner–dog interactions showed relationships between obedience training and reduced prevalence of competitive aggression, separation-related problems, and escaping and roaming. There were further relationships between the timing of dogs' mealtimes and the occurrence of territorial-type aggression; between sleeping close to the owner and increased prevalence of competitive aggression and separation-related problems; and between first-time ownership and the prevalence of dominance-type aggression, separation-related problems, fear of loud noises, and various manifestations of excitability. There were also relationships between owners' initial reasons for acquiring a dog and the prevalence of dominance-type, competitive and territorial aggression. This study found more frequent behaviour problems in dogs belonging to first-time owners.[11]

There may be a number of reasons for this. First-time owners may lack experience of handling and communicating effectively with dogs, and their inappropriate responses to canine behaviour patterns and signals may, inadvertently, help to initiate problem behaviour.[12] Another difficulty first-time owners have is a lack of experience in selecting a dog. The expression of many behaviour patterns involves strong genetic influences,[13] and inexperienced owners may be less aware of breed differences in behaviour, and less sensitive to possible inherited problems.

In relation to possessive aggression, separation-related defecation and urination, and escaping and roaming, owners of obedience-trained animals reported fewer behaviour problems. This would imply that either owners who opt for obedience training tend to perceive their pets' behaviour as less problematical, or that obedience training does actually help to ameliorate these kinds of problems.

Reports have emerged of a reduction in aggression in dogs undergoing obedience training,[14] and obedience training can help to reduce separation-related anxiety.[15] In both cases, the differences are attributed to qualitative changes in the relationship between the dog and the owner. The anomalously high prevalence of over-excitement and disobedience in dogs who underwent formal, as against informal, obedience training was probably due to the use of formal training as a means to control these problems. Formal obedience training is commonly recommended for dogs showing over-excitement and owners tend to take their dogs to obedience classes because they perceive them to be exceptionally disobedient and over-excitable.[16] If this interpretation is correct, the present findings suggest that formal training may not in fact be an effective treatment for this particular type of problem.

In general, social dominance in groups of wild dogs involves priority of access to important resources such as food or sleeping sites.[17] This fact has prompted some behaviour counsellors to propose that the timing of a dog's meals relative to the owner's mealtimes, the tendency to allow the dog to 'win' in competitive games, as well as the proximity of the dog to the owner while sleeping, may all contribute to the development of owner-directed dominance aggression.[18] James Serpell found no evidence that feeding dogs before their owner's mealtimes contributes to the prevalence of dominance-type aggression. He did, however, detect significantly more territorial aggression in dogs fed consistently after their owners. Differences in general arousal may offer a possible explanation for this finding, although making a dog wait for its dinner may also increase its perception of the value of the food resource, and hence its tendency to defend that resource from possible intruders.[19]

With respect to sleeping arrangements, it has been suggested that a dog which is allowed or encouraged to sleep close to the owner may develop an unbalanced attachment to that person, and react adversely to separation. It seems equally plausible to argue that the owner has been forced to accept an over-attached canine sleeping partner in order to avoid nocturnal separation-related problems.

Some pets react badly to changed family circumstances. Few dogs will adapt well to being left alone in an empty house while all its occupants go out to work or school. Such animals may become home wreckers, bark excessively or misbehave in other unpleasant ways.

Control over Pets

In developing a controlling manner with a pet, early handling experiences are important. Proper care and attention in the crucial early days may produce an animal that is more stress resistant in later life. Certainly, this last observation is true with dogs, cats and rodents. Early socialization experiences can shape later behaviour. Pups that have no contact with their own species during their first few weeks of life show a marked preference for contact with human beings in later life.

Gail Clark and William Boyer assessed the effects of obedience training and canine behaviour counselling on the relationship between humans and dogs.[20] Thirty adult participants provided perceptions of their dog's behaviour and were then randomly assigned to one of three groups: the Obedience group, which received obedience training and canine behaviour counselling; the Time-instructed group, which was asked to spend 20 minutes a day interacting with their dog; the No-instruction group, which did not receive any instructions.

After assignment, the Obedience group completed an eight-week obedience and canine behaviour counselling class where all the participants again provided information about their dog's behaviour. In addition, all participants were asked to keep daily logs of the time spent with their dogs in training, play, exercise and other activities. A video camera was used to obtain pre-test and post-test measures of obedience behaviour, proximity, tactile behaviour and separation anxiety exhibited by each dog.

Owners and dogs were observed in a 3m by 6m room on five occasions. Measures were taken of the extent to which the dog stayed close to the owner. Tactile behaviour between the two was also measured. Separation anxiety was gauged by the dog's behaviour when the owner left the room – such as pawing and scratching the door, barking or whining.

Obedience classes were provided on a weekly basis. All classes were 90 minutes long. Training took place in a large room. Reinforcement such as food and praise was used for correct responses from the dog.

The dogs had to complete exercises on sitting, lying down, staying and coming to the owner. Outside classes, owners in the obedience condition were instructed to work with their dog for 15 to 20 minutes a day on the exercises. The Time-instructed group were told to spend 20 minutes a day interacting with their dogs.

Results indicated that the Obedience group showed the most improved obedience behaviour and the highest improvement in the human–canine relationship. The Obedience group also showed lower separation anxiety than the No-instruction group. Contrary to expectation, the Time-instructed group also displayed improvement in obedience behaviour and improvement in the relationship. The Time-instructed group showed lower separation anxiety than the No-instruction group. The No-instruction group revealed higher separation anxiety, no improvement in obedience and no change in the relationship.

The animals in the obedience group demonstrated a more significant improvement in their obedience performance than did dogs in either the Time-instructed or No-instruction groups. Participants in the obedience group reported fewer behavioural problems with the animals.

Treating the Pet Like Another Person

Various types of relationship can emerge between pets and their owners. Very often the pet fulfils a special need for the owner and vice versa. With dogs, a common problem is that the owners go out to work and leave the dog alone in the house during the day. Such social deprivation may produce all kinds of psychological and behavioural problems in the animal as time goes by.

Keeping a pet to fulfil some emotional need for companionship, security, protection, status and so on is ethically acceptable provided that, in the relationship with the pet, the animal does not suffer physically or psychologically. Failure to feed the animal a proper diet, or indulgence to the point where the animal becomes over-dependent or undisciplined and unstable, and potentially dangerous to other people or children, can produce all kinds of problems and a generally unhappy animal and owner.

People often have illusory and unreal expectations about companion animals, knowing and caring little about their basic needs or natural behavioural tendencies. Dogs like to bark and to roam. They do not like to be left in the house on their own for long periods. Cats like to claw furniture and sometimes to spray in certain parts of the house. Human expectations can get in the way of appreciating the animal for itself independent of the owner's needs and demands.

Some pet owners buy non-essential accoutrements for their pets, and treat the animals like little people.[21] This is perfectly acceptable, so long as it is not carried too far. Many animals treated in this way may thrive.

There is more concern when people become too strongly attached to their pets and depend upon them for emotional fulfilment and satisfaction. In some cases, a pathological over-attachment to the pet can develop. Such individuals may over-indulge their animal companion, dominating and smothering it. Others may find themselves being controlled by the animal who, on becoming accustomed to having exclusive attention, will accept nothing less.

The tendency for some owners to treat their companion animals as if they were people is illustrated in the way they often talk to their pets. Female dog owners, for example, have been observed to use the kind of language when speaking to their dogs, sometimes referred to as 'doggerel', which resembles that used by mothers in speaking to children, sometimes known as 'motherese'. The structural properties of doggerel have been found to bear striking similarities to those of motherese.[22] Elsewhere, it has been found that people may attribute to their pets characteristics they would also associate with people, such as love and jealousy. The great majority of cat and dog owners are able to infer such emotions in their pets from the way the animals behave in different situations.[23]

There seem to be mixed views about whether treating a pet as another person is a good idea or not. It all probably depends on the degree to which such anthropomorphic behaviour is carried out. Owners are often advised by professionals and others whose occupation brings them into frequent contact with dogs that one should never treat a dog like a person because such dogs will develop serious behaviour problems. Owners are advised, for example, never to let a dog sleep on the bed or feed it snacks because spoiling the animal in this way will create behaviour problems later on.

At least one writer has disagreed with this point of view: 'I do not believe there is much wrong in an owner being somewhat anthropomorphic in his or her regard for the pet since there is now good scientific evidence to support the contention of many owners that cats and dogs have emotions and sensations comparable to our own – fear, pain, anxiety, jealousy, guilt, joy, depression, anger' (p.38).[24] Apparently similar brain centres underpin such emotional states in man and cats and dogs.[25]

One study was conducted to find out whether dogs that were treated like a person or that had not been obedience trained were more likely to exhibit problem behaviour, as reported by their owners. A survey of dog owners asked them about the way they treated their pets, whether the animal had had any formal obedience training, and whether it had displayed difficult behaviour.[26]

Problem behaviours were not shown to be associated with a lack of formal training and a tendency by the owner to treat the dog as another person. Owners who spoiled their dogs did not experience more trouble with their pets than anyone else. Anthropomorphic behaviours included sharing food with their dog, taking the dog along on trips or errands, and providing extra creature comforts for the animal.

Dominance in Pets

When a person acquires a pet, there is generally an expectation that their future relationship will be a happy one. For the majority of pet owners, this is true. A close bond may be formed between owner and animal to the benefit of them both. Unfortunately, this happy outcome does not always occur.[27]

There may be a number of reasons for the failure of the relationship between pets and owners. Feeding and care of the animal may pose an unexpectedly severe burden upon owners, the animal may compete more than was anticipated with the social and business commitments of the owner, or the behaviour of the animal may cause problems for the owner, the owner's family or neighbours. One study was of 125 dog owners and five cat owners in London who had been referred to the researcher by vets. Some referrals were because vets were concerned about owners' attitudes regarding their pets, others because owners wanted to have their pet put down or neutered because of behavioural problems.[28] One of the key sources of problems is centred on how well the pet has been disciplined and who between pet and owner has control.

There are occasions when the pet gains the upper hand and can become the controlling influence in the household. This phenomenon has been observed to occur with dogs for instance. The genetic predisposition of an individual dog, combined with how specific people have related to it, can result in the dog assuming a dominant role with respect to one, several, or sometimes all family members. A dominant dog may be completely non-aggressive towards strangers yet frequently threaten family members. Such a dog asserts itself in many ways. A dominant animal insists on primary access to food, sleeping places, right of way, objects of interest, or favourite individuals.

The dominant dog refuses to obey commands; it interprets commands as threats and reciprocates with a threat. An order from an owner, usually accompanied by a direct look at the dog, frequently escalates into a growling confrontation with the owner often backing down, thus confirming the dog's dominant position. The dog objects by growling on being disturbed, insists on access to favoured areas, resists being displaced from its resting place (which may be the seat or bed of the owner), will not relinquish objects, often objects to prolonged petting, frequently violently objects to being hugged, and refuses to lie down on command. If the dog did obey any of these commands, it would be complying with a submissive animal's role. Instead, the dominant dog objects. It does so with threats, growls or by biting until its owner backs down.

This situation does not have to occur. Owners can take steps to ensure that their relationship with the animal is positive and caring, but with the pet developing a healthy respect for the owner's ultimate dominance within the household. Problems can arise in the way many owners relate to dogs when they are puppies. They often treat the animal as a person or a child, and as a result the lines of reasoning they use in trying to cope with problematic situations and behaviours do not work. People who are given pets for therapeutic reasons or as a prophylactic measure to combat loneliness may be even more likely than the general populace to find themselves playing the role of a submissive individual relative to a dog. Such a situation is best dealt with by the owner. Owners should routinely interact with the dog in a way that sustains the dominance of the owner.

There are a number of useful tips for obedience training with dogs. Owners should practice obedience tasks several times a week, and rarely give a dog anything for nothing in return. Thus, when feeding, make the dog sit and then make a fuss of it when it obeys. The food then also becomes part of the reward for behaving in a desired way, and is bound up with the receipt of affection from the owner. Another ploy is periodically to take objects way from the dog, and then praise it for being non-aggressive, before returning the object to the dog. Now and again, the owner should displace the dog from a resting place, especially when it is somewhere people would normally rest. Again, the dog should be praised for complying without reacting in a threatening or aggressive way. Owners should also restrain the dog from time to time, and push it over onto its side or back and hold it down for a few moments in a submissive and vulnerable position. This serves further to reinforce the owner's physical dominance over the animal.

Owners should learn to 'read' their dogs' behaviour. They should be able to anticipate in advance when the dog is likely to solicit attention. The owner should then require the dog to sit or lie down – both submissive postures – before giving attention. This again follows the basic principle of not giving anything for nothing. More positive relationships have been observed to occur between owners and their dogs when the owners develop an understanding of their dogs' thought processes, emotional reactions to situations, and their unique personalities.[29]

Destructive Behaviour

Another of the leading problems owners have with dogs involves the destruction by the dog of household items, or even the house itself; excessive whining, howling, or barking; and defecating when the owner is absent from the house. Histories of such cases usually reveal a dog that has been almost constantly with the owner and rarely left alone in its early years, but which then through a set of changed circumstances is left alone for long periods.

Treatment of this problem involves getting the animal progressively accustomed to longer and longer periods without the owner being present. Within the first week the owner has acquired the dog, he or she should begin leaving it for very short periods of time. Initially, this might be for just a minute or two. Gradually, the period of absence should get longer, eventually up to several hours. It is also helpful to provide the dog with an indestructible or slowly destructible chew toy for those periods for which the owner is absent. In addition, if the dog does start howling or barking at the door upon the owner's return, the owner should be quiet and not enter until the dog stops the undesirable activity for at least 15 consecutive seconds. If the owner were to enter while the dog was in the midst of engaging in undesirable behaviour, the dog would associate the owner's return with the behaviour. The behaviour would therefore be reinforced.

In the end, problems with dogs can be traced to the owner's attitude towards the animal and the nature of the relationship which the owner has allowed to develop with it. Evidence has emerged that obedience training which uses the kinds of techniques referred to already in this chapter can reduce behaviour problems in dogs, such as excessive attention seeking, aggressiveness and destructive tendencies. Obedience training on the part of owners results in pets which display fewer problem behaviours, reduced separation anxiety, and a more immediate response to the owner's commands.[30] Whilst it is important that owners care for and show affection towards their animal companion, neither pet nor owner should lose sight of who is ultimately in control.[31]

Trouble with Cats

Cat owners may have problems too. The most common cat behaviour problems are urine spraying, urinating and defecating in inappropriate places. Not only do these pets stop using the litter box, but they may select items of clothing to eliminate upon. These behaviours are frequently associated with environmental events in the household.

Spraying is a method of urinating by a cat while standing with its tail held straight up and quivering. The cat ejects the urine backwards onto a vertical surface. Spraying is a form of territorial marking and communication. Male cats are most likely to spray, but females may also do so. Spraying is most likely to occur in an environment where there are several cats, or when there has been a dramatic change in the living situation such as a house move, acquisition of a new pet, the presence of a visitor, placement of new furniture, and if someone in the household does not like the cat or the cat does not like a member of the household.

Some cats, male as well as female, react to these environmental situations by urinating in a squatting position or defecating in various locations of the house. It is interesting that cats often eliminate on items belonging to people whom the cat does not particularly like.

Cats' relationships with their owners may often depend on how much time they spend together. The closeness of the relationship is affected by the owner's disposition towards the cat. Cats are sensitive to whether people like them or not. They also develop their own people preferences. Whether the cat is permitted to live indoors or is made to stay outdoors most of the time need not adversely affect the relationship the animal establishes with its owners, but the amount of time the owner is present at home does seem to make a difference. Owners who are at home more often will tend to establish a closer bond with their cat.[32]

Fear of Animals

We have seen that pets are generally treated as friends or even as part of the family. Adult pet owners often refer to their pet as being like a child, whilst children may regard a pet on the same basis as a brother or sister. We may look upon our own domestic pet as a trusted and loyal companion who will not only provide comfort and support when we are troubled, but also will look after us or protect us from danger. In contrast with this experience, animals that are unknown to us or with which we do not have a close relationship can be a source of fear. It is known, for example, that animals such as snakes, lions and tigers are among the things children are most likely to say they fear.[33] It is not only wild animals, known for their big teeth, sharp claws and poisonous fangs, that cause fear in children. Even animals kept as domestic pets, most especially dogs, are also frequently mentioned as something to be afraid of. Very often, these fears remain with us even after we have left childhood behind. Most adults who are afraid of dogs report that their fears began while they were children.[34]

Fear of animals has been offered a number of explanations by psychologists and psychoanalysts. Freudian theory links this kind of fear to the Oedipus complex. This theory applies to sons who fear their fathers will retaliate for an allegedly incestuous desire they have for their mothers. During the oral stage of development while the child is still being breast fed, sons supposedly fear being eaten because they feel guilt about their desire to eat (or bite) their mother's breast. This Oedipal triangle must eventually be resolved as the child matures, otherwise residual anxieties stemming from these primitive fears of the father may persist and become manifest in other ways later in life – perhaps through projection onto animals, which come to be regarded as dangerous.[35] The Oedipal theory focuses principally upon the sources of anxiety among sons. It is less clear how such a theory might be used to explain fear of animals among girls.

Behavioural psychologists offer a different kind of explanation for children's fear of animals. Such fears are believed to be triggered through the association of an animal (e.g. a dog) with a traumatic experience. This experience would not necessarily have to take the form of actually being bitten by an animal. Loud barking, for example, could frighten a young child especially when he/she has had no previous contact with dogs. Barking would represent a strange noise perhaps signifying possible danger.[36]

Jungian analysts explain our fear of animals as a vestigial reaction left over from our primitive ancestors' fears of animal predators which posed real dangers and a threat to survival. During such times, wolf packs represented such a real danger. The descendants of wolves, now tamed as domestic pets, may still invoke primal fears which have been inherited over the generations, and persist within us despite the relative safety of modern society.[37]

Bad experiences with dogs may not be sufficient to explain why some of us are frightened by them. People who have no fear of dogs may report as many painful or frightening encounters as do people who are very afraid of dogs.[38] Thus simple conditioning of fear through association with bad experiences does not entirely explain fear of dogs. Nor may it be enough to explain why a traumatic incident with a dog gives rise to a long-lasting fear. Indeed, some people develop a phobia about dogs even though they have not had a bad experience themselves.

A survey of university students and children in Birmingham, England found that those individuals who were afraid of dogs had generally had less contact with dogs prior to the onset of their fear than was true of respondents who reported no fear of dogs. Adults who were fearful of dogs were much more likely than those who felt comfortable around dogs to express fears of being bitten, a dog jumping up, loud barking, sudden movements by dogs, and dogs snapping, snarling or growling. Children who were afraid of dogs were also more worried about dogs snapping or growling. Children who feared dogs were also more likely to report being warned by their parents to stay away from strange dogs.[39]

High-fear adults were less willing to approach and stroke a friendly dog, whereas high-fear children were less likely to display such apprehension. Evidence emerged to suggest that a lack of exposure to dogs was linked to apprehensive reactions. In contrast, prior positive experiences with dogs might inoculate a person against developing dog phobia even after a traumatic experience with an aggressive, unfriendly animal.

Further evidence seemed to indicate that bad experiences with dogs produced enduring fear only in certain susceptible individuals. People who were afraid of dogs also exhibited anxieties about a variety of other things and situations. However, children who were afraid of dogs were no more likely than any of their peers who did not fear dogs to show fear of other animals. Further, dog-fearful children were more likely than dog-fearful adults to recognize the attractiveness of a family dog. Adults with dog phobia were generally reluctant to go near even a friendly dog, as noted earlier. In conclusion, the available evidence suggests that whilst adult fear of dogs usually starts in childhood, not all dog-fearing children grow up to become dog-fearing adults. It is not yet entirely understood why some children lose these fears as they grow up, whereas others do not. Uneventful or positive experiences with dogs might be one explanation, but we do not yet understand why such experiences rid only some children of their fear of dogs.

Are Pets Parasites?

Another aspect of the question of who is in control – the pet or its owner – is a debate about whether pets are really nothing more than parasites who live off their owners without offering any significant return. Some writers have argued that from a strict Darwinian perspective, pet keeping could be classified as maladaptive behaviour. For one species, in this case humans, to privilege another – pets – in an inequitable fashion could be regarded as 'fitness reducing'.[40] People have been observed to form strong attachments to their pet companions. It is argued that pets provide a source of comfort, companionship, loyalty and affection. They can have health-promoting benefits, both physically and psychologically, for their owners. But keeping pets incurs certain costs. Pets have to be fed, given veterinary care and, in some cases, exercised. Owners may have to tolerate damage to their homes caused by young animals and, where the relationship becomes overly mutually dependent, a demanding animal may continue to display costly behavioural problems throughout its life. Psychologist John Archer offers the position that pets can be viewed as manipulating humans. Whilst they first captivate human emotions through their baby features as young animals, they then require varying degrees of care and attention over many years.

How beneficial or detrimental pet ownership in the end turns out to be for people who maintain animal companions depends upon the nature of the relationship. If the relationship is truly symbiotic, then there may be mutual benefits for both species. If these benefits exceed the costs of keeping a pet, the relationship can be regarded as one of mutualism. If the costs and benefits to humans are about equal, it represents a relationship known as commensalism. If, on the other hand, the costs outweigh the benefits, the relationship is parasitism. In other words, pets are parasites who gain benefits for themselves, whilst incurring costs for their human hosts.

Though some writers point to the pleasure people derive from their pets,[41] such feelings by themselves provide no benefits in a Darwinian sense.[42] They do not enhance the fitness of the species to survive. Archer argues that pets manipulate the human species. Although this manipulation may not involve conscious intent, it does nevertheless represent a behavioural pattern designed to bring fitness benefits to the pet rather than to the human host.

What is the Purpose of Attachment?

If pet owners are manipulated by their pets, who represent little more than social parasites, what mechanisms underpin this process? In other cases of parasitic behaviour among animal species, the parasite finds a way of fooling the host that it is actually a member of the host species. In some instances, it is not necessary for the parasite to take on a similar form to the host. Often social parasites are quite different in appearance from the species off which they are living. Sometimes the host species is programmed to respond in a fixed way to specified signals from its own young. If the parasite can mimic these signals, this tactic alone will be suffi-cient to ensure it is treated as a member of the host species. Thus, reed warbler parents will respond by supplying food to any gaping bill in its nest. A cuckoo chick will therefore be fed the same way as a reed warbler chick by opening its bill in the presence of the reed warbler parent.[43]

In another form of social parasitism involving ants and the beetle *Atemeles pubicollis*, the beetle, despite its larger size, will be accepted into the ant nest and cared for because it releases imitation pheromones which control the social behaviour of the host species.[44]

In both of the above examples, the gaping bill of the cuckoo chick and the chemical stimulation of the ant colony by the beetle, host behav-iour is controlled by a simple set of stimuli, known as 'social releasers'. Are there social releasers produced by pets which control the behaviour of human hosts?

The possible existence of social releasers in humans has been debated for a long time. There is agreement that humans respond in a parental way to certain sets of facial and bodily features. Konrad Lorenz originally suggested that these features – a large forehead, large and low-lying eyes, chubby cheeks, short and thick limbs, and clumsy movements – were the human equivalents of the social releasers found in other animals.[45] The young of most bird and mammal species share the same features – thus humans find one-day old chicks, kittens and puppies cute. This mechanism has also been invoked to explain why we are attracted to cartoon characters such as Bambi and Mickey Mouse and to cuddly toys such as teddy bears.[46] Lorenz also suggested that the same facial configuration forms the basis of human attraction to those pets we treat like children. The big baby-like eyes of the young of certain breeds of dog, for example, may play a key part in enhancing their attractiveness to human owners.

There are other characteristics that can influence the acceptability of pets in addition to evidence of baby-like features. A range of background features make some animals acceptable and others not. People tend to choose animals of a certain size and intelligence. Mammals are a popular choice because they are warm blooded and better to the touch. There is also a preference for animals with fur. Furless animals are less appealing, possibly because hairlessness is a fairly recent feature of human evolution.

There are animals who look cute with baby features but cannot be kept as pets because they would be too difficult to look after or would not settle into a human home environment. Examples here might include pandas, penguins and owls. Another important factor about pets is that they must be active at the same time of day that we are.[47] They must be house trained so as not to urinate or defecate in the house, or attack their owners or anyone else who might visit their hosts. Pets must be tame and able to be trained.[48]

The most popular pets are creatures capable of getting in tune psychologically with their human hosts. Dogs and cats, for example, may display emotions and moods that resemble those of humans. They can find ways of appealing to their owners. Dogs show obvious signs of affection and attachment to their owners, and are very attentive to them.[49] Cats are more independent, but many still like to be stroked and petted by their owners. Pets therefore appear to devise ways of appealing to their owners and through this process may in a sense control their human hosts. The most popular pets are those that have been most successful in adapting to the human host environment and reading the needs and expectations of their owners.

Pets are not just favoured companions, they are a responsibility. They need to be cared for, but also trained to behave in appropriate ways while they share our homes with us. Keeping pets therefore can incur certain costs. According to some commentators, the costs of pet keeping outweigh the benefits and thus pets can be considered as little better than parasites. In strict Darwinian terms, pet keeping does not enhance our fitness as a species. In contrast with this school of thought, however, is evidence that has accumulated around the world to show that pets can have real positive benefits. In particular, sharing our lives with animal companions can be good for our physical and psychological health. In the next two chapters, we take a longer look at this evidence to discover if living with pets does yield net benefits.

References

1 Garrity, T.F., Stallones, L., Marx, M.B. and Johnson, T.P. Pet ownership and attachment as supportive factors in the health of the elderly. *Anthrozoos*, 3, 35–44, 1989. Ory, M.G. and Goldberg, G.L. An epidemiological study of pet ownership in the community. In R.K. Anderson, B.L. Hart and L.A Hart (Eds) The Pet Connection. Minneapolis: University of Minnesota. Soares, C.J. The companion animal in the context of the family system. In B. Sussman (Ed.) *Pets and the Family*. London: Haworth, pp. 49–62, 1985.

2 Cain, A.O. A study of pets in the family system. In A.H. Katcher and A.M. Beck (Eds) *New Perspectives on Our Lives with Companion Animals*. Philadelphia: University of Pennsylvania Press, 1983. Voith, V.L. Attachment of people to companion animals. *Veterinary Clinics of North America. Small Animals Practice*, 12, 655–663, 1985.

3 Woodhouse, B. *No Bad Dogs*, Aylesbury: Hazell Watson and Viney, 1978.

4 Serpell, J.A. *In the Company of Animals*. New York: Blackwells.
5 Hart, B.L. and Hart, L.A. Selecting the best companion animal: Breed and gender specific behavioural profiles. In R.K. Anderson, B.L. Hart and L. A. Hart (Eds) *The Pet Connection*. Minnesota: University of Minnesota., pp. 348–354, 1984. O'Farrell, V. *Dog's Best Friend: How Not To Be a Problem Owner*. London: Methuen.
6 O'Farrell, V., 1994, ibid.
7 Voith, V.L., Wright, J.C. and Danneman, P.J. Is there a relationship between canine behaviour problems and spoiling activities, anthropomorphism and obedience training. *Applied Animal Behaviour Science*, 34, 263–272, 1992.
8 Peachey, E. Problems with people. In J. Fisher (Ed.) *The Behaviour of Dogs and Cats*. London: Stanley Paul, pp. 104–112.
9 Borchelt, P.L. and Voith, V.L. Classification of animal behaviour problems. *Veterinary Clinics of North America. Small Animals Practice*, 12, 571–586, 1986.
10 Campbell, W.E. Effects of training, feeding regimens, isolation and physical environment on canine behaviour. *Modern Veterinary Practice*, 67, 339–341, 1986. Clark, G.I. and Boyer, W.N. The effects of dog obedience training and behavioural counselling upon the human–canine relationship. *Applied Animal Behaviour Science*, 37, 147–159, 1993.
11 Jagoe, A. and Serpell, J. Owner characteristics and interactions and the prevalence of canine behaviour problems. *Applied Animal Behaviour Science*, 47(1–2), 31–42, 1996.
12 Peachey, E., 1993, op.cit.
13 Murphree, O.D., Dykman, R.M. and Peters, J.E. Genetically determined abnormal behaviour in dogs: Results of behavioural tests. Conditional Reflex, 2, 199, 1967. Hart, B.L. and Hart, L.A., 1985, op.cit. Serpell, J., 1986, op.cit. 14 O'Farrell, V., 1994, op.cit. Borchelt, P.L. and Voith, V.L., 1986, op.cit.
15 Clark, G.I. and Boyer, W.N., 1993, op.cit.
16 Hart, B.L. and Hart, L.A., 1985, op.cit. O'Farrell, V., 1994, op.cit.
17 Lockwood, R. Dominance in wolves; useful construct or bad habit? In E. Klinghammer (Ed.) *The Behaviour and Ecology of Wolves*. New York: Harland STPM Press, pp. 225–244, 1979. Van Hooff, J.A. and Wensing, J.A. Dominance and its behavioural measures in a captive wolf pack. In H. Frank (Ed.) *Man and Wolf*. Dordrecht: Dr W. Junk, pp.219–251, 1987.
18 O'Farrell, V., 1994, op.cit.
19 Jagoe, A. and Serpell, J., 1996, op.cit.
20 Clark, G.I. and Boyer, W.N., 1993, op.cit.
21 Szasz, K. *Petishism: Pets and Their People in the Western World*. New York: Holt, Rinehart & Winston, 1968.
22 Hirsch-Pasek, K. and Treiman, R. Doggerel: Motherese in a new context. *Journal of Child Language*, 9, 229–237, 1982.
23 Mathes, E.W. and Deuger, D.J. Jealousy: A creation of human culture? *Psychological Reports*, 51(2), 351–354, 1982.
24 Fox, M. Relationships between the human and non-human animals. In B. Fogle (Ed.) *Interrelationships between People and Pets*. Springfield, IL: Charles C. Thomas, 1981.
25 Fox, M.W. *Understanding Your Cat*. London: Bland & Briggs, 1974a. Fox, M.W. *Understanding Your Dog*. London: Bland & Briggs, 1974b.
26 Voith, V.L. et al., 1992, op.cit.

27 Mugford, R.A. The social significance of pet ownership. In S.A. Corson and E.O. Corson (Eds) *Ethology and Non-verbal Communication in Mental Health*. Oxford: Pergamon, 1980.

28 Mugford, R. Problem dogs and problem owners: The behaviour specialist as an adjunct to veterinary practice. In B. Fogle (Ed.) *Interrelationships between People and Pets*. Springfield, IL: Charles C. Thomas, 1981.

29 Sanders, C.R. Understanding dogs: Caretakers' attributions of mindlessness in canine–human relationships. *Journal of Contemporary Ethnography*, 22(2), 205–226, 1993.

30 Clark, G.I. and Boyer, W.N., 1993, op.cit.

31 Jagoe, A. and Serpell, J., 1996, op.cit.

32 Mertens, C. Human–cat interactions in the home setting. *Anthrozoos*, 4, 214–231. 1991

33 Maurer, A. What children fear. *Journal of Genetic Psychology*, 106, 265–277, 1965.

34 Doogan, S. and Thomas, G.V. Origins of fear of dogs in adults and children: The role of conditioning processes and prior familiarity with dogs. *Behaviour Research and Therapy*, 30(4), 387–394, 1992.

35 Freud, S. Analysis of a phobia in a five year old boy. *Collected Papers*, Vol III. London: Hogarth Press, pp. 149–288, 1925.

36 Watson, J.B. *Behaviourism*. Chicago: University of Chicago Press, 1959.

37 Jung, C.G. *The Archtypes and the Collective Unconscious*. Collected Works – Bollinger Series. New York: Pantheon Books, 1962.

38 Di Nardo, P.A., Guzy, L.T., Jenkins, J.A., Bak, R.M., Tomasi, S.F. and Copland, M. Etiology and maintenance of dogs fears. *Behaviour Research and Therapy*, 1988.

39 Doogan, S. and Thomas, G.V., 1992, op.cit.

40 Archer, J. Why do people love their pets? *Evolution and Human Behaviour*, 18, 237–259, 1996.

41 Serpell, J. A., 1986, op.cit.

42 Archer, J., 1996, op.cit.

43 Davies, N.B. and Brooke, M. Cuckoos versus reed warblers: Adaptations and counteradaptations. *Animal Behaviour*, 36, 262–264, 1988

44 Wilson, E.O. *Sociobiology: The New Synthesis*. Cambridge, MA: Harvard University Press, 1975.

45 Lorenz, K. *Studies in Animal and Human Behaviour*, Vol II. London: Methuen, 1971.

46 Gould, S.J. *The Panda's Thumb*. New York: W.W. Norton, 1980. Hinde, R.A. and Barden, L.A. The evolution of the teddy bear. *Animal Behaviour*, 37, 1371–1373, 1985.

47 Serpell, J.A., 1986, op.cit.

48 Messent, P.A. and Serpell, J.A. An historical and biological view of the pet–owner bond. In B. Fogle (Ed.) *Interrelations Between People and Pets*. Springfield, IL: Charles C. Thomas, pp. 5–22, 1981.

49 Smith, S.L. Interaction between pet dog and family members: An ethological study. In A. H. Katcher and A. M. Beck (Eds) *New Perspectives on Our Lives with Companion Animals*. Philadelphia: University of Pennsylvania Press, pp. 29–36, 1983.

Chapter 5
Are pets good for our physical well-being?

Keeping pets can be good for our health. Or at least that is what a growing body of research has shown. The health benefits of living with animal companions are both physical and psychological. The precise nature of these benefits can sometimes depend upon the nature of our relationship with our pets. Close attachments represent emotional bonds which in themselves can be a source of emotional comfort. We have seen already that pets represent companions who are often regarded as members of the family. For those of us who lack emotional support from our families, a pet may provide a substitute source of affection.[1] For some owners pet ownership has benefits on a more spiritual level, serving to decrease feelings of alienation in an increasingly impersonal and fragmented, technology-driven society, and providing a closer link with nature.[2] Establishing a bond with animals enables us to regain emotional harmony and stability.[3]

Pet owners will often admit that they experience positive health benefits and subjectively feel better having a pet around. Quite apart from these personal feelings and the anecdotal evidence volunteered by pet owners, there is more objective scientific evidence that pets can help us cope with stress and that physical contact with an animal can produce measurable physiological changes such as reduced heart rate and blood pressure. Pets have also been found to help patients recover from illness after hospitalization, and have even been associated with extending the life expectancy of the old and infirm. In this chapter, we will examine evidence for the benefits pets may have on our physical well-being. The next chapter will look at how companion animals have been used in a therapeutic context to treat psychological problems.

One writer reported seven functions of companion animals which might influence physical health. Pets represented something to decrease loneliness, to care for, to keep us busy, to touch and fondle, to watch, to make us feel safe and to provide a stimulus for exercise.[4] Some of these aspects of pet involvement could have direct and immediate physical effects, while others acted indirectly upon our physical well-being by facilitating the reduction of psychological problems. The first three were expected to decrease depression and feelings of loneliness and social isolation. The second three functions would be expected to decrease anxiety. Any factor that decreases or prevents feelings of depression, anxiety, loneliness and helplessness would be likely to have a positive benefit on physical health and decrease the incidence of a broad spectrum of chronic disease including, most importantly, heart disease.

Pets, Stress and Health

One potential benefit of pet ownership, according to some writers, is that interaction with a pet can relieve stress. The evidence for this effect derives both from what pet owners themselves report about their personal experiences with their pets as well as from more direct physiological measures which have shown actual physical changes in a person to accompany contact with a companion animal.

Pet ownership can yield real clinical benefits. Several studies in the United States have indicated that pet ownership can yield positive health benefits by helping people to cope with distressing and stressful life events. The effects of pets on people's well-being are not always simple and straightforward, and often depend upon other factors in a person's life such as the degree of social support they receive from other people. Enjoying a close attachment to a companion animal certainly seems to be able to alleviate or assist in coping with emotionally distressing and painful experiences in a person's life, or with physical illness. Pet ownership *per se* is not the only important factor in this context. The nature of a person's relationship with his/her pet, as well as the type of pet, is also significant. The importance of pet ownership in relation to health-related benefits is also moderated by the extent to which the individual maintains a vibrant social network of friends and relatives from whom much social support is received. It is perhaps the significance of these variables that underlies the greater observed dependency upon and benefits obtained from pets among older than among younger people.[5]

Further research in the United States among people enrolled in a health-care programme found that pet ownership moderated the effects of stressful life events. In this survey, interviews were carried out with people who were enrolled in a Medicare health programme. Information was collected from them about potentially stressful life events they had recently experienced, how many doctor's visits they had made, and also, in the case of pet owners, about their relationship with their pets.

Compared with non-pet owners, pet owners who enjoyed a close relationship with their pets needed fewer doctor's visits and experienced fewer stress-related health problems.[6] After controlling for the sex, age, race, education, income, employment status, number of family and friends with whom contact was regularly made, and even chronic health problems, respondents with pets reported fewer doctor contacts during the past year than those without pets. Pets seemed to help their owners in times of stress. The accumulation of stressful life events was associated with increased doctor contacts for respondents without pets; however, this relationship did not emerge for pet owners. An analysis of the kinds of events which were the most likely causes of stress indicated that these mostly involved the loss of a close friend or family member in the six months or so prior to interview.

The benefits of pet ownership which respondents themselves identi-fied were that the pet provided companionship and feelings of security and affection. It would seem that distressing life events can create needs for companionship and social support which pets, to a great extent for many of these people, were able to satisfy. Often, in times of great distress, people turn to doctors for psychological support as well as for physical diagnosis and treatment. For pet owners, their companionship needs were being met at least partially by their pets. Pet owners there-fore do not seem to show such a strong need for regular contact with their physician.

The same research compared pet owners on the basis of the type of pet they had: a dog, cat or bird. Dog owners were found to experience greater health benefits from their pet than did either cat or bird owners. Dog owners, compared with cat or bird owners, spent more time outdoors with their pet, more time talking to their pet and overall spent more time with their pet. Dog owners were also generally more attached to their pet than were cat or bird owners. Dog owners were more likely than other pet owners to report that their animal made them feel secure. Other pet owners were more likely to make reference to the fact that their pet entertained them. It was clear that dog owners had a different kind of relationship with their pet from that of other pet owners. In many ways, dog owners enjoyed a deeper relationship with their animal companions that did owners of other pets.

Physiological Effects of Pets

Pets may represent a pleasant and absorbing distraction for many pet owners that are capable of reducing anxiety and other physical symptoms of stress. Interacting with a cat or dog, or contemplating an aquarium, can have a calming effect on the human system, resulting in lowered heart rate and blood pressure. Such effects may be even more powerful than conversing with another person or watching an involving television programme.[7]

Pets and Blood Pressure

What effects does pet ownership have on physiological responses such as blood pressure? Many observations have shown that both participants and experimenters believe animals are beneficial to health, but very few have measured physiological changes in owners of pets, and even fewer have made measurements in the owners' homes.[8]

In the early 1980s a pioneering study of 92 patients, who had been hospitalized for either severe angina pectoris or myocardial infarction in a coronary care unit, showed that there was a survival rate benefit in those patients whose families owned a pet compared with non-pet owners. The benefit was maintained even when they excluded dog owners, which suggested that exercise was not a contributory factor.[9] A further study reported that the survival rate benefit was independent of the personality of pet owners, which supported the hypothesis that the benefit was the effect of the pet on the owner's physiology.[10] Verbal communication between people has been shown to raise blood pressure significantly, whereas it was lowered when people were allowed to talk to and touch their pets.[11]

In another context, researchers found that looking at aquarium fish lowered blood pressure in a comparable way to hypnosis.[12] Among children, the presence of a dog could also affect blood pressure. In this case blood pressure and heart rate changes were monitored in two groups of children who were resting and reading, with an unfamiliar dog present for half the experiment.[13] It was found that blood pressure and heart rate were reduced during both resting and reading if the dog was present, even without obvious interaction between the dog and the children. Heart rate, systolic blood pressure, diastolic blood pressure and mean arterial blood pressure were significantly higher during reading compared with resting, whether the dog was present or not. Also, the order of appearance of the dog influenced the results; the relaxing effect of the dog was greater in the children who had the dog present at the first testing period. It was suggested that the effect could have been mediated by the children associating the dog with less stressful conditions.

Elsewhere, researchers recorded reductions in people's blood pressure, heart rate and respiratory rate when they petted their own dogs or read quietly.[14] Blood pressure and respiratory rate also fell when participants petted strange dogs. In a further study, researchers were unable to duplicate these results when a similar experiment was carried out in the participant's home. To explain the lack of effects of the pet upon its owner's physiological response, the researchers suggested boredom may have overtaken the subjects after about 10 min of testing time, and also, not all subjects received all tests.[15]

An extensive Australian study compared the cardiovascular risk factor of blood pressure, cholesterol and triglyceride concentrations in pet owners and non-pet owners. It was concluded that pet owners had lower levels of accepted risk factors, which was not explicable on the basis of diet, body mass index, cigarette smoking or socioeconomic profile. Exercise did not appear to be causative.[16] It was noted by the researchers that the difference in systolic blood pressure (SBP) between male pet-owners and male non-owners was similar to the reported lowering of SBP associated with a reduction of salt intake, which is a recognized first-line treatment for hypertension.[17]

In a further study, researchers recorded systolic blood pressure, diastolic blood pressure, heart rate, mean arterial blood pressure and relaxation in six people with and without their pets over two testing periods and two free periods in one day in order to ascertain any effect their pet may have had on these variables. Two non-pet owners were also tested. Having a pet did not appear to significantly alter blood pressure or heart rate in the testing periods. However, heart rate and mean arterial blood pressure were the physiological responses most closely associated with pet ownership. In their own homes, relaxation had a significant effect upon individuals' heart and mean arterial blood pressure. There was no strong indication, though, that the presence of a pet made any difference to cardiac measures.[18]

Pets and Recovery from Illness

Among patients who have had heart operations, pet ownership has been found to speed up recovery rate and enhance overall chances of full recovery. In the course of a study of the social psychological and physiological factors affecting coronary heart disease patient survival, pet ownership was related to one-year survival. In one piece of research conducted in the United States, only three of 53 pet owners died within one year of admission for coronary heart disease (severe angina pectoris or myocardial infarction) to a large urban university hospital, while 11 of the 39 non-pet owners died in this same period. As was expected, the most important predictor of survival was the physiological status of the patient. The effect of pet ownership was independent of the physiological severity of the illness; the combination of pet ownership and physiological severity was better at predicting survival than was physiological severity alone. Furthermore, the beneficial effect of pet ownership was not limited to socially isolated individuals. These findings led to the conclusion that the effects of pets on health were distinct from the effects of other people.[19]

The effects of pets in this illness recovery context has been explained in a number of ways. There is little doubt that the ability of pet animals to help their owners to relax and cope with stressful situations is important.[20] Pet owners are less likely to worry about getting ill in the first place than are non-pet owners. Pet owners are also known to have fewer visits to the doctor.[21] Thus, pet ownership seems to be associated in a general sense with a healthier and more robust constitution. In addition, pet animals can have a direct impact on how we feel. Stroking a furry animal can have immediate and beneficial effects on our state of well-being, by reducing physical tension in our bodies.

An alternative viewpoint has been offered that the differences in illness recovery outcomes between pet owners and non-pet owners could be due to inherent differences in their personalities rather than to the pets themselves. However, this hypothesis has been checked out and found to be wanting. In one American survey conducted with over 300 college students, researchers found no differences between pet owner-ship groups in terms of how much they experienced a variety of positive and negative mood states such as tension, depression, anger, vigour, fatigue, anxiety and confusion. Pet owners and non-owners also exhib-ited few differences on other measures of personality such as their sensation-seeking tendencies or tendency to exhibit reactions to stress known to be related to the onset of heart disease.[22] The acquisition of a pet, such as a dog or a cat, has been found to produce general improved health over the following year.[23]

Pets as Direct Stress Reducers

The presence of pets in anxiety-arousing situations can help their owners cope with the pressure they are under at the time. Pets seem to have the ability to act directly upon their owners' distress in a threat-ening situation. This effect can occur among young as well as old pet owners. Interacting with a friendly dog was found to have a calming effect, as measured physiologically and psychologically, among under-graduate students, which was similar to the level of relaxation that could be achieved by reading quietly.[24]

An even better demonstration of the stress-relieving effects of pets was provided by an experiment in which a sample of adult women were required to perform a stressful experimental task either in a laboratory setting in the presence only of the experimenter, or in their own home, with a female friend present, a pet present, or no one present. The level of physiological arousal caused by the task was enhanced even further in the presence of a female friend and task performance was generally poorer. However, in the presence of a pet, much less physiological arousal was registered. The additional anxiety that occurred in the presence of another person was believed to have been caused by the fact that the person performing the task felt her performance was being evaluated and this added to the stress of the situation. In the presence of an animal, there was no feeling that someone was there looking over your shoulder at how well you were doing. Pets provide unconditional, non-evaluative support. In this particular study, subsequent interviews with the women who participated in it revealed that they were all devoted to their pet dogs. Although many had spouses, children and friends, they described the relationship they had with their dogs as special and different from all others. All of the women were lifelong animal enthusiasts and had experienced pets in their lives since early childhood. Dogs were often described as members of the family. Some of these women appeared, on the surface at least, to have more devotion to their dogs than to their husbands.[25]

The Importance of Touching

We have seen that mere presence of a pet can reduce tension in an otherwise stressful situation. However, touching a pet can invoke an even more powerful relaxation response. As well as being a means of expressing affection, touching an animal companion can have a direct effect on the owner's cardiovascular system. Direct interaction with a pet, which involves talking to the animal and touching it, can be highly relaxing as compared with talking to another person, which can increase heart rate and stress levels.[26]

Attachment and Reduction of Stress

Considerable interest has been stimulated by findings that appear to demonstrate that some people experience beneficial psychological effects from positive social interaction with pet animals. As we have seen already these effects include short-term reductions in heart rate and blood pressure and a variety of long-term physiological benefits.[27] The extent to which a pet animal can produce this physiological calming effect may depend upon the nature of the bond between owner and animal. The mere presence of an albeit friendly animal may not be sufficient to produce stress or anxiety reduction. Once a close attachment has been formed with the pet, however, the owner may then experience some real, health-promoting, physical benefits. Whether children, young adults, middle-aged or elderly people, pet owners exhibit lowered heart rate and blood pressure while stroking their pet dogs, and this calming effect is all the more pronounced as the bond between animal and owner gets deeper.[28] Petting an unknown but friendly dog does not appear to influence heart rate or blood pressure to the same degree as petting a familiar dog.[29]

One interesting study compared the effects on people's blood pressure of stroking a dog with whom a bond had been developed, stroking an unknown dog, and reading quietly. The participants were people aged from their mid-20s to their mid-70s. Results showed that interacting with a familiar dog with whom a bond had been established produced significantly lower blood pressure than did interacting with a previously unknown dog. The effect of being with the familiar dog was similar to that of reading quietly in the degree to which it lowered an individual's blood pressure. The same study also observed a 'greeting response' associated with raised blood pressure at the moment of first meeting the dog again after a period of absence. The same effect did not occur on first meeting the previously unknown dog.[30]

The nature of a person's physiological response to being with a pet animal has been found to vary with the kind of interaction being engaged in. The so-called 'pet effect' of lowered blood pressure, for example, may be contingent upon what the owner and pet are doing together. Blood pressure seems to be lowered most of all when stroking or petting a pet with which a bond of attachment has been established. When simply talking to the animal, blood pressure may be lowered slightly though not to the same extent as when physical contact occurs between animal and owner. Touch appears to be the key factor in the 'pet effect', despite the fact that on a more social or psychological level, companionship can be enjoyed from the mere presence of the pet.[31] In fact, blood pressure (arterial, systolic and diastolic measures) can be significantly reduced while stroking and touching a pet animal such as a friendly dog, to a greater extent than other relaxing activities such as talking to another person or reading. Furthermore, the more positively disposed we are towards pets in general, the greater the calming effect experienced while interacting with friendly animals.[32]

Touching a warm, furry animal has been observed to bring relief to patients recovering from heart operations.[33] Of particular interest is the possibility that a pet can cause decreases in specific physiological responses such as blood pressure.[34] While it is known that blood pressure can become lowered during reading, introducing a friendly dog into the situation can produce a further fall in blood pressure.[35] However, the strength of this pet effect does seem to depend on how well we know the dog in the first place. Petting an unknown dog may have a less pronounced effect on blood pressure.[36] Having said that, evidence has emerged that even people who do not own pets can nevertheless experience reduced heart rate and blood pressure while interacting with an approachable and friendly dog.[37]

According to some researchers, in the absence of tactile contact, the mere physical presence of a pet such as a dog may exert little effect on physiological indicators of anxiety level such as heart rate or blood pressure.[38] This last conclusion has not been universally supported, however. In another laboratory-based experiment, nine- to 16-year-olds had their heart rate and blood pressure monitored while on their own and then in the presence of a friendly dog. The dog produced lower blood pressure readings in these children and teenagers gradually over the course of the experiment. The researchers concluded that as the dog became more familiar, it helped to make the experiment less threatening.[39] In another study, interacting with an unknown dog was found to have a similar set of physiological effects to reading quietly, reducing to a modest extent blood pressure and heart rate levels. These effects were found for individuals who scored high or low on a psychological test of trait anxiety, although anxiety test scores themselves were unaffected by interaction with the friendly animal.[40]

Pets are good for our health. They provide psychological comfort through their companionship and unconditional loyalty and affection. But more than this, pets can bring real, measurable physical benefits to their owners' health. How well we are can depend on so many factors, with social and economic status, lifestyle and activity levels being among the most important. People who lead a healthier lifestyle, are careful about their diet, take exercise and have a positive outlook, possibly fuelled by success professionally and in their personal lives, tend to be less likely to succumb to illness. Pets add to the ingredients which result in a healthier life. A friendly pet, such as a dog or cat, can provide a source of comfort and companionship for many people. The benefits of keeping a pet extend beyond mere social support. A well-established relationship with a pet can have definite health-promoting consequences for the owner. Pets represent one of life's social assets and can contribute to a healthier lifestyle.

Having a pet can bring real clinical benefits. Pet ownership has been found to be a good predictor of survival for one year after a period of hospitalization after serious illness.[41] Such pet effects are not due either to the better health of pet owners from the start. Nor is the pet effect due to the better social status of pet owners. Pet owners may not have significantly more social assets than non-owners. Yet, despite controlling for a range of other demographic, social and economic factors, pet ownership generally retains its significant association with better health or faster recovery from ill-health. Pets may have important effects on the lives of people today that are independent of and supplementary to human relationships. Pets may never represent complete compensation for a lack of other human contact, but they often offer a kind of relationship that other people do not provide.

This chapter has examined the physical health benefits that have been observed to accrue from pet ownership or from being placed in a situation with a friendly, though unfamiliar animal. In addition to physical side-effects of close associations with animals, are there any psychological benefits? In the next chapter, evidence is examined for the impact of animals on our mental well-being. Not only do such benefits occur as an incidental side-effect of pet ownership, but also interesting results have emerged from clinical trials in which animals have been used in therapy contexts.

References

1 Friedmann, E. and Thomas, S.A. Pets and the family. In B. Sussman (Ed.) *Pets and the Family*. London: Haworth Press, pp. 191–203, 1985.
2 Levinson, B.M. The child and his pet. A world of nonverbal communication. In S. A. Corson and E.O. Corson (Eds) *Ethology and Nonverbal Communication in Mental Health*. New York: Pergamon, pp. 63–81, 1980.

3 Levinson, B.M. *Pet-oriented Child Psychotherapy*. Springfield, IL: Charles C. Thomas, 1969.

4 Katcher, A. Interaction between people and their pets: Form and function. In B. Fogle (Ed.) *Interrelations Between People and Pets*. Springfield, IL: Charles C. Thomas, pp. 41–67, 1981.

5 Stallones, L., Marx, M.B., Garrity, T.F. and Johnson, T.P. Quality of attachment to companion animals among US adults 21 to 64 years of age. *Anthrozoos*, 3, 171–176, 1990.

6 Siegel, J.M. Pets and the physician utilisation of behaviour of the elderly. Paper presented at the 6th International Conference on Human–Animal Interactions, Montreal, 1992.

7 Katcher, A. H., Friedmann, E., Beck, A.M. and Lynch, J.J. Talking, looking and blood pressure: Physiological consequences of interaction with the living environment. In A. H. Katcher and A.M Beck (Eds) *New Perspectives on Our Lives with Companion Animals*. Philadelphia: University of Pennsylvania Press, pp. 351–359, 1983.

8 McCulloch, M. Animal-facilitated therapy: Overview and future directions. In A.H. Katcher and A.M. Beck (Eds) *New Perspectives on Our Lives with Companion Animals*. Philadelphia: University of Pennsylvania Press, 1983.

9 Friedmann, E., Katcher, A.H., Lynch, J.J. and Thomas, S.A. Animal companions and one-year survival of patients after discharge from a coronary care unit. *Public Health Reports*, 95, 307–312, 1980.

10 Friedmann, E., Katcher, A.H., Thomas, S.A., Lynch, J.J. and Messent, P.R. Social interaction and blood pressure: Influence of companion animals. *Journal of Nervous and Mental Diseases*, 171, 461–465, 1984.

11 Katcher, A., 1981, op.cit.

12 Katcher, A. et al., 1984, op.cit.

13 Friedmann, E. et al., 1984, op.cit.

14 Baum, M.M., Bengstrom, N., Langston, N.F., and Thoma, L. Physiological effects of human/companion animal bonding. *Nursing Research*, 33(3), 126–129, 1984.

15 Oetting, K.S., Baum, M.M. and Bergstrom, N. Petting a companion animal, dog and autogenic relaxation effects on systolic and diastolic blood pressure, heart rate and peripheral skin temperature. Paper presented at the annual Delta Society Conference, Denver, CO, 1985.

16 Anderson, W.P., Reid, C.M., and Jennings, G.L. Pet ownership and risk factors for cardiovascular disease. *Medical Journal of Australia*, 157, 298–301, 1997.

17 Law, M.R., Frost, C.D. and Wald, N.J. But how much does dietary salt reduction lower blood pressure? III – Analysis of data from trials of salt reduction. *British Medical Journal*, 302, 819–824, 1991.

18 Moody, W.J., Fenwick, D.C. and Blackshaw, J.K. Pitfalls of studies designed to test the effect pets have on the cardiovascular parameters of their owners in the home situation: A pilot study. *Applied Animal Behaviour Science*, 47(1–2), 127–136, 1996.

19 Freidmann, E. et al., 1984, op.cit.

20 Bergler, R. The contribution of dogs to avoiding and overcoming stress factors. Paper presented at the 6th International Conference on Human–Animal Interactions. Animals & Us, Montreal, 1992.

21 Siegel, J.M. Stressful life events and use of physician services among the elderly: The moderating role of pet ownership. *Journal of Personality and Social Psychology*, 58, 1081–1086, 1990.

22 Friedmann, E.et al., 1984, op.cit.

23 Serpell, J.A., Beneficial effects of pet ownership on some aspects of human health and behaviour. *Journal of Royal Society of Medicine*, 84, 717–720, 1991.

24 Wilson, C.C. A conceptual framework for home–animal interaction research: The challenge revisited. *Anthrozoos*, 7(1), 4–24, 1994.

25 Allen, K.M., Blascovich, J., Tomaka, J. and Kelsey, R.M. Presence of human friends and pet dogs as moderators of autonomic responses to stress in women. *Journal of Personality and Social Psychology*, 61(4), 582–589, 1991.

26 Baum, M.M. et al., 1984, op.cit. Friedmann, E., Katcher, A.H., Lynch, J.J. and Thomas, S.A. Animal companions and one-year survival of patients after discharge from a coronary care unit. *Public Health Reports*, 95(4), 307–312, 1980. Katcher, A.H., 1981, op.cit.

27 Katcher, A.H., 1991, op.cit. Brown, L.T., Shaw, T.G. and Kirkland, D. Affection for people as a function of affection for dogs. *Psychological Reports*, 31, 957–958, 1972. Mugford, R.A. and M'Comisky, J. Some recent work in the psychotherapeutic value of cage birds with old people. In R.S. Anderson (Ed.) *Pet Animals and Society*. London: Bailliere Tindall, pp.54–65, 1974. Delafield, G. Self-perception and the effects of mobility training. Unpublished doctoral dissertation, University of Nottingham, 1976. Kidd, A.H. and Feldman, B.M. Pet ownership and self-perceptions of older pets. *Psychological Reports*, 48, 867–875, 1981.

28 Jenkins, J.L. Physiological effects of petting a companion animal. *Psychological Reports*, 58(1), 21–22, 1986

29 Wilson, C.C. Physiological responses of college students to a pet. *Journal of Nervous and Mental Disease*, 175(10), 606–612, 1987.

30 Baum, M.M. et al, 1984, op.cit.

31 Vormbrock, J.K. and Grossberg, J.M. Cardiovascular effects of human–pet dog interactions. *Journal of Behavioural Medicine*, 11, 509–517, 1988.

32 Grossberg, J.M. and Alf, E.F. Interaction with pet dogs: Effects on human cardiovascular response. *Journal of the Delta Society*, 2, 20–27, 1985.

33 Lynch, J.J., Thomas, S.A., Paskewitz, D.A., Katcher, A.H., and Weir, L.O. Human contact and cardiac arrhythmia in a coronary care unit. *Psychosomatic Medicine*, 39, 188–199, 1977.

34 Wilson, C.C., 1987, op.cit.

35 Friedmann, E., Katcher, A.H., Lynch, J.J. and Messent, P.R. Social interaction and blood pressure. *Journal of Nervous and Mental Diseases*, 171, 461–465, 1983.

36 Baum, M.M. et al., 1984, op.cit.

37 Moody, W.J. et al., 1996, op.cit.

38 Grossberg, J.M., Alf, E.E. and Vormbrock, S.K. Does pet presence reduce human cardiovascular response to stress? *Anthrozoos*, 2(1), 38–44, 1988.

39 Friedmann, E. et al., 1983, op.cit.

40 Wilson, C.C., 1987, op.cit.

41 Katcher, A., 1981, op.cit.

Chapter 6
Are pets good for our mental well-being?

The importance of pets in our society is demonstrated repeatedly through frequent accounts of pets in the popular press, movies and books. Prior to the 1970s there were few scientific studies of the benefits of interactions between people and pets. In fact, what research had emerged tended to focus upon health problems caused by pets rather than the importance of animal companions.[1]

Pets are not only good for our physical health, they can also provide enormous benefits to our psychological well-being. Mental health and physical health are often closely intertwined. Pets, as we have seen already, can provide emotional comfort and help to alleviate stress and distress. It appears, however, that such is the power of animal companionship to bring comfort and stability into our lives, that they can be effectively deployed as a deliberate form of treatment for certain psychological and behavioural problems.

Pet owners who have been compared with people who are similar in other respects except for having a pet have been found to suffer fewer episodes of depression,[2] enjoy life more,[3] are generally more satisfied with their lives, and experience more happiness.[4]

There is abundant evidence that loneliness causes increases in both morbidity and mortality.[5] A pet can cause a decrease in loneliness, and decreases in the pathological effects of lack of support from family members and close friends; pets can act as companions for their owners. In numerous surveys of pet owners, results have shown that the great majority of pet owners considered their pets to be family members. Furthermore, a great many pet owners talked to their pets regularly, treated them as if they were people, and thought their pets were sensitive to their moods.[6] With the companionship of animals, humans have the comforts of a needed close-contact relationship,[7] develop a sense of self-respect, independence and responsibility,[8] maintain contact with reality,[9] and enjoy greater self-esteem.[10]

It is known that the presence of pets can make people feel better about themselves. Research in Australia, for example, has indicated that cat owners of all ages exhibited better general psychological health, as measured by a battery of tests. Cat owners compared with non-owners has fewer psychiatric problems, were less likely to get depressed, experienced less sleep disturbance, had a more positive attitude towards animals in general, and were generally less stressed.[11]

Such findings have not always been reproduced. Some studies have found limited or negative effects from pet ownership. In a study of the relationship between pet ownership and perceived happiness in elderly women, the results indicated a limited relationship between the presence of pets in the household and reported happiness. However, happiness derived from pet ownership was found to increase as socioeconomic status increased. Not only that, but the same authors reported on another occasion that psychological health benefits of pet ownership depended importantly on how strongly the owner was attached to the animal.[12]

Erica Friedmann found no evidence for psychological and physiological differences between college student pet owners and non-owners.[13] Likewise, other comparisons revealed no significant differences for upper-middle-class adults between casual pet owners and non-owners regarding feelings of well-being.[14] Elsewhere considerable overlap was found to exist between owners and non-owners along selected psychological dimensions, although the differences suggested that pet owners are less psychologically healthy than non-owners.[15] However, the studies showing negative effects, like many of those showing the positive effects of pet ownership, can be hard to interpret because the level of subjects' attachment to their pets was not adequately measured.

There have usually been extenuating circumstances to explain why pets apparently did not produce a therapeutic effect. One study of working women, some of whom were cat owners, found that there were no marked differences between cat owners and non-owners in levels of emotional distress experienced. The explanation given for this result was that the working women in question were so busy with their jobs that those with cats had insufficient time to spend with their pets to develop the level of attachment usually needed to experience physical and psychological benefits.[16]

Support for psychological benefits as a result of naturally occurring pet ownership has emerged elsewhere, however. Such an effect has been particularly likely to occur among older people.[17] Although a later chapter will examine the benefits of pets for the elderly, it is worth mentioning at this point the important finding that people aged 65 and over who owned pets suffered less depression.[18] The stronger the bond of attachment between owner and pet, the greater the physical and psychological benefits experienced.

Pet-facilitated Therapy

The specifically psychotherapeutic role pets can serve has received increasing professional attention since a pioneering paper by Boris Levinson on the subject called 'The dog as co-therapist' was published in the early 1960s.[19] In this review, it was reported that a dog can help to establish a relaxed and non-threatening relationship between therapist and patient. It can produce an atmosphere in which patients become more willing or able to respond. The idea of pet-facilitated therapy had been around for a long time before this paper appeared.

In 1800, pets were provided at the 'York Retreat' when it was believed they were of therapeutic value.[20] In a series of papers, Levinson furthered the idea that pets are of therapeutic value in institutions, in therapists' offices, and in the homes of the disturbed.[21] In institutional research, Judith Siegel outlined a programme for using pets in treatment of severely withdrawn schizophrenics.[22] Levinson, meanwhile, noted that for emotionally disturbed and retarded patients, pets provided stimulation and could be used to reduce the incidence of maladaptive behaviours.[23]

Pets have successfully been used as co-therapists in their work with severely withdrawn children.[24] Some observers have noted what they called the 'social lubricant' effects of pets. Elizabeth Corson and her colleagues used pet dogs in psychotherapy with hospitalized mental patients who had not responded to traditional therapies and found notable improvement with pet-facilitated therapy.[25] The presence of pets led to increased social interaction among these patients.

The psychotherapeutic value of pets in the home has been seen from two viewpoints. Erika Friedmann noted that observation of the relationship between family members and house pets added to the understanding of family relationships.[26] In addition, American therapist Boris Levinson reported that dogs could serve the disturbed or normal child as a playmate, defender, companion, and a source of learning. Further, he reported that pets helped children develop a sense of responsibility and minimized the impact of emotional traumas, that the death of a pet could help prepare children for other deaths, and that a pet could help serve as emotional support for a child following the death of a parent.[27]

The term 'pet-facilitated therapy' (PFT) has been used loosely to describe a therapeutic intervention that involves an animal. PFT may indicate anything from the use of animal visitors in nursing homes (during which no structured interaction takes place between humans and animals) to attempts to lower blood pressure through the contemplation of fish swimming in an aquarium. The term has also been used to describe situations in which contact with an animal is a prescribed component of psychotherapy (such as instructing withdrawn children to stroke a rabbit). Given the range of activities that fit under the banner of PFT, it is not surprising that the advantages and disadvantages of the approach are unclear.

The Psychotherapeutic Benefits of Pets

Evidence on the psychotherapeutic impact of animals has been derived from largely clinical impressions. The problem with this sort of evidence is that it derives from investigations in which there are no control points of comparison against which to compare the patients upon whom animals have supposedly had a beneficial clinical effect. One of the seductive aspects of PFT is that the animals are often highly appealing and elicit positive responses from the researchers themselves.

A number of different types of animal-assisted therapy programmes have been instigated over the years. The main types of programme include: (1) service animal programmes; (2) institutional programmes; (3) pet programmes for the elderly; (4) visitation programmes; (5) equine programmes; and (6) wild animal programmes. These programmes have met with varying degrees of success in terms of the psychological well-being of recipients of such therapy. There are also a number of ethical issues connected with these programmes which centre on the implications for the well-being of the animals.[28]

Service Animal Programmes

Service animals include guide dogs for the blind, hearing dogs for the deaf, and assistance animals for the handicapped. In some programmes, animals are bred especially for the purpose, whilst in others animals are taken from local shelters and trained for the specialized tasks they will have to perform for their disabled human partners. These programmes have become increasingly popular. Dogs can not only be trained to be the eyes or ears of visually- or hearing-impaired people, they can also be trained to carry personal items or assist with the mobility of physically handicapped people confined to wheelchairs. There have been concerns in some cases that the animal's welfare is not always given as much consideration as it should be. Dogs have been known to suffer physical injuries when required to carry or pull loads that are too heavy.

Institutionally Based Residential Programmes

These programmes may be set in long-term care hospitals, nursing homes, psychiatric hospitals and prisons. These programmes have also become very popular and this growth in prevalence reflects the degree of success they have often enjoyed. There are problems of animal fatigue and even of abuse in these programmes. It is important to allow the animals time to rest despite the demand there may be among residents in institutional settings to each spend some time with them. In prisons and psychiatric institutions incidents or animal abuse have been recorded that underline the need for the animals to be closely guarded.

In an experiment involving placement of a rabbit on a psychiatric inpatient unit, results showed that a uniformly positive response occurred across even the more seriously ill patients. Even patients who displayed deep psychological regression from everyday reality had been able to include the rabbit as a part of their own individual private world and used it as a bridge to the real world. Other patients who showed irritation at the rabbit's presence nevertheless were prompted to interact with other people in venting their annoyance.[29]

PFT sessions at one institution in the United States involved the introduction of a dog and cat. A number of the psychiatric patients showed marked improvements in behaviour as a function of contact with a pet animal. Some patients volunteered to walk the dog, and others got involved in grooming it. They benefited both from the exercise and the emotional satisfaction of being involved in an activity which was different from their usual daily routine. The significance of these results was underlined by the fact that they occurred among patients for whom other forms of psychotherapy and treatments had been largely unsuccessful.[30]

The use of small birds in a state mental hospital has also proved effective in producing an improvement in several patients who had not responded to other therapies, by increasing the need and desire to speak, by teaching responsibility and lessening anxiety, and by giving patients charge of living beings to which they could relate.[31] Results indicated that the presence of companion animals reduced mediation levels by 50% and the number of 'incidents' among inmates by 84%.

Pet Therapy for the Elderly

A number of pet-assisted therapy programmes have been developed especially for use with the elderly. Although the elderly tend to have a lower rate of pet ownership than the rest of the population they have nevertheless been targeted as one group whom therapists believe could benefit from the company of animals.

One study reported that the presence of a dog at an old people's home occupied by residents suffering from Alzheimer's disease resulted in increased numbers of social behaviours such as smiling, laughing, physical movement, talking and calling out names. Once the dog had been present for a time, such behaviours continued even when it was taken away again. In another study, elderly residents at a long-term care facility were found to respond more actively to a caged puppy than to a plant in terms of how often they looked at it, smiled and talked to others about it.[32]

Problems have been experienced with pet-assisted therapy programmes aimed at the elderly in care. One difficulty can be ensuring that the animal selected and trained for the purpose is temperamentally suited to the task. Dog breeds vary in personality with some being more aggressive and less placid than others. Highly strung breeds which cannot tolerate constant demands for attention or are prone to react aggressively to unwanted touching will not be suited to this kind of programme. In some cases, the animals have been spoiled and have even died through over-feeding. It is also important to ensure that animals on these programmes receive adequate exercise. The demand from residents who are confined indoors for the dog to be ever present with them may result in it not getting the exercise it needs to stay fit and healthy.

Visitation Programmes

These are the most widespread type of animal-assisted therapy programme. They tend to be run either by the staff of institutions such as nursing homes or hospitals, or by volunteers. Some programmes even provide for visits to private homes. As with other programmes the animals, usually dogs, must have the right temperament. They must also receive some training in how to behave with strangers. Although dogs are the species used most often in these programmes, cats and birds have been used as well.

The difference between visitation programmes and the previously mentioned residential therapy programmes is that the animals do not live in residence in the former, but make temporary visits and then return to their private home again.

The presence of pets can bring great comfort to people who are seriously ill. The presence of cats and dogs in a nursing centre for terminally ill cancer patients has been found to reduce patients' feelings of anxiety and despair and helped them to cope more readily with progressive stages of dying. The presence of animal companions helped patients to come to terms with leaving loved ones behind. The more the patients developed a relationship with an animal, the greater were the psychological benefits they obtained from it.[33]

In another study of terminally ill people, the introduction of a miniature poodle into a hospice produce measurable improvements in patients' attitudes and behaviour. These improvements were noted by patients and staff alike. The poodle appeared to facilitate more positive interactions between carers and patients, better reactions from patients when they had visitors, and generally boosted everyone's morale.[34] Another therapist suggested a useful emotional benefit when he noted that a turtle provided living companionship and seemed to produce a sense of responsibility and focus of interest for women bedridden with tuberculosis.[35]

Equine Programmes

Animal-assisted programmes involving horses have achieved good results with the handicapped. Therapeutic riding provides an opportunity for an otherwise physically disabled person, unable to walk, to experience the sensation of movement under their own control. Though there may be some physical benefits of such an experience, there are certainly psychological benefits.

One therapist summarized the therapeutic benefits of horse ownership or use when he noted that patients suffering from muscular, neurological and neuromuscular damage and disease demonstrated improved circulation and were more physically relaxed after a series of riding lessons.[36] They also displayed reciprocal motion with both sides of the body working together more smoothly than prior to such therapy. Such programmes were also associated with a reduction in the number and severity of seizures among epileptics by using horses to assist with relaxation techniques. Mentally retarded and emotionally disturbed individuals showed both physical gains and increased self-esteem and the ability to concentrate on social stimuli external to themselves through such programmes.

Wild Animal Programmes

Animal-assisted programmes have been developed using undomesticated animals. Although there are those who believe that such programmes can bring positive psychological benefits to individuals suffering from various disabilities, there are others who have expressed ethical concerns about the well-being of the animals and concerns, in some cases, for the safety of those receiving this type of therapy. Among the best known programmes are those involving swimming with dolphins and using monkeys in care assistance roles. In the dolphin swim programmes, those receiving therapy either get in the water with the animals or interact with them at the water's edge. This may take place in an aquarium or lagoon. Concern has been voiced about the confinement of dolphins in captivity. But even in programmes where the dolphins are not confined there are critics who warn that, despite their reputation, not all dolphins are well behaved. Some dolphins enjoy startling or bumping into human swimmers and such is their power that they can do real physical damage if they connect. Other question-marks hanging over dolphin swim programmes, however, query their real therapeutic value, which has yet to be systematically demonstrated.

Monkey assistance programmes have involved the use of capuchin monkeys as personal care assistants for quadriplegics. These wild animals are specially trained to accept living in a human household and to perform tasks such as picking up dropped items, playing a cassette recorder, and even spoon-feeding the quadriplegic. These programmes have not been widely adopted, and where they have occurred the results have been mixed.[37] The training process begins when the monkeys are just a few weeks old.

The animals are placed with individuals who live alone and who have been disabled for at least a year. Strong bonds have been observed to develop between some monkeys and their owners with psychological as well as practical benefits for the human partners.[38] Ethical questions have once again been asked about the morality of keeping wild animals in captivity in a human domestic environment. There have also been question-marks raised about some of the training methods with allegations of the use of electric-shock treatment on the monkeys. The animals also routinely have all their teeth pulled before they are placed with a human partner. There have been calls for a thorough and independent review of the effectiveness of these programmes.[39]

Other Therapeutic Uses of Pets

Pets have been used in a number of other psychotherapeutic contexts not so far mentioned. One intriguing application was the use of a kitten in a sex therapy context. This case involved a married couple who, after three years together, had not developed sexual intimacy in their relationship. The couple were engaged in a systematic desensitization treatment that consisted of playing with and stroking a pet kitten in order to induce relaxation and make them feel more comfortable about physical contact with another being.[40]

It seems that pets can provide emotional benefit in psychotherapy by distracting patients' attention from the causes of their anxiety. If a person is exposed to a situation which normally provokes anxiety attacks, the severity of the attacks can be reduced or brought under more effective control if at the same time the individual is distracted slightly by the presence of a pet, such as a dog or a cat. The animal's presence may help the patient to relax.[41]

Pets and Child Welfare

Dogs have been found to bring particular benefits in child welfare cases. Chronically rejected children, or those who spend their entire youth in care, tend to develop a withdrawn, depressed and suspicious posture toward their relations with other people. Such a posture ultimately results in their failure to respond to conventional treatments. Under these circumstances, the use of dogs may prove to be a valuable adjunct and help to make conventional therapeutic approaches more effective.[42]

Many animals can make excellent pets for handicapped children and can provide social, emotional and recreational benefits. Pet selection should be carefully matched to the child's skills, maturity and interests.

Parental opinion, location of residence and the animal's susceptibility to training should also be considered.[43]

A number of studies have noted cases in which mute autistic children began speaking to a pony and then communicating verbally with people.[44] The potency of pets in the therapeutic context for mentally or emotionally handicapped children is that the responsibility of caring for a pet can lead to the child gaining in self-esteem and obtaining recognition from others for looking after an animal. It gives the child a sense of self-worth and adds meaning to his or her life, improving their entire outlook.[45]

The treatment of autistic children has been found to be enhanced by the inclusion of a pet dog in the therapeutic sessions. The presence of the dog along with the therapist resulted in a decrease in autistic children's self-absorption and produced improved social behaviour. After a number of sessions with the dog present, the children's behaviour remained much improved even when the dog was no longer present.[46]

Pets and other animals, both domesticated and wild, can bring psychological benefits to individuals placed in close proximity to them. These mental health side-effects can occur for owners as a function of sharing their lives with an animal companion. More significantly, however, therapeutic benefits can be obtained through animal-assisted treatments where no prior bond has been formed between human patient and animals involved in therapy. This type of therapy has been found to be especially effective with children. This finding underlines the wider significance animals can have in children's lives. In the next chapter, we examine the evidence for why children can benefit from an early introduction to animals through pet care.

References

1 Beck, A. Public health implications of urban dogs. *American Journal of Public Health*, 65, 1315, 1975.

2 Francis, G., Turner, J. and Johnson, S. Domestic animal visitation as therapy with adult home residents. *International Journal of Nursing Studies*, 2293, 201–206, 1985. Katcher, A. and Friedmann, E. Potential health value of pet ownership. *Compendium on Continuing Education for the Practicing Veterinarian*, 2, 117–122, 1980.

3 Francis et al., 1985, op.cit. Mugford, R.A. and M'Comisky J. Some recent work on the psychotherapeutic value of cage birds with old people. In R.S. Anderson (Ed.) *Pet Animals and Society*. London: Baillière Tindall, 1975.

4 Francis, G. et al., 1985, op.cit. Connell, M.S. and Lago, D.J. Favourable attitudes toward pets and happiness among the elderly. In T.K. Anderson, B.L. Hart and L.A. Hart (Eds) *The Pet Connection*. Minneapolis: University of Minnesota Press, 1983.

5 Cobb, S. Social support as a moderator of life stress. *Psychosomatic Medicine*, 38, 300–314, 1976.

6 Cain, A.O. A study of pets in the family system. In A. H. Katcher and A. M. Beck (Eds) *New Perspectives on Our Lives with Companion Animals*. Philadelphia: University of Pennsylvania Press, 1983. Friedmann, E., Leather, A.H., Eaton, M. and Berger, B. Pet ownership and psychological status. In R.K. Anderson, B.L. Hart and L.A. Hart (Eds) *The Pet Connection*. Minneapolis: University of Minnesota Press, 1984. Katcher, A.H., Friedmann, E., Goodman, M. and Goodman, L. Men, women and dogs. *California Veterinarian*, 37, 14–17, 1983.

7 McCulloch, M. The pet as prosthesis – defining criteria for the adjunctive use of companion animals in the treatment of medically ill, depressed outpatients. In B. Fogle (Ed.) *Interrelations between People and Their Pets*. Springfield, IL: Charles C. Thomas, 1981.

8 Corson, S.A., Corson, E.O. and Gwynne, P. Pet-facilitated psychotherapy in a hospital setting. In J.A. Masserman (Ed.), *Current Psychiatric Therapies*, Vol.15. New York: Grune & Stratton, pp. 277–286, 1975.

9 Levinson, B.M. *Pets and Human Development*. Springfield, IL: Charles C. Thomas, 1972.

10 Savishinsky, J.S. Pet ideas: The domestication of animals, human behaviour and human emotion. In A.H. Katcher and A.M. Beck (Eds) *New Perspectives on Our Lives with Companion Animals*. Philadelphia: University of Pennsylvania Press, 1983. Katz, S., Atlas, J., Walker, V. and Crossman, E. Pet-facilitated therapy: Potential benefits. *Community Animal Control*, September/October, 1982. Messent, P.R. Social facilitation of contact with other people by pet dogs. In A.H. Katcher and A.M. Beck (Eds) *New Perspectives on Our Lives with Companion Animals*. Philadelphia: University of Pennsylvania Press, 1983.

11 Straede, C.M. and Gates, G.R. Psychological health in a population of Australia cat owners. *Anthrozoos*, 6(1), 30–42, 1993.

12 Ory, M.G. and Goldberg, E.L. An epidemiological study of pet ownership in the community. In R.K. Anderson, B.L Hart and L.A. Hart (Eds) *Pet Connection* Minneapolis: University of Minnesota Press, 1984.

13 Friedmann, E. Pet ownership and psychological status. In R.K. Anderson, B.K. Hart and L.A. Hart (Eds) *Pet Connection*. Minnesota: University of Minneapolis Press, 1984.

14 Martinez, R.L. and Kidd, A.H. Two personality characteristics in adult pet owners and non-owners. *Psychological Reports*, 47, 318, 1980.

15 Cameron, P. and Mattson, M. Psychological correlates of pet ownership. *Psychological Reports*, 30, 286, 1972

16 Watson, N.L. and Weinstein, M. Pet ownership in relation to expression, anxiety and anger in working women. *Anthrozoos*, 6(2), 135–138, 1993.

17 Lawton, M.P., Moss, M. and Moles, E. Pet ownership: A research note. *The Gerontologist*, 24(2), 208–210, 1984. Ory, M.G. and Goldberg, E.L., 1984, op.cit. Robb, S.S. and Stegman, C.E. Companion animals and elderly people: A challenge for evaluators of social support. *The Gerontologist*, 23, 277–282, 1983.

18 Garrity, T.F., Stallones, L., Marx, M. and Johnson, T.P. pet ownership and attachment as supportive factors in the health of the elderly. *Anthrozoos*, 3, 35–44, 1989.

19 Levinson, B. The dog as co-therapist. *Mental Hygiene*, 46, 59–65, 1962.

20 Siegel, A. Reaching the severely withdrawn through pet therapy. *American Journal of Psychiatry*, 118, 1045–1046, 1962.

21 Levinson, B.M. 1962, op.cit. Levinson, B.M. Pets: A special technique in child psychotherapy. *Mental Hygiene*, 48, 243–244., 1964. Levinson, B.M. The veterinarian and mental hygiene. *Mental Hygiene*, 49, 320–323. Levinson, B.M. The pet and

the child's bereavement. *Mental Hygiene*, 51, 197–200, 1967. Levinson, B.M. Household pets in residential schools: Their therapeutic potential. *Mental Hygiene*, 52, 411–414, 1968. Levinson, B.M., 1972, op.cit.

22 Siegel, J., 1962, op.cit. Siegel, J. The journal investigates: Pet therapy, an unlighted path. *Journal of Small Animal Practice*, 5, 275–279, 1964.

23 Levinson, B.M. The value of pet ownership. *Proceedings of the 12th Annual Convention of the Pet Food Institute*, 12–18, 1969b.

24 Rice, S., Brown, L. and Caldwell, H. Animals and psychotherapy. *Journal of Community Psychology*, 1, 323–326, 1973.

25 Corson, S.A., Corson, E.O., Gwynne, P. and Arnold, L. Pet-facilitated psychotherapy. In R.S. Anderson (Ed.) *Pet Animals and Society*. London: Bailliere Tindall, pp.19–36, 1974. Corson, S.A., Corson, E.O. and Gwynne, P. Pet-facilitated psychotherapy in a hospital setting. In J.H. Masserman (Ed.) *Current Psychiatric Therapies*, Vol.15, New York: Grune & Stratton, pp. 277–286, 1975.

26 Friedmann, E. *Psychotherapy for the Whole Family*. New York: Springer.

27 Levinson, B.M., 1962, op.cit. Levinson, B.M. Pets, child development and mental illness. *Journal of the American Veterinary Associaiton*, 157, 1759–1766, 1970. Levinson, B.M., 1972, op.cit.

28 Iannuzzi, D. and Rowan, A.N. Ethical issues in animal-assisted therapy programmes. *Anthrozoos*, 4(3), 154–163, 1992.

29 Doyle, M.C. Rabbit-therapeutic prescription. *Comprehensive Psychiatry*, 18, 61–72, 1975.

30 Corson, S.A., Corson, E.O. and Gwynne, P. Pet-facilitated psychotherapy in a hospital setting. *Current Psychiatric Therapy*, 15, 277–286, 1975.

31 Trussel, V.L. Lima State Hospital: People helping animals...animals helping people. *American Humane Magazine*, 6696, 27–29, 1978. Lee, D. Birds as therapy at Lime State Hospital for the criminally insane. *Bird World*, February–March, 1(6), 14–16, 1979.

32 Robb, S.S., Boyd, M. and Pritash, C.L. A wine bottle, plant and puppy. *Journal of Gerontological Nursing*, 6, 721–728, 1980.

33 Muschel, I.J. Pet therapy with terminal cancer patients. *Social Casework*, 65(8), 451–458, 1984.

34 Chinner, T.L. and Dalziel, F.R. An exploratory study on the viability and efficacy of a pet-facilitated therapy project within a hospice. *Journal of Palliative Care*, 7(4), 13–20, 1991.

35 Ross, S.D. The therapist use of animals with the handicapped. *International Child Welfare Review*, 56, 26–39, 1983.

36 Iannuzzi, D. and Rowan, A.N., 1992, op.cit.

37 Quiejo, J. Faithful companions. *Bostonia*, January–Febrary, 35–39, 1989.

38 Willard, M.J., Levee, A. and Westbrook, L. The psychosocial impact of simian aides in quadriplegics. *Einstein Quarterly Journal of Biology and Medicine*, 3, 104–108, 1985.

39 Iannuzzi, D. and Rowan, A.N., 1992, op.cit.

40 Pichel, C.H. and Hart, L.A. Desensitization of sexual anxiety: Relaxation, play and touch experience with a pet. *Anthrozoos*, 2(1), 58–61, 1988.

41 Brickel, C.M. Pet-facilitated psychotherapy: A theoretical explanation via attention shifts. *Psychological Reports*, 50, 71–74, 1982.

42 Ganski, Y.A. The therapeutic utilisation of canines in a child welfare setting. *Child and Adolescent Social Work Journal*, 2(2), 93–105, 1985.

43 Frith, G.H. Pets for handicapped children: A source of pleasure, responsibility and learning. *Pointer*, 27(1), 24–27, 1982

44 Mason, H. How horses are helping the handicapped. *Kiwanis Magazine*, 65(8), 25–27,1980a. Mason, H. A ride to health: Horseback riding helps Browndale students. *Special Education in Canada*, 54(4), 28–29, 1980b.

45 Ross, S.D. 1983, op.cit.

46 Redefer, L.A. and Goodman, J.F. 1989. Redefer, L.A. Brief report: pet-facilitated therapy with autistic children. *Journal of Autism and Developmental Disorders*, 19, 3–5.

Chapter 7
Are pets good for children?

Pets can play an important role in human development. The existence of a healthy child–animal bond can have important consequences for the child's social and emotional development. According to one writer, animal companions have their strongest impact during middle childhood and old age.[1] The significance of pets to old people is the subject of the next chapter. In this chapter, we will examine the evidence on the importance of pets for children.

There is a growing opinion that having a pet can be good for the child. Whether or not a pet is essential for personality development, it is assumed to be beneficial to it.[2] A pet may fulfil many different roles and functions in the family context. It may act as a proxy with whom a child can practise a variety of interactions which are later incorporated into other social relationships. Caring for a pet may encourage a sense of responsibility and provide naturalistic examples of problems concerning toilet training and sexuality.[3] Large pets may give children a feeling of strength through identification. They can also be a source of continuity. Not only does the pet always have time to spend with the child, when the parent may not, but the pet is believed to be permanent. It does not go out for the evening but, more importantly, it does not file for divorce. A pet may provide a sense of continuity during the adjustment of separation and divorce: it is one 'parent' the child can count on.[4]

Pets and the Family

Pets have been especially valued for their role in family life. By the early 1980s, one writer observed that over half of all households in the English-speaking world kept pets.[5] Pets are most common in households with children.[6] Most children express a desire to own a pet at some time.[7] In addition, the few studies that have considered parents' opinions concerning pet keeping have found a broad consensus of belief that pets are, in general, good for children and beneficial for their development.[8] The role of the pet in family households depends on the family structure, the emotional strengths and weaknesses of each family member, and the social climate of the family.[9] One writer believed that there are two complementary dimensions of pet ownership which exist for the family itself. First, a pet can be a means by which a family can widen its social network. Pets can be a source of interest beyond the family and may bring the family into contact with other people who also hold favourable attitudes towards animals. Second, an animal can create a climate within a family in which different feelings and rivalries among family members can be played out, with the animal often used as a target or catalyst in testing out different roles and relationships.[10] This particular function of the pet may be especially important for children, for whom the pet may become a more significant 'relative' or 'friend' than other family members.[11]

The last two decades have witnessed an unprecedented increase of research interest in the phenomenon of pet keeping and the role that animals might have in determining the social, physical and psychological well being of people, and especially children.[12] The majority of studies that have attempted to investigate the effects of pet ownership on children have used cross-sectional comparisons between pet owning and non-owning families.[13] A few others have used correlational approaches in which pet ownership levels or pet attachment levels have been analysed in relation to measures of particular hypothesized effects of childhood pet ownership.[14] The findings of such studies have offered suggestions that pet keeping in childhood may have important effects on children's self-esteem, social skills and empathy.[15] These psychological benefits have been illustrated by adolescents' reports that pets such as dogs, cats and rabbits or hamsters represent friends from whom they can receive and give love and affection. In addition, keeping pets gives their young owners a sense of responsibility. As Table 7.1 shows, these feelings of friendship and responsibility can vary in the extent to which they are experienced by adolescent pet owners depending on the type of animal.

None of this research, however, has demonstrated any firm causal relationships between childhood pet ownership and alterations in the social and psychological well-being of children, or the quality of their development. Prospective and longitudinal research designs are needed to assess the impact of pets on children's lives. The few studies that have used this approach have focused on institutional settings, children with special needs, or relatively short 'experimental' exposures to a variety of animals.[16] What is also of interest, however, is the impact of pets on their family owners within natural living conditions. In this context, research has found that adult cat and dog owners exhibit significant improvements in their self-reported physical and psychological health, compared with non-pet owners during the first 10 months of owning their pet. But are similar effects experienced by children?

Table 7.1: What do adolescents gain from keeping pets?

Type of pet	% saying 'Friendship'	% saying 'Responsibility'
Dog	87.8	78.4
Cat	57.9	53.8
Rabbit/hamster	40.5	41.7
Fish/bird	38.1	35.8
Large animal	17.9	17.5
Horse	23.8	13.7

Source: Adapted from Covert, A.M., Whiren, A.P., Keith, J. and Nelson, C. Pets, early adolescence and families. In B. Sussman (Ed.) *Pets and the Family*. New York: Hawarth Press, 1985, pp. 95–108.

When a pet is introduced into a family, the entire climate of family interaction can change and become more complex. Not only does each member of the family interact with the animal in his or her own characteristic way, but family members interact with each other over the pet. Feelings of rivalry, possessiveness and jealousy can emerge just as with the advent of a new child or sibling.[17] Well handled by the parents, this situation can provide an opportunity for working through similar feelings about siblings which have hitherto not been dealt with. Similarly, the promotion of a nurturant, considerate attitude toward the pet can involve the entire family in a cooperative enterprise aimed at the good of the animal which at the same time promotes the closeness of the family members. Children who become the 'parents' of a pet may develop a more realistic view of their own parents and parenting functions, not only nurturant but disciplinary in nature. In this way, pets can serve what many parents have observed to be a valuable educative purpose for children as well as providing a little furry companion for them to play with.[18]

According to one writer, pets become part of the 'undifferentiated ego mass' of the family.[19] Many people consider their pet as a member of the family.[20] Pet-owning families often include their pets in family photographs.[21] Family members not only interact with their pet in their own characteristic manner, but they also interact with each other in relation to the pet. In some families, pets become the major focus of attention and assume a position even more important than that of human family members.[22]

One American survey of the impact of obtaining a new pet dog on the lives of 27 children in the eight to 12 years range during the first year of ownership found that the effects of pets on children could vary quite a bit. There was no indication that the presence of a dog was associated with changes in the extent to which members of the family spent time together. It did emerge that children in dog-owning families were more

sociable and better behaved than children in households that did not
have a dog. However, these differences were also true of the children in
the new dog-owning households before they had acquired the dog. Even
so, the children who had got a pet dog reported that they received more
visits from friends, which they attributed to the dog. Dog-owning
families also engaged in more leisure activities at home together during
the early days of having the pet.[23]

Understanding Animals

It was observed elsewhere in a study in Canada that children develop a
better understanding of animals when brought up around them. They
become more confident and skilled at dealing with animals as a result of
having a pet as a member of the family.[24]

Acquiring a Sense of Responsibility

For many pet-owning family households, pets are regarded as members
of the family, being treated as people and representing an important
aspect of the family's social network beyond the home.[25] People with
pets claim to talk to their animals and find that they often make new
friends because of them. Pet owners tend to meet one another while out
walking their dogs, and enjoy swapping anecdotes about their pets.

The individual child who is old enough to take responsibility for the
care and training of a pet can benefit in a variety of ways. A pet is an
accepting creature. It holds up no ego for the child to meet, as do
parents, but unstintingly gives acceptance and affection without strings.
The pet may accept the child for what he or she is, not for what they
might be or ought to be. Complete acceptance by a pet can therefore
provide a child with a sense of worth which he or she might not be
getting sufficiently from the rest of their social environment.

Boris Levinson suggested that responsibility for pet care by children
should be introduced gradually and that parents should recognize that
there will be periods when even for a conscientious child the care of a
pet will be too much.[26] Teenagers living in normal family environments
frequently share pet care responsibilities with the adults of the household and obtain great pleasure from doing so.[27] The successful care of a
valued pet will promote a sense of importance and being needed.

If the child can train a pet to behave acceptably and even perform
tricks, the child will have a feeling of competence which enhances his/her
self-esteem. This is particularly true when parents acknowledge the
child's accomplishments with the pet. Success of this kind can often
enhance a child's self-confidence in general so that he or she tackles with
a positive attitude other tasks appropriate to his/her developmental stage.

Relationships with peers may also benefit from owning and handling
pets. Having a pet, particularly one which can be taught tricks and that

openly demonstrates loyalty and affection, can enhance a child's prestige in the eyes of his/her peers and cause them to seek him/her out. It can also help a shy child break the ice with other children, particularly if he/she is a newcomer to the situation.

Relating to an animal in an empathic way is good preparation for relating to other people in a similar way. For children living in isolated areas in which there are few peers, animal companionship may have to be a substitute for human friendships. Whilst certainly not equivalent, association with a loved animal can greatly reduce a child's sense of isolation and give him or her something other than the adult world in which to develop.

Boris Levinson concluded that 'closeness to animals can reduce alienation' (p.1031), based on the argument that people and companion animals evolved together. According to Levinson, children's empathy, self-esteem, self-control and autonomy could be promoted by raising pets.[28] This is not restricted to children – people of all ages can benefit from nurturing animals. The value of pets in children's lives can be measured in terms of many different kinds of learning experience, including the giving and receiving of affection, taking responsibility for another creature's well-being, understanding about animals and how they behave, and learning about concepts such as life and death and how to cope with loss.[29]

Early and Later Pet Ownership

Early pet ownership tends to be associated closely with the likelihood of pet owning later in life. People who own pets as adults are generally more likely to have been brought up with family pets as children.[30] Positive relationships with animal companions during childhood are remembered for life. Pet preferences may also become established early in life. The pets we choose to own as grown-ups tend to be the same species as those we befriended as children.[31] Adult dog lovers were much more likely to have been brought up as children with pet dogs than pet cats, whereas adult cat lovers were more likely to have lived with pet cats than pet dogs when they were young.[32] In some cases, of course, people own pets continuously throughout their lives, never knowing what it is like to be without an animal companion. For these people, the initial experiences of living with an animal will have been continually reinforced throughout different stages of their own lives.

The earlier in life we are introduced to pets, the stronger is the lifelong bond of attachment we develop with whichever species it is whose company we keep. For instance, our attitudes towards pet cats or dogs as adults are more positive if we had our first pet before we were six years old than if we were older than 10 before first having a pet.[33] The strength of the bond we form with pet animals as adults, including how physically affectionate we are towards our pets, is directly linked to the age at which we first had a pet as children. If we developed a strong bond of friendship with an animal companion when very young, we are much more likely to form strong bonds with our pets when we have grown up.[34]

The results of another survey on pets showed that pet owners were happier than people who did not own pets, albeit that this result was confounded by demographic differences between owners and non-owners in their sample. Pleasure or companionship were the main reasons given for pet ownership.[35] In addition, further evidence emerged that childhood pet ownership predisposes us to have family pets again when grown up. Approximately 90% of the respondents had owned pets as children and felt that pets were important for children. Once we have learned how to relate to pets as children, we are more likely to take pleasure from them again as adults.[36]

Undoubtedly, early positive experiences with pets cultivate positive attitudes about animals which persist throughout life. Nevertheless, we may not always have had positive experiences with animals: any of us who has been bitten by a dog or scratched by a cat will testify to that. If such incidents occur when we are very young, they could condition our feelings towards animals for a long time. There are also some animals, such as snakes and spiders, which invoke deep-seated and uncontrollable fears or even phobias, even though we may, in some instances, never have directly come into contact with them. Even so, living with pets when children can help us overcome our fear of animals, by improving our understanding of what makes them tick.[37]

Pets and Child Development

Animals can play an important part in child development. Some writers have suggested that children who have never had an opportunity to get involved with animal life would be deprived.[38] Involvement with animals provides a great depth and breadth of emotional experience. This does not mean that every family should own a pet, because there are so many ways in which nature and animal life can be enjoyed.

Awareness of the need to provide intelligent care and to take responsibility for animals and the ability to feel genuine warmth towards them do not depend on one-time ownership of an animal. Parents of families who do accept companion animals into their homes should supervise the care of the animals, set boundaries to the intimacy between children and animals, and not permit the animals to infringe upon the freedom of neighbours or the community.

The benefit to children of having pets as companions is not derived solely from the animals, but depends largely on the parents' psychological awareness of the child's friendship with the animal concerned. No good will come when parents force a child to take responsibility beyond his/her ability, make a child's relationship with the animal appear ridiculous, or ignore the child's concern when the animal is ill or dies. Normally, parents allow their children to grieve after the death of a companion animal. It might also be a good practice for the vet to help the child express sadness and remove any unnecessary guilt the child may feel because of the death of an animal.

Children will quite spontaneously interact with pets by playing with them, talking to them or stroking them. Indeed, children have been found to be much more proactive than reactive in their dealings with family pets. A child will seek out the family's pet dog and initiate communication with it, more often than the dog seeks out the child. This has been observed to happen even among very young children under five years of age.[39]

A child's sensitivity to the world of animals is often developed through reading and storytelling. Through such a fantasy world the child can become aware of certain values, principles and moral truths. The various fictional animal characters are anthropomorphized and thus children confront qualities that are both animal and human. Characters such as Walrus in Lewis Carroll's *Alice in Wonderland*, Mole and his companions in Kenneth Grahame's *The Wind in the Willows*, C.S. Lewis's lion and mythic characters of *The Chronicles of Narnia*, and Rudyard Kipling's Rikki-tikki-tavi in *The Jungle Book* represent introductions to fictional creatures with 'human' personalities and characteristics.

The process of making children sensitive to not only the animal world but the moral consequences of the actions of animals (and by implication, similar human actions) is an important first step in establishing the animal–human bond. A child's sensitivity to and appreciation for animals is further broadened through fictional accounts of animals in a more realistic setting such as Lassie the dog or Flicka the horse.

Research has shown that children's attitudes towards animals develop through a number of stages. Between the ages of six and nine years, there is a marked increase in the level of affection children show towards animals, assuming they have been given opportunities to get to know animals at all. During the 10 to 13 years period children's knowledge and understanding of animals can show significant growth. During the mid-teens (13 to 16 years) a dramatic increase in ethical concerns about animal species, as part of a wider awareness of ecological and environmental issues, becomes evident.[40]

Some writers have recommended a role for schools in helping children to understand the world of real animals.[41] Schools can fill the gap in understanding by teaching about the environment and characteristics of real animals. By routinely caring for animals in the classroom or the home, children learn the rudiments of responsibility of people for animals and also the bond from animal to humans that comes from the quiet delight of holding something warm and furry. It is important at this early stage that children have actual hands-on experience with several animal species. It is also important to expose them early to the importance of wild animals to society and the importance of letting them be wild and not trying to make them into pets.

Pets and Self-identity

Having pets as children and throughout childhood and adolescence may play a part in establishing our self identity. In other words, living with a pet helps us to become clearer about the type of person we are. For one thing, having a pet such as a dog with which we establish a close and affectionate relationship can help us feel better about ourselves. We not only find out that we can give affection which is gratefully received but also that we are able to command affection unconditionally from our loyal pet.[42] Being able to give and receive affection is a crucial element in the development of a healthy self-concept. If we feel good about ourselves, knowing we are capable of being loved, it gives us more confidence in life generally.

Empirical support for the effects of pet ownership on adolescents' empathy and interpersonal trust has been reported elsewhere, but the same research found no significant effects on adolescents' self-esteem measures.[43]

Pets function particularly for adolescents as transitional objects much like the blanket or teddy bear does for infants. As transitional objects, pets help children feel safe without the presence of parents. Pets are more socially acceptable as transitional objects for older children than are inanimate objects. Adolescence brings with it a changing relationship to pets, in large part due to this emergence of pets as transitional objects. At this period, pets can be a confidant, an object of love, a protector, a social facilitator or a status symbol.[44] Moreover, the bond between children and pets is enhanced by its animate quality. The crucial attachment behaviour of proximity and caring between children and pets forms an active reciprocating alliance.[45] The relationship is simpler and less conflicted than are human relationships.

Like other transitional objects, most of the shared behaviours between animals and children are tactile rather than verbal. Pets can satisfy the child's need for physical contact and touch without the fear of entanglements that accompany contact with human beings. Pets can become special friends and that friendship can always be trusted and depended upon.[46]

Pets as Children

One aspect of identity development is learning to distinguish between various family and social roles in order to be able to learn about the responsibilities and expectations that such roles carry with them. For children, pets can sometimes come to occupy the role of a 'child', while children themselves try out the role of 'parent'. One researcher noted that pets can elicit maternal behaviours in children as young as three.[47] Other writers have observed that much of the usual activity that occurs between children and pets resembles parent–child relationships, with the animal representing the child as infant.[48]

Children unconsciously view their pets as an extension of themselves and treat their pets as they want to be treated themselves. This process is what Desmond Morris has called 'infantile parentalism' suggesting that this is one way children learn to cope with the loss of their own childhood.[49]

One writer discussed the case of a five-year-old insecure boy referred for psychiatric care owing to his habit of petting his goldfish. For this boy, petting the fish helped him feel both caring and cared for. Gradually he was able to transfer his affection toward a dog. With increased parental nurturance he became more confident and outgoing.[50] Another case was reported of a nine-year-old girl whose pets became symbolic substitutes for her ideal self. The sick pets that she care for and nursed back to health represented the cared-for, protected and loved child that she longed to be. The girl's mother was a vain woman concerned with appearances who turned most of her maternal instincts toward the family pet rather than her daughter. The girl's behaviour toward her pet was an unconscious effort to model 'good enough' mothering to her own mother.[51]

Many children grow up with parents unable to care for them properly or incapable of showing them affection, often because of their own emotional shortcomings, but who nevertheless show affection to an animal. The child then grows up thinking that if only he or she were an animal then they might receive parental love.[52] In one case in which this kind of animal identity was carried to an extreme, a seven-year-old boy with very low self-esteem took on the identity of a cat and meowed to his psychiatrist.[53]

Pets as Parents

It has been suggested that as children get older, the pet acquires many of the characteristics of the ideal mother.[54] The pet is devoted, attentive and loyal and much of the communication with the pet is non-verbal – all elements of the primary symbolic relationship with the mother. From a developmental point of view, a major task of childhood is the movement away from the primary symbolic relationship with the mother and the establishment of a separate and distinct identity.[55] This process of separation and individuation creates feelings of 'separation anxiety' that occur throughout the life process, particularly at stressful times of loss or during new experiences.[56]

Pets and Family Identity

Children in homes with pets show a wider range of interests in animals and animal-related subjects. They are more likely than non-pet owning children to read about animals, to enjoy animal stories, to watch programmes about animals on television, and to visit wildlife parks.[57] Pet-owning children also define their family structure differently from children with no pets. We have seen already that pet owners frequently regard their pets as members of the family. This idea has been found to surface in the way children perceive their families. Indeed, children may see themselves as closer to their pets than to other family members.

When asked to draw pictures of themselves and other family members, children may place their pets in closer proximity to themselves than other human family members. One reason for this may be that children's relationships with pets are seen as more accepting and less complex than those with other family members. Pets do not scold, criticize or demand changes to behaviour. They serve as playmates and companions, giving and receiving affection unconditionally and always greeting owners with enthusiasm.[58] The same research showed no differences in closeness of apparent relationships with dogs and cats, supporting the idea that closeness to pets is based on animals' characteristics in general rather than on the specific characteristics of a particular type of animal.

The distance between the self-figure in these drawings and the other figures was greater for younger children than for older children. Further, some younger children separated themselves from their pets by inserting a family-member figure between the self-figure and the pet figure. Older children did not do this. Younger children also tended to draw pet figures further away from their self-figures than did older children. Some young children may fear separation from a family member, usually the mother, so they situate themselves closer to her in their drawings. Moreover, some young children may harbour fears of animals which have not yet been conditioned out of them through positive relationships with pets. Whilst dogs and cats were drawn equally close to the self-figure of the child, pet fish tended to be placed further away indicating that there may be less close personal attachments to fish than to cats and dogs.

Which Pet Qualities do Children Like?

As we have seen already, children obtain many different gratifications from pets. But apart from general needs for companionship or affection, are there any specific physical qualities of pets that influence children's reactions? One interesting study observed how very young toddlers aged 6–30 months reacted to a toy dog that barked and moved like a real dog, a toy cat that purred and meowed when stroked, and a real family pet. The researchers were interested in finding out which qualities the toddlers responded to most of all. Did they seem to like these pets because of their tactile qualities, the sounds they made, the way they moved, or some other attributes? In the first place, these very young children showed the earliest signs of attachment either to the live or toy pets from the age of one year. Dogs were generally preferred to cats by both boys and girls, although boys exhibited more attachment behaviours than did girls.[59]

The Pet's Friendship Role

Perception of a pet's friendship role has been explored from several perspectives. Children aged 11 and 12 years have been reported as particularly likely to emphasize the importance of a pet's companionship attributes.[60] Among slightly younger children aged seven to 10 years old, the family dog tended to be regarded as a special friend.[61] In conclusion, pre-adolescent dog owners perceived their dogs as very much like a person and largely believed that the animals liked them very much.[62]

Early adolescents have been found to rate a pet as something that makes them feel good and satisfied about themselves.[63] In a study of latchkey children who called an after-school hotline, it was found that pet companionship was an important coping resource for loneliness and boredom.[64]

Pet friendship has been suggested as particularly important during pre-adolescence.[65] Over the pre-adolescent years, between nine and 14 years of age, an individual is in transition between childhood and puberty.[66] As the pre-adolescent prepares for the coming demands of adolescence and friends become increasingly important, pre-adolescents seek empathic, supportive friendship within the peer group.[67] The pre-adolescent generally chooses friends of the same sex who complement his or her personal needs. Inadequate friendship relationships can result in feelings of loneliness and isolation.

An investigation of aspects of children's friendship with the family pet during pre-adolescence revealed that children viewed the family pet as a friendly companion.[68] There was a generally positive regard for the pet. The friendship with the pet had two components: emotional reciprocity and caring responsibility. Significant affiliation responses included strong affective statements such as 'I love you' along with 'I make you feel liked'. The pleasurable socialization aspect of the pre-adolescent's emotional investment in the family pet was illustrated by the statement 'I think you are funny' or 'I like spending time with you', or 'like playing with you'. The caring responsibility aspect of the pre-adolescent pet friendship was reflected in the responses 'I take care of you' and 'I protect you'.

Perceived Ownership among Family Members

Ideas about pet ownership can vary from one family to the next. In some pet-owning households, the pet is seen as everyone's property, whereas in others, it is regarded primarily as belonging to one family member. In some families, the idea of the pet as 'property' is not consistent with the alternative notion of the pet as 'family member'. One study which tried to shed more light on this issue surveyed a number of parents and their children in the United States from dog-owning households. Out of 31 households who returned questionnaires, in seven cases the dog was described as belonging to the child and in 21 cases to the family as a whole. Among the children, most (20) thought that the dog was intended to be a companion or friend, whilst a smaller number (six) described the animal as an object for giving and receiving affection. In about half these households, the dog slept in the child's room.

Another sign of who was closest to the dog was who in the family spent most time with the animal. Most of the children in this small sample played more frequently with the dog than did any other family member but in regard to another important part of the relationship between human and animal, at feeding time it was generally the mother who fed the dog. The dog was exercised mainly by the child, however, in the 23 cases out of 31. Thus, through playing with the dog, exercising it and talking to it, children established a close bond of attachment. The dog was regarded as a cherished companion who gave as well as received affection.[69]

Problem Behaviour Associated with Children and Pets

Usually, unfavourable attachments are formed when a child has nowhere else to turn for understanding or affection, perhaps in situations of isolation, loneliness or depression. On occasions the child's need for animal companionship can reach pathological proportions. On the death of a pet, for example, the child refuses to let go and accept that the pet is never coming back.[70]

Under some circumstances, the normal formation of attachments can go wrong and result in anxious attachments and compulsive care-giving. In situations where children have failed to establish emotional bonds with parents or sense that their parents are rejecting them, an intense displacement of emotional attachment to a pet can occur. Subsequent separation and loss of such a pet can create complicated psychiatric reactions.[71]

A quite different reaction occurs, which can also reach pathological proportions, when children develop a fear of animals. Fear of animals may be very real. There are many situations in which we cannot blame a child for being afraid of cats, dogs or other animals because he or she has had a disturbing experience, such as, for example, being bitten. However, when a child refuses to go to school for fear of seeing even an innocent dog or panics in the presence of a little kitten, there is a good chance that the fear is out of proportion to reality and has become a phobia.

Cruelty to Animals and Children

Disturbances in children may also involve cruelty to animals. Van Leeuwen indicated that a certain degree of careless manipulation of small animals is not necessarily a sign of disturbance, particularly when the child is very young or inexperienced. But actions like setting fire to animals, tying the tails of animals together or killing companion animals are sure signs of trouble and warrant psychiatric assessment because such behaviour equals a desperate cry for help.[72]

A Dutch therapist recounted a case of a nine-year-old boy of normal intelligence who had stuffed sand into the mouth of an infant, pinched a piece off his pet rat's tail, maltreated his dog, tried to strangle his cat, put clothes pins on his little brother's fingers, and shaved his guinea pig. The boy was angry about a muscular weakness which was the first sign of a slowly progressive illness that would lead to death in about 10 years.[73]

Therapeutic Use of Pets with Children

Pets can meet the mental needs of children in different ways. To begin with, a pet is an active and energetic playmate. The child can release pent-up energy through playing with the pet.[74] In general, a child who is physically active is less likely to be tense than one who is not. A pet can also make a child feel safe. This may create a condition in which an anxious child may be more likely to explore new situations which he/she would otherwise be afraid to approach. A pet can also help the child make friends. A new pet can be the source of much interest among other children. For those children living in situations where they have little contact with others of their own age, pets can become substitute friends. One group of researchers quoted a child whom they interviewed as saying that 'pets are important especially for kids without brothers and sisters. They can get close to this animal and they both can grow up to love one another'.[75]

The presence of pets can also prove to be useful when dealing with children in more formal therapeutic situations. Children have been found to be relaxed and comforted by the therapist's dog.[76] It may break the ice with a shy child, otherwise reluctant to talk. The child may find reciprocal affection, including physical touch and tenderness, without getting caught up in an exchange of physical affection between therapist and patient.

Another therapist recounted the case of an 11-year-old girl who was deeply upset about her father's death, believing, wrongly, that she had caused it. The mother acquired a dog, on the psychotherapist's advice, to which the girl became attached. Sadly the dog was run over and killed. The girl grieved for the dog and through this experience was able also to grieve for her father, which, in turn, enabled her to master her feelings of depression.[77]

Pets can have a number of benefits for children. In the family context, pets can provide companions on which children can depend. They provide company for isolated youngsters and a source of social attention for more gregarious children. Pets also have potentially important developmental benefits. They can help to instil in the child a sense of responsibility and introduce the child to the concept of death. In a therapeutic context, animals can produce results where other forms of treatment have failed. Our introduction to pets during the earliest years of our lives can also lay the foundations of a generally positive disposition towards companion animals and increase the likelihood that we will own pets as adults. In the next chapter, we switch attention to the effects of pet ownership and animal companionship in later life.

References

1 Levinson, B.M. Pets and personality development. *Psychological Reports*, 42, 1031–1038, 1978.

2 Veevers, J.E. The social meaning of pets: Alternative roles for companion animals. In B. Sussman (Ed.) *Pets and the Family*. New York: Haworth, pp. 11–130, 1985.

3 Bossard, J.H. Domestic animals: Their role in family life and child development. In J. Bossard (Ed.) *Parent and Child: Studies in Family Behaviour*. Philadelphia: University of Pennsylvania Press, pp. 236–252, 1953.

4 Schowalter, J.E. The use and abuse of pets. *Journal of the American Academy of Child Psychiatry*, 22, 68–72, 1983.

5 Fogle, B. *Pets and Their People*. Glasgow: Williams, Collins, Sons, 1983.

6 Godwin, R.D. Trends in the ownership of domestic pets in Great Britain. In R.S. Anderson (Ed.) *Pets, Animals and Society*. London: Bailliere Tindall, pp.96–102, 1975. Griffiths, A.D. and Brenner, A. Survey of cat and dog ownership in Champaign County, Illinois. *Journal of the American Veterinary Medical Association*, 170(11), 1333–1340, 1977. Messent, P.R. and Horsfield, S. Pet population and the pet owner bond. In *The Human–Pet Relationship*. Vienna: IEMT [Institute for Interdisciplinary Research on the Human–Pet relationship], Austrian Academy of Sciences, pp. 9–17, 1985.

7 Salomon, A. Montreal children taking the test of animal affinities. *Annals of Medical Psychology*, 140(2), 207–224, 1982. Kidd, A.H. and Kidd, R.M. Children's attitudes about pets. *Psychological Reports*, 57, 15–31, 1985.

8 Macdonald, A. The pet dog in the home: A study of interactions. In B. Fogle (Ed.), *Interrelations between People and Pets*. Springfield, IL: Charles C. Thomas, 1981. Solomon, A., 1982, op.cit.

9 Levinson, B.M. Pets: A special technique in child psychotherapy. *Mental Hygiene*, 48, 243–244, 1964. Levinson, B.M. Household pets in residential schools: Their therapeutic potential. *Mental Hygiene*, 52, 411–414, 1968.

10 Bridger, H. The changing role of pets in society. *Journal of Small Animal Practice*, 1876, 17, 1–8.

11 Macdonald, A., 1981, op.cit.

12 Covert, A.M., Whiren, A.P., Keith, J., and Nelson, L. Pets, early adolescents and families. In B. Sussman (Ed.) *Pets and the Family*. New York: Haworth Press, pp. 95–108, 1985. Bergeson, F.S. The effects of pet-facilitated therapy on the self-esteem and socialisation of primary school children. Paper presented at Monaco '89 5th International Conference on the Relationship Between Humans and Animals, 1989. Paul, E.S. and Serpell, J.A. Why children keep pets: The influence of child and family characteristics. *Anthrozoos*, 5(4), 231–244, 1992.

13 Covert, A.M. et al., 1985, op.cit.

14 Poresky, R.H. and Hendrix, C. Developmental benefits of pets for young children. Paper presented at the Delta Society 7th Annual Conference *People, Animals and the Environment: Exploring Our Interdependence*, 1988.

15 Covert, A.M. et al., 1985, op.cit. Poresky, R.A. and Hendrix, C., 1990, op.cit.

16 Bailey, C.M. Exposure of pre-school children to companion animals: Impact on role taking skills. *Dissertation Abstracts International*, (8-A), 48, 1988. Mader, B., Hart, L.A. and Bergin, B. Social acknowledgements for children with disabilities: Effects of service dogs. *Child Development*, 60, 1529–1534, 1989.

17 Cain, A.O. A study of pets in the family system. In A.H. Katcher and A.M. Beck (Eds) *New Perspectives on Our Lives with Companion Animals*. Philadelphia: University of Pennsylvania Press, 1983.

18 Pedigree Petfoods. *Pet Ownership Survey*. Leicester, Melton Mowbray: Author, 1977.

19 Bowen, M. Family psychotherapy with a schizophrenic in the hospital and in private practice. In I. Borzormenyi-Nagy and I.C. Framo (Eds) *Intensive Family Therapy*, New York: Harper & Row, 1965.

20 Cain, A.O., 1983, op.cit.

21 Ruby, J. Images of the family: The symbolic implications of animal photography. In A.H. Katcher and A.M. Beck (Eds) *Perspectives on Our Lives with Companion Animals*. Philadelphia: University of Pennsylvania Press, 1983.

22 Levinson, B.M. *Pet-oriented Child Psychotherapy*. Springfield, IL; Charles C. Thomas, 1969.

23 Cain, A.O., 1983, op.cit

24 Salomon, A. 1982, op.cit.

25 Cain, A.O. A study of pets in the family system. *Human Behaviour*, 8(2), 24, 1979.

26 Levinson, B.M. *Pets and Human Development*. Springfield, IL: Charles C. Thomas, 1972.

27 Robin, M., ten Bensel, R., Quigley, J., and Anderson, R. Childhood pets and the psychosocial development of adolescents. In A.H. Katcher and A.M. Beck (Eds) *New Perspectives on Our Lives with Companion Animals*. Philadelphia: University of Pennsylvania Press, pp. 436–443, 1983.

28 Levinson, B.M. Pets and personality development. *Psychological Reports*, 42, 1031–1038, 1978.

29 Blue, G.F. The value of pets in children's lives. *Childhood Education*, 63, 84–90, 1986.

30 Kidd, A.H. and Kidd, R.M. Factors in children's attitudes towards pets. *Psychological Reports*, 46, 939–949, 1980.

31 Serpell, J.A. Childhood pets and their influence on adults' attitudes. *Psychological Reports*, 49, 651–654, 1981.

32 Kidd, A.H. and Kidd, R.M. Personality characteristics and preferences in pet ownership. *Psychological Reports*, 46, 939–949, 1980.

33 Poresky, R. Analysing human–animal relationship measures. *Anthrozoos*, 2, 236–244, 1989.

34 Poresky, R., Hendrix, C., Mosier, J. and Samuelson, M. The companion animal semantic differential: Long and short-form reliability and validity. *Educational and Psychological Measurement*, 48, 255–260, 1988.
35 Horn, J.C. and Meer, J. The pleasure of their company. *Psychology Today*, August, 52–57, 1984.
36 Brickel, C.M. Pet-facilitated psychotherapy: A theoretical explanation via attention shift. *Psychological Reports*, 50, 71–74, 1985.
37 Bowd, A.D. Young children's beliefs about animals. *Journal of Psychology*, 110, 263–266, 1982.
38 Van Leeuwen, J. A child psychiatrist's perspective on children and their companion animals. In B. Fogle (Ed.) *Interrelations Between People and Pets*. Springfield, IL: Charles C. Thomas, 1981.
39 Filiatre, J.C., Millot, J.L., and Montinquer, H. New findings on communication behaviour between the young child and his pet dog. In *The Human–Pet Relationship*. Vienna: IEMT, Austrian Academy of Sciences, 1985.
40 Kellert, S.R. and Westervelt, M.O. Attitudes toward animals: Age-related development among children. In R.S. Anderson, B.L. Hart and L.A. Hart (Eds) *The Pet Connection*. Minneapolis: University of Minnesota Press, 1983.
41 Busted, L.K. and Hines, L. Historical perspectives of the human–animal bond. In R.K. Anderson, B.L. Hart and L.A. Hart (Eds) *The Pet Connection*. Minneapolis: University of Minnesota Press, pp. 241–250, 1984.
42 Davis, J.H. Preadolescent self-concept development and pet ownership. *Anthrozoos*, 1, 91–94, 1987.
43 Hyde, K.R., Kurdek, L. and Larson, P. Relationships between pet ownership and self-esteem, social sensitivity and interpersonal trust. *Psychological Reports*, 52, 110, 1983.
44 Fogle, B., 1983, op.cit.
45 Bowlby, J. *Attachment and Loss*, Vol I: *Attachment*. London: Hogarth Press, 1969.
46 Levinson, B.M., 1969, op.cit.
47 Fogle, B., 1983, op.cit.
48 Beck, A. and Katcher, A. *Between Pets and People: The Importance of Animal Companionship*. New York: G.P. Putnam & Sons, 1983.
49 Morris, D. *The Naked Ape*. New York: McGraw-Hill, 1967.
50 Schowalter, J.E., 1983, op.cit..
51 Sherick, I. The significance of pets for children. In *Psychoanalytic Study of the Child*, 36, 193–215, 1981.
52 Searles, H.E. *The Nonhuman Environment*. New York: International University Press, 1960.
53 Kupferman, K. A latency boy's identity as a cat. *Psychoanalytic Study of the Child*, 32, 193–215, 1977.
54 Beck, A. and Katcher, A., 1987, op.cit.
55 Erickson, E. *Identity and the Life Cycle*. New York: W.W. Norton, 1980.
56 Perin, C. Dogs as symbols in human development. In B. Fogle (Ed.) *Interrelations Between People and Pets*. Springfield, IL: Charles C. Thomas, 1983.
57 Kidd, A.H. and Kidd, R.M. 1990, op.cit.
58 Kidd, A.H. and Kidd, R.M. Children's drawings and attachments to pets. *Psychological Reports*, 7791, 235–241, 1995.
59 Kidd, A.H. and Kidd, R.M., 1987, op.cit.
60 Solomon, A. Animals and children: The role of the pet. *Canada's Mental Health*, June, 9–13, 1981.

61 Bryant, B.K. The relevance of family and neighbourhood animals in social-emotional development in middle childhood. Paper presented at the Delta Society International Conference *Living Together, People, Animals and the Environment*, Boston, MA, 1986.

62 Davis, J.H., 1987, op.cit.

63 Juhasz, A.M. Problems toward animals: Age-related developments among children [Cited in David and Juhasz]. In M.B. Sussman (Ed.) *Pets and the Family*. New York: Howarth Press, pp. 79–94, 1985.

64 Gurney, L. An investigation of pets as providers of support to latchkey children. Unpublished manuscript, 1987, cited by Davis, J.H. and Juhasz, A.M. The preadolescent/pet friendship bond. *Anthrozoos*, 8(2), 78–82, 1995.

65 Levinson, B.M., 1972, op.cit.

66 Thornburg, H.D. Early adolescents: Their developmental characteristics. *The High School Journal*, 63, 215–221, 1980.

67 Youniss, J. *Parents and Peers in Social Development*. Chicago: University of Chicago Press, 1980.

68 Davis, J.H. and Juhasz, A.M. The preadolescent/pet bond and psychosocial development. In M.B. Sussman (Ed.) *Pets and the Family*. New York: Haworth Press, pp. 79–94, 1985.

69 Macdonald, A. The pet dog in the home: A study of interactions. In B. Fogle (Ed.) *Interrelations Between People and Pets*. Springfield, IL: Charles C. Thomas, 1981.

70 Keddie, K.M.G. Pathological mourning after the death of a domestic pet. *British Journal of Psychiatry*, 131, 21–25, 1977.

71 Rynearson, E.K. Humans and pets and attachment. *British Journal of Psychiatry*, 133, 550–555, 1978.

72 Hellman, D.S. and Blackman, N. Enuresis, firesetting and cruelty to animals: A triad predictive of adult crime. *American Journal of Psychiatry*, 122, 1431, 1966. Justice, B., Justice, R. and Kraft, I.A. Early warning signs of violence: is a triad enough? *American Journal of Psychiatry*, 131, 457, 1974.

73 Van Leeuwen, J., 1981, op.cit.

74 Feldman, B.M. Why people own pets. *Animal Regulation Studies*, 1, 87–94, 1977.

75 Robin, M. et al., 1987, op.cit.

76 Levinson, B.M., 1969, 1970, op.cit.

77 van Leeuwen, J., 1981, op.cit.

Chapter 8
How do pets keep you young?

A rich anecdotal lore exists in support of pets as companions to old people. Observational studies suggest that introducing pets into the lives of terminal cancer patients or the lives of patients in a geriatric ward brings about significant positive social and psychological consequences.[1] Bird placement among pensioners has been found to lead to positive psychological effects in comparison with pensioners who received a plant.[2] At least one evaluation of a companion animal programme, however, failed to show positive gains for those who acquired pets relative to a comparison group.[3] Even then, among pet owners who exhibited affection for their pets, there was a real benefit in respect of morale.

Surveys of elderly pet owners have indicated that pets are believed to contribute to feelings of physical and emotional well-being. This effect seems to operate principally through improving morale among people who are perhaps unwell or disabled and unable to get around very much.[4] Pets can help their owners in times of stress. Research with elderly people has found that pet owners are less likely to seek help from their doctor than are non-pet owners even when they have suffered from a number of stressful life events. Dogs can prove to be particularly effective stress relievers. Dog owners enjoy social companionship with their pets, obtain support and comfort from a loyal friend, and benefit from the physical exercise involved in taking their pet for a walk.[5]

The evidence for the positive benefits pets can have for older people derives from two main strands of research. The first of these has investigated the physical and mental health benefits of pets for old people who remain independent and live in their own homes. The second strand of evidence derives from the adoption of pet residential or visitation programmes for institutionalized elderly people. For the non-institutionalized older person, pets have been found to bring a range of social, mood-enhancing and life expectancy benefits.

The Social Benefits of Pet Ownership

There is a social function of pet ownership as well as physical and emotional pay-offs. For some people, pets have social status which rubs off on their owners. Furthermore, owning a pet can provide a source of conversation with other people, especially other pet owners with whom a social network may become established.[6] Elderly people, whether living independently in their own homes or in special housing with others of their age, have often identified the companionship that animals can provide as a primary reason for having pets. However, whether they prefer to care for their own pet or to have someone else's pet come to visit often depends on where they live and how much space they have. Avoiding direct involvement in caring for a pet is also affected by the physical well-being of the elderly person.[7] Another important factor, however, was the extent to which old people had enjoyed prolonged contact with animals earlier in life. The more this had been the case, the more enthusiastic they were about having their own pet again. It was certainly clear that many of the elderly are interested in maintaining some sort of contact with animals. But they do not all want the responsibility of being the primary carer. Despite the practical difficulties of being able to cope with a pet themselves, many elderly people display a deep-rooted tendency to want to maintain some form of direct contact with animals.

Pets can play a central role in the social interactions of elderly people. Research with individuals aged 65 to 78 years in the United States found that a pet dog would often feature as the focal point of conversation for owners. Conversations were monitored while these elderly pet owners were walking their dogs. The owners talked *to* their dogs when on their own and in the presence of other people, and invariably talked *about* their dogs to others. When speaking to their dogs, owners would frequently repeat what they were saying. Passers-by often joined in talking to the dogs as well, confirming the social acceptability of such conversations.[8]

Pets may serve to buffer and normalize ageing persons' sense of social isolation. In a study of elderly New Zealand women, pet cats appeared to reduce loneliness by substituting for some aspects of social interaction with others.[9] In Rhode Island, USA, attachment to pets was found to be especially high among those people who had been widowed or who had never married.[10] In several North American studies, pet ownership or attachment has been shown to be associated with the maintenance of physical or emotional health during bereavement.[11]

In a British study, researchers gave birds or plants to a small number of elderly pensioners who were living alone.[12] They compared changes in attitudes toward people and toward their own psychological health over the course of the study among six people given birds, six given begonias and six who were given nothing. Those individuals who received birds showed improvements in their general state of health over a five-month observation period. In contrast, neither of the other two groups exhibited any change in their health.

A number of surveys of pet satisfaction among elderly rural pet owners in the United States found that companion animals are more beneficial for some elderly than for others. Factors such as people's gender, economic situation, marital status and degree of attachment to their pets all have to be taken into account in determining how important pet ownership *per se* is to an elderly person's physical and emotional well-being.[13] In shedding further light on this subject, an Australian survey showed that divorced, separated, widowed and childless people – that is, individuals lacking a normal family network – had more of their needs satisfied by pet dogs than was the case among dog owners at other stages of the family life cycle.[14]

Non-pet owners reported a deterioration of health after the loss of a spouse, whereas dog owners who had formed a bond with their dogs reported no such deterioration if their health was generally good anyway.[15] Particularly when it involves a close attachment, pet ownership among elderly individuals has been associated with less depression among bereaved persons who have recently lost a spouse and who have few or no confidants.[16]

In documenting the fact that elderly people are at risk from social isolation, researchers have shown that in New York City, elderly people receive less favourable treatment by physicians.[17] Some elderly people in the United States have no human friends in whom they confide.[18] In one study of the relationships of 92 elderly people and their dogs, the dog was found to be the only friend for a large majority of the men and women.[19]

Other studies have provided clear evidence that pets stimulate social interactions. Dogs were found significantly to enhance the number of friendly approaches in studies of people walking their dogs in a London park.[20] American adults or children who use wheelchairs and are accompanied by a service dog attracted more conversation from others.[21] This socialization would be most valuable for individuals who are feeling isolated, including elderly people, who are often discounted or rejected.

Walks with a dog represent routine events in an elderly person's life, giving them something to look forward to each day. The same routes are taken and the same people encountered on the walks. These people often become friends. In talking to and about the dog, the walker and passers-by had near at hand a comfortable companion and a target of conversation. Even small animals such as rabbits or turtles become a major topic of conversation for unfamiliar passers-by who approach.[22]

In addition to facilitating social contact with people, dogs are willing companions who are virtually always available. One writer has proposed seven alternatives for how pets might affect social interaction including as (a) a basis for making social judgements, (b) a source of envy or self-esteem, (c) a novelty, (d) an innate release mechanism, (e) a source of common interest, (f) a social facilitator, and (g) an 'ice breaker'.[23] All but the first two could play a role in conversation.

Dog owners talk regularly to their dogs during walks. Most North American dog owners reported that they talk to their dogs.[24] As if conversing with people, dog owners often ask their dogs questions.[25] Pets other than dogs may also be the targets of human conversation. Pet owners often speak to their birds. When doing so, they typically adopt a quieter style of conversation using a softer voice and speaking in shorter sentences. Often words are used that are reminiscent of baby talk.[26] Even convicts use a stereotyped style of discourse with their pets, lowering their voices, decreasing the rate of speech, asking their pets questions and pausing, as if the animals were going to reply.[27]

Companionship with pets tends to be lifelong. People with a sustained lifetime predilection for animals will continue to seek contact with them as long as they are healthy and the physical environment in which they live allows pets to be kept.[28]

The Mood-enhancing Effects of Pets

Pets can lift their owners' moods, making them feel better about themselves and happier with life. To some degree, this observation may be the result of old people with more positive personality dispositions being drawn to pets in the first place. But there is no doubt that pet ownership has distinctly positive benefits for old people in its own right. Certainly, pet owners exhibit much more positive personality and mood profiles than do non-pet owners among older people. Such pet owners differ from non-pet-owning counterparts by rating higher in terms of wanting or needing to care and take responsibility for other things, whereas they tend to score lower in terms of their need to be looked after by others. Pet owners also had higher self-esteem and had greater self-confidence, but were not as self-centred as non-pet owners. Pet owners have been found to have a more optimistic outlook on life, although the one area where they did worry was over their pet's health and well-being.[29]

People of pension age who own a pet show a generally more positive outlook on life. They exhibit more positive moods, more ambition, and retain stronger feelings than do non-pet owners of being perfectly able to fend for themselves. In so many ways, then, pet ownership seems to bring the best out in older people.[30]

People whose social circumstances are already reasonably stable and more affluent may benefit all the more from pet ownership. In one survey, elderly women who owned pets expressed greater personal happiness than did non-pet owners. This effect was most pronounced, however, among women of higher socioeconomic status. Further investigation revealed, however, that the relationship between pet ownership and feelings of personal well-being was even more complex. The degree of attachment between pet and owner was another important factor. Owners who did not have a strong attachment to their pet were often unhappy, whilst those who had developed a strong bond with their animal companion were happiest of all.[31]

Pets and Life Expectancy

In helping older people feel better about themselves, there may be a very significant knock-on effect of pet ownership of extending the expected life span of a person. The benefits obtained from pets may be lifelong. A number of writers have suggested that independent older people who keep pets may live longer and healthier lives than those without animals,[32] although contradictory and inconclusive findings have also been reported on this issue.[33] Individuals who bond with pets in early life often retain a positive disposition towards them into later life. The continued presence of pets throughout life not only helps the individual cope with all kinds of stresses, but may actually contribute to an extended life span. Several different pieces of research into pet ownership by the elderly have confirmed that having animal companions around helps old people live longer.[34] The ownership of companion animals has been positively associated with better health status among people receiving medical treatment,[35] and has been related to enhanced survival rates among former patients or coronary care units.[36]

Having a pet encourages the older person to become more physically active. The responsibility of looking after an animal gives the individual a sense of purpose and, in the case of some pets of course, the owner has to make arrangements to give it exercise. Walking the dog not only exercises the pet, but the owner too.

Reports have noted that in geriatric institutions pet ownership helps to reduce loneliness, isolation and withdrawal of the inhabitants, thereby lowering the life-threatening depression so characteristic of many geriatrics. Owning a pet can help slow deterioration in terminal geriatrics by helping them get more involved in life through keeping them out of bed and moving around.

Pet research casts a special light on two issues that have drawn the attention of many people in gerontology, namely reminiscing and disengagement. In the psychology of ageing, reminiscence is no longer perceived of as a harmless, pointless activity. Rather, it is a healthy and productive process through which the elderly integrate the threads of their existence and come to an appreciation of what has been meaningful in their lives. Reminiscing is therefore a development task that marks an older person's continued growth and present adjustment.[37] Several observers have noted that pets facilitate this activity by triggering memories from childhood and other life stages, thereby contributing to the fulfilment of a significant endeavour.[38]

A number of factors appear to underlie this connection. First, animals are directly associated with real events in the personal histories of people who are lifelong pet owners. Second, pets encourage individuals to engage in regressive forms of play that characterized earlier stages of their development.[39] Third, childhood experiences with pets have been shown to shape the adult patterns and relationships that people later establish with animals.[40] Fourth, as Carl Jung recognized over half a century ago, the elderly resemble children in that these two age groups are most readily in touch with the unconscious, a side of ourselves that animals symbolize. As tokens and symbols, pets may therefore foster communication with this part of the human psyche.[41]

Disengagement is another process that has been linked with the elderly.[42] It explains their status as a result of a mutual withdrawal by the aged and those who once associated with them. Critics point out that many older people do not want to dissociate themselves from social and cultural life, but are cut off from once satisfying experiences by the geographic mobility of other family members, the death of spouses and contemporaries, the institutionalization that they and significant others undergo, their poverty or reduced financial resources, the limitations imposed by their declining health and vigour, and cultural attitudes which stereotype and stigmatize elderly people in negative ways.[43]

Pet Therapy among the Elderly

Pets have been used with growing popularity in certain parts of the world in therapeutic contexts with the elderly. In a therapy context, pets can be used as an adjunct to the therapist, as sole therapeutic agent, as a catalyst for change, and as a means of facilitating contact with nature. Each of these applications has been used with some success.[44]

The work of Boris Levinson and Elizabeth Corson popularized the modern trend towards animal-facilitated therapy. Levinson suggested there were benefits for patients in a clinical psychological setting when companion animals were present during therapy sessions.[45] The Corsons' early work involved providing suitable dogs for psychiatric patients to form loving relationships with and for the patients to develop social skills.[46] They also encouraged patients to take care of the animals and ultimately to take better care of themselves. These pioneers of pet-facilitated therapy were also the first to try and evaluate pet therapy programmes. Their evaluation methods, which involved questionnaires on patient progress being recorded by nurses and videotaped recordings of resident–staff interactions, enabled quantification of patient responses.

Pets have been found to provide valuable, morale-boosting companionship for elderly patients living on their own and to have a range of positive benefits for elderly patients in clinical settings such as nursing homes, rehabilitation centres and hospitals. The benefits of human–animal bonding include a positive physiological effect on the heart, a reduced need for medication, and assistance for people with disabilities. Pets in these conditions can give love and friendship that boosts feelings of self-worth among individuals who might otherwise fade away from feelings of depression.[47]

In a controlled study of the treatment of clinical depression among elderly patients, the introduction of a dog to the therapy session was found to enhance the willingness of participants to engage in conversation with the rest of the group and the therapist. The dog served as a catalyst for disclosure by giving the patients a non-threatening object to focus upon and talk about. Once they had begun to open up and engage in conversation in this way, the therapist was able to direct the conversation onto other matters more central to the patients' problems.[48] The ability of animals to relax elderly people has been demonstrated in studies with institutionalized and non-institutionalized people. Groups of elderly people who were introduced to the new hobby of keeping fish aquariums were found to experience reduced blood pressure and conscious feelings of being happier and more relaxed.[49]

In a nursing home setting, residents were, for the purposes of an experiment, divided randomly into different groups, whereby some residents received a wild-bird feeder which was placed outside their window. In some of these cases an additional instruction was given to residents to take personal responsibility for ensuring that food was placed in the dispenser, while others were not told to do so. After a time, all residents were questioned about how happy and how satisfied with life they were. The placement of a bird feeder over which residents were invited to take personal charge was associated with much more positive feelings about their personal circumstances.[50]

In another controlled study the efficacy of animal companionship as a therapy intervention for hospitalized elderly patients was investigated. In this context, patients were randomly assigned to conditions in which they enjoyed contact with dogs who were allowed to visit, or received brief talks about dogs, or engaged in an exercise programme. Direct contact with dogs was found to produce some positive changes in that the patients became less irritable and withdrawn and made more effort to help themselves rather than waiting for others to assist them.[51]

Allocating companion pets to the wards where elderly hospitalized inpatients are housed has also been found to have a measurable effect on morale and levels of social interaction. The dogs served as talking points, personal companions, and a distraction from everyday concerns.[52] Whilst hospital inpatients can be cheered up by visitors, one study found that when volunteer visitors also brought a dog with them this could achieve an even more powerful effect. One of the reasons for this positive effect was that the dogs created an air of domesticity for elderly residents who had been cut off from their homes and families by illness and geographical distance. The common interest that inpatients and visitors had in the dogs resulted in the visitors coming to see themselves and to be seen by patients as friends rather than volunteers.[53] Sometimes, such visits could trigger childhood memories among elderly inpatients who had owned pets themselves as children. For other residents as well, the presence of dogs helped to replace the loss of companionship in later life from their pets who were now being cared for by other family members.[54]

Visiting Dog Programmes in Nursing Homes

One suggestion is that the role of a pet in a nursing home could be to relieve feelings of loneliness, depression and boredom.[55] Companion animals, in this context, could decrease anxiety, loneliness and depression because they can be touched and exercised and provide a sense of protection for nursing home residents.[56] Other research has also addressed the problem of depression in a nursing home and tried to evaluate the effects of animal-facilitated therapy by using psychological tests. This study showed that there were significant treatment effects between the study groups on their depression scores after implementation of the pet programme; also, the group involved with the pet displayed a greater frequency of social interactions.[57]

Animal visits to semi-institutionalized elderly have been found to have a marked positive impact on the well-being of occupants. A study in which two experimental groups were compared comprised one with weekly visits of animals and the other with visits by humans only. The research found improvements in the visiting animal group on a number of dimensions; however, only the humans-only group did not display any changes.[58] It is also possible that the human handlers who accompanied the pets when they visited the nursing homes could have a confounding effect on research into visiting pet programmes.[59]

In another analysis of the effects of pets on chronically ill, confused, elderly patients in an institutional setting, the patients were cognitively impaired and had negligible capacity for socialization and communication, owing to their confused state.[60] Two scales were used for the evaluation of therapeutic and behavioural changes in patients, and they concluded that puppies did not have any effects on the severely debilitated patients, who were unable to remember the pups after they were out of contact with them. This suggested that visiting animals did not offer enough stimulation for the subjects. An important limitation of this study was the lack of a standard behavioural rating scale to measure quality of life or enjoyment.

One visiting dog programme reported benefits including decreased verbal response time to questions and increased interactions between residents. As a consequence of the visiting dog programme resident friendships were enhanced, loneliness and isolation were decreased and there was an enhanced atmosphere of community feeling among residents.[61]

Joel Savishinsky reported an anthropological study of pet visiting programmes to three nursing homes to reveal five aspects of how elderly residents dealt with their past and present ties to their families.[62] This study used participant observation, unstructured interviewing and the collection of life-history materials on residents. Pet sessions were found to achieve their basic goal of fostering human–animal contact, but they accomplished this goal in distinct ways in each of the homes studied. At two of the homes with just over 70 residents each, people were seen by small numbers of volunteers and animals in a group format. At the third nursing home with more than 250 residents, a greater number of pets and volunteers moved around the building separately and at their own pace, usually visiting individual residents in their own rooms or lounge areas.

Pet visiting sessions could trigger childhood memories and family reminiscences associated with animals. Pet loss and human loss were spoken about as interrelated experiences. Animal visits highlighted and helped counteract the decline of domesticity that people go through in institutions. Residents also explored their ties to pets they had tried to give up and their relationships with family members currently caring for these animals. Occasional visits of relatives during pet sessions indicated the role of animals in domestic interaction and the reaction of family members to the situation of their institution-dwelling relatives.

The weekly pet visits promoted a great variety of social, physical and verbal interactions at the facilities. Residents enjoyed the tactile stimulation of contact with animals, an experience that restored an element of touch to the lives of people who are more often handled than led. Furthermore, pet sessions involved social encounters not only between volunteers and residents, but between the latter and staff, and between individuals and their fellow residents. By providing a shared source of approved interest, animals thus crystallized an increase in sociability among several categories of people.

The presence of pets also made animals an obvious and easy topic of conversation. More noteworthy and more unexpected was the frequency with which certain other subjects were voluntarily raised by residents. Many of their conversations, initially centred on the animals, eventually shifted to a concern with their former pets and, from this, their reflections on a range of personal and family issues. The latter included: (a) childhood memories and family reminiscences associated with animals; (b) pet loss and human loss as interrelated experiences; (c) the decline of domesticity that people go through as a result of being institutionalized; and (d) residents' ties to pets they had to give up when moving into the home, and their relationships with those family members currently caring for these animals.

The perception that animals promote the fulfilment of human needs has led to an increase in pet-facilitated therapy programmes. Elderly people are among the prime recipients of these efforts, and programmes have been geared both to aged individuals who live in their own homes,[63] and to those who reside in retirement communities, geriatric facilities, or nursing homes.[64]

Contacts with pet animals are designed to address some of the significant losses that elderly people commonly experience, including diminishing companionship, a decrease in tactile experience, a decline in stimulating leisure activities, and reduced ties with family and friends. As many elderly people have also had to give up their own pets on moving into housing units or institutions designed for their age group, animal visitations are also meant to fill part of the gap created by this additional, involuntary loss. Pet programmes thus centre on the disruptions in family and personal life that accompany ageing, and they constitute one social attempt to reconstruct a balance of domestic experiences caused by the diminution of earlier family relationships.

Another research group measured the impact of visiting or resident dog programmes in three nursing homes in Brisbane, Australia. Tension and confusion were found to be reduced in the nursing home with a resident dog.[65] The resident dog group showed significant decreases in depression. Resident and visiting dogs enhanced vigour and decreased fatigue levels. Confusion scores also reduced over time for residents who kept company with a dog.

Positive Benefits

In later life, as we become less mobile and more socially isolated, pets can provide a valuable source of companionship and encouragement to continue to lead an active life. Having a creature that is dependent on our care and attention gives us a sense of purpose and can make us feel worthy. Pets that require exercise also create opportunities for social contact with other pet owners and encourage us to take exercise as well. All of these positive side-effects of pet ownership contribute to a more active lifestyle and, in turn, an increased probability of a longer life. Even among elderly people who have lost their independence through being institutionalized, keeping pets or experiencing visits from animals can produce important physical and psychological benefits. As we grow older and lose those close to us, pets can provide important emotional support. Eventually, of course, even our most loved animal companions leave us. At that point we must learn to cope with a loss which for many pet owners can be as upsetting as losing a family member or close friend. In the next chapter, we explore the significance of pet loss, and also the strength that having a pet can give us following the loss of close human companions.

References

1 Brickel, C.M. Pet–facilitated psychotherapy: A theoretical explanation via attentional shifts. *Psychological Reports*, 50, 71–74, 1982.
2 Mugford, R.A. and M'Comisky, J. Some recent work on the psychotherapeutic value of cage birds with old people. In R. S. Anderson (Ed.) *Pet Animals and Society*. London: Bailliere Tindall, pp. 54–65, 1974.
3 Lago, D., Connell, C. and Knight, B. The effects of animal companionship on older persons living at home. *Proceedings of the International Symposium on the Occasion of the 80th Birthday of Nobel Prize Winner Professor Konrad Lorenz*, pp. 34–36. Vienna, Austria: Austrian Academy of Sciences, Institute for Interdisciplinary Research on Human–Pet Relationships, 1983.
4 Lago, D., Kafer, R.J., Delaney, M. and Connell, C. Assessments of favourable attitudes toward pets: Development and preliminary validation of self-report pet relationship scales. *Anthrozoos*, 1(4), 240–254, 1987.
5 Siegel, J.M. Stressful life events and the use of physician services among the elderly: The moderating role of pet ownership. *Journal of Personality and Social Psychology*, 58, 1081–1086, 1990.
6 Netting, F.E., Wilson, C.C. and Fruge, C. Pet ownership and non-ownership among elderly in Arizona. *Anthrozoos*, 2, 125–132, 1988.
7 Verderber, S. Elderly persons' appraisal of animals in the residential environment. *Anthrozoos*, 4(3), 164–173, 1991.
8 Rogers, J., Hart, L.A. and Boltz, R.P. The role of pet dogs in casual conversation of elderly adults. *Journal of Social Psychology*, 13393, 265–277, 1993.
9 Mahalski, P.A., Jones, R. and Maxwell, G.M. The value of cat ownership to elderly women living alone. *International Journal of Aging and Human Development*, 27, 249–260, 1980.
10 Albert, A. and Bulcroft, K. Pets and urban life. *Anthrozoos*, 1, 9–25, 1987.
11 Akiyama, H., Hotlzman, J.M. and Batz, W.E. Pet ownership and health status during bereavement. *Omega: Journal of Death and Dying*, 17, 181–193, 1987. Lund, D.A., Johnson, R., Baraki, N. and Dimond, M.F. Can pets help the bereaved? *Journal of Gerontological Nursing*, 10, 6–12, 1984.
12 Mugford, R.A. and M'Comisky, J., 1975, op.cit.
13 Connell, M.S. and Lago, D.J. Favourable attitudes toward pets and happiness among the elderly. In R.K. Anderson, B.L. Hart and L.A. Hart (Eds) *The Pet Connection*. Minneapolis: University of Minnesota Press, 1983. Lago, D.J. et al., 1983, op.cit.
14 Salmon, P.W. and Salmon, I.M. Who owns who? Psychological research into the human–pet bond in Australia. In A.H. Katcher and A.M Beck (Eds) *New Perspectives on Our Lives with Companion Animals*. Philadelphia: University of Pennsylvania Press, pp. 244–265, 1983.

15 Bolin, S.E. The effects of companion animals during conjugal bereavement. *Anthrozoos*, 1(1), 26–35, 1987.

16 Garrity, T.F., Stallones, L., Marx, M. and Johnson, T.P. Pet ownership and attachment as supportive factors in the health of the elderly. *Anthrozoos*, 3, 35–44, 1989.

17 Greene, M.G., Adelman, R., Charan, R. and Hoffman, S. Ageism in the medical encounter. An exploratory study of the doctor–elderly patient relationship. *Language and Communication*, 6, 113–124, 1986.

18 Garrity, T.F. et al., 1989, op.cit.

19 Peretti, P.O. Elderly–animal friendship bonds. *Social Behaviour and Personality*, 18, 151–156, 1990.

20 Messent, P.R. Social facilitation of contact with other people by pet dogs. In A.H. Katcher and A.M. Beck (Eds) *New Perspectives on Our Lives with Companion Animals*. Philadelphia: University of Pennsylvania Press, 1983.

21 Eddy, J., Hart, L.A. and Holtz, R.P. The effects of service dogs on social acknowledgements of people in wheelchairs. *Journal of Psychology*, 122(1), 39–45, 1988. Mader, B., Hart, L.A. and Bergin, B. Social acknowledgements for children with disabilities: Effect of service dogs. *Child Development*, 60, 1519–1534, 1989.

22 Hunt, S.J., Hart, L.A. and Gomulkiewicz, R. The role of small animals in social interactions between strangers. *Journal of Social Psychology*, 132, 245–256, 1992.

23 Messent, P.R. Correlates and effects of pet ownership. In R.K. Anderson, B.L. Hart and L.A. Hart (Eds) *The Pet Connection*. Minneapolis: University of Minnesota Press, 1984.

24 Katcher, A.H. Interrelations between people and their pets: Form and function. In B. Fogle (Ed.) *Interrelations Between People and Their Pets*. Springfield, IL: Charles C. Thomas, 1981.

25 Stallones, L., Marx, M.B., Garrity, T.F. and Johnson, T.P. Attachment to companion animals among older pet owners. *Anthrozoos*, 2, 118–124, 1988.

26 Katcher, A. Physiologic and behavioural responses to companion animals. *Veterinary Clinics of North America: Small Animal Practice*, 15, 403–410, 1985.

27 Katcher, A., Beck, A. and Levine, D. Evaluation of a pet programme in prison – the PAL project at Lorton. *Anthrozoos*, 2, 175–180, 1989.

28 Verderber, S., 1991, op.cit.

29 Kidd, A.H. and Kidd, R.M. Personality characteristics and preferences in pet ownership. *Psychological Reports*, 46, 939–949, 1980.

30 Kidd, A.H. and Feldman, B.M. Pet ownership and self-perceptions of old people. *Psychological Reports*, 48, 867–875, 1981..

31 Ory, M.G. and Goldberg, E.L. Pet possession and life satisfaction among elderly women. In A.H. Katcher and A.M. Beck (Eds) *New Perspectives on Our Lives with Companion Animals*. Philadelphia: University of Pennsylvania Press, 1983. Ory, M.G. and Goldberg, E.L. An epidemiological study of pet ownership in the community. In R.K. Anderson, B.L. Hart and L.A. Hart (Eds) *The Pet Connection*. Minnesota: University of Minneapolis Press, 1984.

32 Bustad, L.K. and Hines, L. Placement of animals with the elderly: Benefits and strategies. *California Veterinarian*, 36, 37–44, 50, 1982. Messent, P.R., 1983, op.cit.

33 Robb, S.S. and Stegman, C.E. Companion animals and elderly people: A challenge for evaluators of social support. *The Gerontologist*, 23, 277–282, 1983. Lago, D., Connell, C.M. and Knight, B. A companion animal programme. In M.A. Sanyer and M. Gatz (Eds) *Mental Health and Aging*. Beverly Hills, CA: Sage, 1983.

34 Thompson, M.K. Adaptation of loneliness in old age. *Proceedings of the Royal*

Society of Medicine, 66, 887, 1973. Corson, S.A., Corson, E.O. and Gwynne, P. Pet-facilitated psychotherapy in a hospital setting. In J.H. Masserman (Ed.) *Current Psychiatric Therapies*, Vol. 15. New York: Grune & Stratton, pp. 277–286, 1975. Corson, S.A. and Corson, E.O. Pets as mediators of therapy in custodial institutions for the aged. In J.H. Masserman (Ed.) *Current Psychiatric Therapies*, Vol.18. New York: Grune & Stratton, pp. 195–205, 1078.

35 Katcher, A.H. and Friedmann, E. Potential health value of pet ownership. *The Compendium on Continuing Education for the Practising Veterinarian*, 2, 112–122, 1980. Robb, S.S. and Stegman, C.E., 1983, op.cit.

36 Friedmann, E., Katcher, A.H., Lynch, J.J., and Thoma, S. Animal companions and one-year survival of patients after discharge from coronary care unit. *Public Health Report*, 95, 307–312, 1980.

37 Butler, R.N. The life review: An interpretation of reminiscence in the aged. In B.L. Neugarten (Ed.) *Middle Age and Aging*. Chicago, IL: University of Chicago Press, 1968. Myerhoff, B. *Number Our Days*. New York: Simon & Schuster, 1978.

38 Levinson, B.M. *Pets and Human Development*. Springfield, IL: Charles C. Thomas, 1972. Bustad, L.K. *Animals, Aging and the Aged*. Minneapolis, MN: University of Minnesota Press, 1980. Brickel, C.M. Pet-facilitated psychotherapy: A theoretical explanation via attention shifts. *Psychological Reports*, 50, 71–74, 1984.

39 Corson, S.A. and Corson, E.O. Pet animals as non-verbal communication mediators in psychotherapy in institutional settings. In S.A. Corson and E.O. Corson (Eds) *Ethology and Non-Verbal Communication in Mental Health*. New York: Pergamon Press, 1980.

40 Messent, P.A., 1983, op.cit.

41 Jung, C.G. *Modern Man in Search of a Soul* (W.S.Dell & C.F. Baynes, trans.) New York: Harcourt, Brace & World, 1933.

42 Cumming, E. and Henry, W. *Growing Old*. New York: Basic Books, 1961.

43 Watson, W.H. and Maxwell, R.J. *Human Aging and Dying: A Study in Sociocultural Gerontology*. New York: St Martin's Press, 1977.

44 Levinson, B.M., 1972, op.cit.

45 Levinson, B.M., 1972, op.cit.

46 Corson, E.O. et al., 1975, op.cit. Corson, S.A., Corson, E.O., Gwynne, P.H., and Arnold, L.E. Pet dogs as nonverbal communication links in hospital psychiatry. *Comprehensive Psychiatry*, 18, 61–72, 1977. Corson, S.A. and Corson, E.O., 1980, op.cit.

47 Hoffman, R.G. Companion animals: A therapeutic measure for elderly patients. *Journal of Gerontological Social Work*, 18(1–2), 195–205, 1991.

48 Brickel, C.M. Depression in the nursing home: A pilot study using pet-facilitated psychotherapy. In R.K. Anderson, B.L. Hart, and L.A. Hart (Eds) *The Pet Connection*. Minnesota, MN: University of Minneapolis Press, pp. 407–415, 1984.

49 Riddick, C.C. Health, aquariums and non-institutionalised elderly. In B. Sussman (Ed.) *Pets and the Family*. New York: Haworth Press, pp. 163–173, 1985.

50 Banziger, G. and Roush, S. Nursing homes for the birds: A control-relevant intervention with bird feeders. *The Gerontologist*, 23, 527–531, 1983.

51 Zisselman, M.H., Rovner, B.W., Shmuely, Y. and Ferrie, P. A pet therapy intervention with geriatric psychiatry inpatients. *American Journal of Occupational Therapy*, 50(1), 47–51, 1996.

52 Haughie, E., Milne, D. and Elliott, V. An evaluation of companion pets with elderly psychiatric patients. *Behavioural Psychotherapy*, 29(4), 367–372, 1992.

53 Savishinsky, J.S. Intimacy, domesticity and pet therapy with the elderly: Expectation and experience among nursing home volunteers. *Social Science and Medicine*, 34(2), 1325–1334, 1992.

54 Savishinsky, J. Pets and family relationships among nursing home residents. *Marriage and Family Review*, 8, 109–134, 1985.

55 Andrysco, R.M. PFT in an Ohio retirement nursing community. *The Latham Letter*, Spring, 1982.

56 Fogle, B., 1981, op.cit.

57 Brickel, C.M., 1982, op.cit

58 Francis, G. and Odell, S. Long-term residence and loneliness: Myth or reality? *Journal of Gerontological Nursing*, 5, 9–11, 1979.

59 Hendy, H.M. Effects of pets on the sociability and health activities of nursing home residents. In R.K. Anderson, B.L. Hart and L.A. Hart (Eds) *The Pet Connection*. Minneapolis, MN: University of Minnesota Press, pp. 430–437, 1984.

60 Jendro, C., Watson, C. and Quigley, J. The effects of pets on the chronically ill elderly. In R.K. Anderson, B.L. Hart and L.A. Hart (Eds) *The Pet Connection*. Minneapolis, MN: University of Minnesota Press, pp. 430–437, 1984.

61 Torrence, M.E. The veterinarian's role in pet-facilitated therapy in nursing homes. In R.K. Anderson, B.L. Hart and L.A. Hart (Eds) *The Pet Connection*. Minneapolis, MN: University of Minnesota Press, pp. 423–429, 1984.

62 Savishinsky, J., 1985, op.cit.

63 Mugford, R.A. and M'Comisky, J. Some recent work on the psychotherapeutic value of cage birds with old people. In R.S. Anderson, (Ed.) *Pet Animals and Society*. London: Baillière Tindall, pp. 54–55, 1974.

64 Corson, S.A. and Corson, E.O., 1980, op.cit. Bustad, L.K., 1980, op.cit.

65 Crowley-Robinson, P., Fenwick, D.C. and Blackshaw, J.K. A long-term study of elderly people in nursing homes with visiting and resident dogs. *Applied Animal Behaviour Science*, 47, (1–2), 137–148, 1996.

Chapter 9
How to cope with the loss of a pet

We have seen that strong attachments can develop between owners and their pets. Attachment is of crucial importance in all social animal species. Human development, however, inevitably brings with it a distrust of permanent unwavering attachments. The unmitigated attachment that a baby has for its mother must finally yield to permit the independence necessary for intellectual and healthy emotional development. As we saw in Chapter 3, owners and pets can develop a similar bond. Furthermore, such attachments can be so strong that the owner may be reluctant to let go. The owner, under extreme circumstances, becomes as dependent on the pet as the pet is on the owner. At times of stress, some pet owners turn to their animal companions in preference to close family members. Indeed, where personal relationships at home are unhappy or unsatisfactory, the pet becomes a substitute confidant. Owners who display anxious attachments to their pets have, in some cases, been found to display severe, although usually treatable, psychological problems when the pet eventually dies.[1]

Attachments between owners and their pets, in contrast, may remain in their purest form. The strength of this attachment is a central factor determining the nature of the owner's reaction upon loss of a pet. The death of pet animals can be distressing even to those who witness more such deaths than most. When asked to describe the degree of loss felt when they had lost a pet, who had died, been killed or simply disappeared, the overwhelming majority of pet owners experience a considerable sense of loss.[2] Families are known to experience a range of emotions and frequently report a deep sense of sadness, grieving, crying, mourning and even depression after losing a pet.[3] Even practising vets report experiencing various forms of emotional distress in response to animal deaths, whether these deaths were caused by euthanasia or by the progress of illness.[4]

The depth of emotional bonds between humans and pet animals comes dramatically into focus when the pet dies. Individuals and families react in a variety of ways to such an eventuality. On a positive note, as we saw in the chapter on children and pets, a child can come to understand something about the meaning and significance of death as well as learn to cope with personal suffering when a loved one dies, knowing that a pet will not live as long as he or she will. Experiencing the death of a pet can force the child to face the ultimate reality. It may therefore have indirect benefits for children. Knowing that all things that live will die can give a clarity and significance to relationships with other living things and a reverence for life. This effect may extend to coping with the loss of members of the child's own family. Pets may become very significant in the lives of children as close companions and this friendship in many ways resembles the kind of relationship a child may form with other people.[5] The loss of a pet may therefore be every bit as painful for the child, for a time, as the loss of a family member might be.

Antecedents of Pet Attachment

The significance of pets in the context of our mental well-being became firmly established with the industrialization of society and the movement of the population from rural towards urban environments. Not only did this remove many people from regular, direct contact with nature, but also the disruption and fragmentation that resulted to close-knit family communities meant that there was an increased likelihood of more people experiencing social isolation. Pets served a fundamental role in plugging, at least partially, both of these gaps. Sharing one's home with a pet animal provided a reminder of and substitute for traditional contacts with nature which form part of everyday rural surroundings. Further, pets provide companions and support to those individuals who are otherwise socially isolated.

In these circumstances, domestic animals such as dogs, cats, birds and fish have important social and psychological functions. Such pets may be regarded by their owners not simply as companions but even as surrogate relatives.[6] The particular role imposed upon the animal will vary with the position and needs of the owner. It may represent a surrogate parent, child, sibling or spouse. As we have seen already, a pet may have special significance in old age and can make the difference between tolerable life and intolerable misery.[7]

Several factors have been identified as contributing to the growing importance of the bonds that can exist between pets and their owners. First, the classic family unit of two parents with children is no longer the dominant unit in western society. With its demise goes the security this brings. Second, other aspects of family life are also changing. The extended family of grandparents, parents, children and relatives living in proximity to one another is almost a thing of the past. Third, religion is no longer a significant force in the community. These things provided people with companionship, security and, above all, human contact. As they have been lost, pet animals have slipped into the void.[8]

Other factors include the lengthening survival time of dogs and cats.[9] The longer one has a dog or a cat as a pet, the greater the attachment can become. A pet can be with its owner for 15 years or more.

Many pet owners can be distinguished by the fact that they have grown up with companion animals and pets have always featured in their lives. Studies of elderly pet owners and non-pet owners have confirmed that many more of the former than the latter had pets as children, in their teens and during all the earlier stages of adulthood. Furthermore, elderly pet owners tended to exhibit stronger attachments to pets in their earlier years than did elderly non-pet owners.[10]

The closeness of owners and their pets can lead to the animal being regarded as another person. This fact is manifest in the elaborate ceremonies that may mark the loss of a pet. People grieve for their pets in much the same way as they do for the deaths of other friends.[11] Whilst this grief is usually less than it would be for the passing away of an intimate human companion, in some instances it can be excessive or even pathological.[12] Many pet owners report being unable to concentrate properly on their everyday lives for quite some time after the death of a pet.[13] As human-like creatures, dead pets must be treated with respect. They cannot be recycled into pet food.[14] Cities have special pet cemeteries which allow grieving owners to remember their lost animal companions. Such facilities may be more important than most of us realize given that at least one report indicated that three-quarters of bereaved pet owners had some kind of funeral for their dead pet.[15]

The Distress of Pet Loss

As with any attachment bond, the bond between human owners and their pets can be and often is broken. The life span of most species of pet is relatively short, making separation by death a more frequent occurrence than is usually experienced in human–human relationships. Pets also run away or become lost. In addition, some individuals are forced to give up their pets for many reasons, including a move to housing where pets are not allowed or a previously undetected allergy of a family member. Whatever the cause of the separation, the loss of a pet, when a close attachment has been formed, can be a profoundly upsetting experience.

For children, the death of a pet may be their first encounter with a permanent separation. Because young children often think of the family pet as similar to themselves,[16] the death of the animal can be confusing and frightening. It can be interpreted by children as a punishment, and if so, they may ask why the pet was punished and if a similar punishment might ever occur to them. As most young children think that death is reversible,[17] they may at times wish the pet dead, thinking that they can resurrect it. Then when the animal does die and the finality of death becomes a reality, some children may experience extreme feelings of guilt and even nightmares in which the pet appears as a threatening, ferocious animal.[18]

For those who are retired, time takes on a new, often less important meaning. The absence of a rigid daily routine can lead to disorganization and occasionally, disorientation. According to Aaron Katcher and Erika Friedmann: 'The presence of an animal, especially an animal that makes demands on the owner, provides a stimulus for maintaining a daily routine' (p.199).[19] With the loss of the pet, reality may become clouded as social contacts lessen and days become seemingly endless. In a study of pet bereavement in older owners, another writer has noted that '97% of them reported experiencing some disruption in their daily living routines; most often eating and sleeping schedules became erratic.... Socialization diminished for 82% of the elderly bereaved owners and 61% of the elderly bereaved' (p.295). In addition, a significant difference can be observed between the elderly owners and non-owners in terms of job-related problems following the death of a pet. Those older persons who suffered the death of their pet generally experienced bereavement-related problems which impeded their ability to concentrate at work.[20]

As recipients of care and unconditional companionship, pets can play a major role in the lives of both young and old. Children and adults may accept an animal as a confidant and a source of emotional support as well as a source of continuity at times of family stress.[21] To the older child and adolescent, the pet may represent an accepting, non-critical friend, sometimes a rare commodity in adolescence.[22]

Women in the middle years may experience a sense of uselessness if they have devoted their earlier adult years to the care of children. A pet may easily serve as a surrogate for those children who have grown and left home. For the growing population of single adults who live alone, pets can play an integral role in providing companionship. Finally, for people of all ages, but especially for older adults, the pet may also meet the very basic human need of being needed.

Given that pets can satisfy a range of fundamental human needs, pet loss can often give rise to feelings of emptiness, sadness and pain.[23] Guilt is generally defined as anger turned inward. Harris in particular noted that when euthanasia is an issue, the guilt experienced by the pet owner may be overwhelming. Despite the rational awareness that the animal may be suffering, the emotional response to actively terminating a life to relieve suffering is often one of guilt. Owners may question their own motives, knowing that they, rather than the pet, have the sole power to choose life or death. They may also question the adequacy of their previous care of the pet. Did they do all that they could to avoid the illness or accident that brought them to the point of having to choose for or against euthanasia?

Anger may be directed outwardly, however, often towards a convenient scapegoat. This unlucky person is often the vet. In families with young children, anger may be directed by children at their parents who are generally the ones who have to take the decision about putting the animal down. Parents may be accused by their children of failing to do enough to care for the animal and to protect its interests.

Evidence derives from around the world that loss of a pet can cause a great deal of sorrow. Studies in the United States, United Kingdom and Israel of situations in which people say they cry, have revealed substantial numbers of respondents – male and female – who said they would cry after the death of a pet.[24] For many bereaved pet owners the grief they experience on losing a pet may be brief but intense. For others, however, it may be much more long-lasting.[25]

The emotional distress caused by the loss of a pet can be so great that many pet owners, when asked if they would get another pet after their present pet died, say they will not because of the psychological trauma associated with the loss.[26] For some people, who have developed a deep bond with their pet, its loss can trigger the onset of a period of complicated, even pathological grieving. One writer recounted a case of a middle-class teenager, an academic high achiever, whose academic performance deteriorated one month after the accidental death of his pet Alsatian. In 10 weeks after the death, the problem was severe enough to warrant referral for psychiatric evaluation. During this it was discovered that his personality and performance changes were related to his feeling of shame at grieving so deeply over the loss of 'only a dog'.[27] One explanation of this effect is that it is likely to occur in circumstances where there has been undue reliance on the pet for companionship, usually to the detriment of meaningful human relationships.[28] The more the pet fills the place or role of another person, the more severely will it be missed when it dies.

Keddie described three cases of reaction to pet loss which occurred among individuals who had developed close bonds with their pets. These cases illustrated the extreme degree to which emotional breakdown can occur following the death of a loved pet after years of devoted care.

In the first case, a 16-year-old schoolgirl became very upset following the death of her King Charles spaniel for which she had cared for many years. The dog had developed cancer and had to be 'put to sleep'. The girl became very upset at the loss and developed an erythematous rash of the hands. Although prescribed antihistamines by her family she then developed an inability to swallow, even though she suffered no discomfort in her throat. The girl was the product of a broken marriage, and was raised by her grandparents, having been abandoned by her mother at the age of six. She had been given the pet dog to look after on going to live with her grandparents. The patient had developed close attachments to her grandparents and pet dog. Following the death of her dog she suffered an acute depressive reaction. This reaction manifested itself as an acute hysterical conversion symptom in the form of hydrophobia. After one week in a psychiatric hospital she made rapid progress and at one month was symptom free. She indicated that she had been devoting attention to her grandmother's budgerigar and was planning to get another puppy.

A second case involved a woman who became distressed following the death of one of her Yorkshire terriers. The woman had bred these dogs for many years, but became especially upset over the loss of her favourite champion breeder. What added to her distress was that the dog had been pronounced dead after a serious operation, but made a brief recovery when returned to the woman's home prior to burial. The dog survived for just a few hours. As a result the woman suffered a bout of severe depression which was accompanied by physical symptoms including disturbed sleep and breathing difficulties.

The woman had a distant relationship with her husband who exhibited little sympathy towards her distress over the loss of her favourite animal. She threatened to commit suicide, upon which she was admitted to a short-stay unit of a psychiatric hospital. A thorough medical check-up revealed no genuine physical ailments. Psychiatric investigation, however, revealed that the depth of her relationship with her favourite dog may have represented a substitute for the death she had suffered in infancy of a son many years before. Her 'adoption' of an extensive family of dogs provided compensation for the loss to her own family. She had formed a deep emotional attachment to the dog that died, which not only compensated for the loss of her son, but also to some extent for an unsatisfactory relationship with her husband.

In the third case, a middle-aged woman experienced a range of physical symptoms following the death of her 14-year-old poodle. Initial enquiry established a strong emotional attachment between owner and pet. Further investigation revealed that she experienced some regrets at being unable to have more than one child following a hysterectomy at age 30. Her depression following the death of her dog emerged out of a deep sense of loss of an animal companion, which again may have been treated as a surrogate child. Her recovery was aided by psychotherapy and drugs, and accompanied by a decision to buy a new dog.

Once the pet has gone the owner can feel empty and unable to carry on with his/her normal daily routine. This may be particularly problematic when much of the owner's daily routine revolved around the pet. Feelings of loss can be acute in several respects which include having been needed, having a companion to share experiences with, the sense of loss of a family member, and missing the pet's own special qualities.[29]

The degree of grieving for a pet that has died is linked to the depth of the relationship with the pet. Individuals who have established a very close bond with an animal companion experience more intense grief when it dies. This bonding and the grief experienced at pet loss has been found to be much more intense among female pet owners than male pet owners.[30]

Grieving at the death of a pet may appear exaggerated when it is related to a previous death of a friend or relative and that grieving has been suppressed. In circumstances such as these, the owner sometimes sees the pet as an animate link with the person who died. The pet's death triggers off grieving for the deceased relative as well as for the pet.[31] With strong attachments, some owners will need time in which to work through the grief. Friends and relatives who rush out to buy a replacement pet may not necessarily be doing the best thing. Because of the close attachment some people can form with their pets, their grief at the loss of the animal can be every bit as profound as it would be over the loss of a close friend.

The closer the attachment to a pet, the more difficult it can be to get over its loss. This has been found to occur among pet owners of all ages. Elderly pet owners, for example, may become especially dependent on their animal companions. Often they re-orientate their lives around their pets, who occupy centre stage in their diminishing social network. With the death of a pet, the elderly owner who has formed a deep bond with the animal may have difficulty adjusting to life without it.[32]

The suffering experienced by pet owners on losing their pet may be compounded by a reluctance to express their feelings because they believe that others will not understand or be supportive. Very often, owners who have lost a pet do not feel able to bring themselves to talk to anybody about it, even those close to them. Yet it is important that grief is expressed and in some way resolved so that the owner can move on.[33] There is a common perception that other people, especially non-pet owners, will not understand the grief a pet owner experiences upon the death of a loved animal companion and will not be sympathetic to the owner's distress.[34]

The Need for Counselling

The loss of a pet, whether due to the death of the animal or any other cause, can be the trigger for acute grief responses in individuals of all ages.[35] For many pet owners, the death of a companion animal can precipitate a grief that is as intense as that felt after the loss of a human family member. The depth of the human–animal bond can even exceed that between a person and close friends and relatives.[36] Because the relationship is authentic and enduring, bereavement following death of a companion animal may be very distressing and persistent. Some people suffer such distress after the loss of a pet that they need to seek professional help.

Coping with pet loss can be helped by understanding more about the form it takes and the psychological processes which underpin it. Owners who have lost their pets often experience memories of the animal. Whilst some of these may be painful, many people will eventually derive comfort from recalling the pet and particular special times spent with it.[37] One suggestion has been that owners should be encouraged to verbalize and share memories of experiences with the pet. It is through repetitive sharing of memories that energy bound to the pet can be released so that owners may invest in new objects and attachments.[38]

If the pet has died as a result of an accident, a cognitive reliving of the event may be evidenced in the owner. Rumination, or a frequent recall of the same event, is necessary for some bereaved people as it helps in establishing the reality of a shocking event. Thinking about the loss of a pet can also bring to the surface thoughts about the loss of relatives. [39]

The death of a loved one almost always serves as a reminder of our own mortality. [40]

For some, this reminder stimulates fear and this fear can be projected onto the animal. People need to be reassured that animals do not themselves harbour such anticipatory fear responses to death.

The need to make choices in response to both impending and actual pet death is an area that, in many instances, is unique to the human–animal bond. Usually the first choice that faces the owner of a very ill pet is whether or not to have the pet put down. The need to make this choice gives rise to strong ambivalent feelings for most owners and it is usually helpful if these feelings can be discussed with a knowledgeable support person prior to the time the choice is made. According to one writer: 'Such decisions call for the ultimate in unconditional love and caring on the part of the owners. They must care enough for their pets to do what is humanely correct... disregarding personal emotional needs, guilt at playing God in the choice of death for the pet, and fear of death itself.'[41]

It is important to recognize that for some owners who firmly believe euthanasia to be morally wrong, there is no choice. For these individuals, assistance can be provided through teaching them how to care for the ill pet at home. Other pre-death choices that may face owners are who will take the pet to be euthanized and will the owner stay with the pet during the procedure. Owners may sometimes wish to remain with their pets throughout the procedure and should be allowed to do so.[42]

Regardless of who is to bring the animal in for euthanasia or who will or will not remain with the pet, some experts advise that in order to afford some privacy to owners, the appointments for putting pets down be made at a time of day, usually at the end of office hours, when there will be the fewest number of people in the waiting area. Any necessary paperwork and the bill for the procedure should be taken care of prior to the procedure so that the owner or other responsible person will not be bothered with these details after the death.

The post-death choices of bereaved pet owners usually relate to the disposal of the body and replacement of the pet. Some of these thoughts may taken place prior to the death but the final choices often occur after the pet dies. Disposal of the pet's body can range from mass cremation to individual burial in a pet cemetery. Whatever choice is made by the owner, it is often important for those who have loved the pet to experience some form of leave-taking ritual.[43] The ritual may be formal, such as an actual, pre-arranged funeral, or it may consist of family members simply sharing together photographs and memories of the pet. When children are part of the family, a ritual may be especially helpful as the children will begin to learn through adult example how they can cope with grief.

The choice of whether or not to replace the pet, like the other choices, should be an individual decision. Many well-meaning people will encourage the grieving pet owner to go out and get a new pet straight away. However, this may not be an appropriate course of action for a number of reasons. Grieving is a painful, but necessary, human response to loss. If acquisition of a new pet occurs in an attempt to avoid grieving for the lost animal, grief may be repressed or it may be channelled into other negative responses. Repressed grief will, at some future time, resurface and may be more painful than it would have been if the process had not been interrupted initially. Unresolved grief can be a contributing factor in severe depression at a much later time. Some owners who attempt to replace a pet too quickly will find themselves resenting the new animal. They will compare the new animal with the old, only to find that the new animal cannot totally replace the lost pet.[44]

A survey among people living in the north-west of England who had lost a pet found that many referred to an initial feeling of numbness and disbelief. Many allowed themselves to become preoccupied with the loss. They were sometimes drawn towards reminders of the pet; many also felt that the loss was like losing part of themselves. About one in four of these respondents had experienced an urge to search for the pet even though it was dead, and sought to ease their grief by trying to convince themselves that the pet was really nearby.[45]

Pet loss may produce loss of appetite, difficulty in sleeping, and disrupt pet owners' daily routine, causing them to become very unsettled. Sometimes, the grief felt over pet loss is so acute that the bereaved shut themselves away and want to be alone. Not everyone is sympathetic to loss of a pet in the same way they would be to loss of a human companion, close friend or family member. Grieving pet owners sometimes complain that their own family, friends and people they work with display a lack of sensitivity to their loss. This reaction can only make matters worse, and often encourages owners mourning the loss of a close animal companion to avoid social company.[46] There is a growing realization that the death of a pet can be sufficiently severe to require professional support. Grieving pet owners are vulnerable both mentally and physically. Counselling can provide support.[47]

The potential seriousness of pet bereavement has been underlined by media reports of people who have committed suicide following their pet's death. There are further reports from veterinary surgeons in the United States that some clients have said they would rather lose their spouse than their pet.[48]

People often respond to loss of a pet in the same fashion as they would to any other close member of the family. They may continue to think about their pet long after it has passed on, perhaps mistakenly believing they can still hear or see it.[49] Pet loss can brings waves of varied emotions to the surface. Owners feel angry, upset, guilty and disorientated. Their anger can sometimes become projected onto someone else, often, as mentioned earlier, the unfortunate vet.[50] Physical symptoms may follow, including loss of appetite and difficulty sleeping or concentrating.

For some people, loss of a pet represents an experience similar to loss of some other fundamental aspect of the individual's life, such as his/her home, a job or a limb.[51] A different view is that relationships with pets represent an extension of relationships with other family members. Loss of a pet does not therefore produce a similar reaction to the loss of a possession, but rather resembles the loss of a close friend or relative.

The earliest signs that the pet owner is suffering to an extent that his/her health may be affected are often spotted by vets who have to deal with pets when they are very ill or dying. They can play an important role in giving advice to mourning and deeply upset pet owners about where to seek support. Pet owners' distress can be so acute that counselling is advisable, at least in the short term. Through this kind of help, a grieving pet owner can learn to accept the pet's death and start to work constructively to restore order to his/her own life. Such counselling support has been found to produce highly satisfactory results in assisting pet owners to resolve the emotional distress they suffer when their pet dies.

Pet Loss among Children

With children, the loss of a companion animal is probably their first experience with death and bereavement. In fact, it is often stated that one of the most important aspects of pet ownership for children is that it provides the child with experiences of dealing with the reality of illness and death which will prepare them for these experiences in later life.[52] By fully experiencing the grief of losing a pet, the child learns that death is a natural part of the life process. Although pet loss is painful, it can eventually be tolerated and coped with. Nothing lives for ever. A child can learn that death is permanent and that dead animals will not come back to haunt them. Children can also be taught that guilt feelings following the death of a loved object are common and can be overcome.[53]

For some writers on the subject, the death of a pet has been considered an 'emotional dress rehearsal' and preparation for greater losses yet to come.[54] There are strong indicators, however, that the loss of a pet is more than a 'rehearsal' and is a profound experience in itself for many children. In a study of over 500 adolescents in Minnesota, over half had lost their 'special pet' and only two reported feeling indifferent to the loss.[55] Most of the young people whose pets had died had deep feelings of regret and sadness.

In a survey of children in Scotland on their experiences and feelings toward pet loss, the children wrote about their pets and how they felt if or when their pet had died. In all, 44% had experienced the death of a pet and over two-thirds of these children expressed profound grief at their loss. In most cases, the children went over the loss in their own minds, or discussed it with parents. In all the bereavements that seemed to be unresolved, parents had been unwilling to have another animal.[56]

How a child reacts to the loss of a pet depends largely on his or her age and emotional development, the length of time the child had the pet, the quality of the relationship, the circumstances surrounding the loss of the pet, and the quality of support available to the child. Pre-school children are less likely to become deeply attached to their pets, and are less likely to view the pet loss as irrevocable. According to some researchers, children under five years usually experience the pet loss as a temporary absence, and from five years to nine years or so pet loss is not seen as inevitable and is believed to be possible to avoid.[57] School-aged children often express profound grief for a short time, and then seem quickly to adapt to normal, especially if a new animal is introduced. Most young children miss their deceased animals, but more as a playmate than as an object that satisfied basic emotional needs.[58]

It is usually adolescents who have the most profound experiences with pet loss. From early adolescence on, children begin to develop an adult perception that death is final, permanent and inevitable.[59] Adolescents tend to take longer to get over their grief, in part because their relationships with pets tend to be more intense at this age.[60] How a young adolescent will react to pet loss will depend on the circumstances surrounding the death. A pet may be lost in a variety of ways such as old age or illness, being run over, theft, being given away or traumatic death. One study found that most of those youngsters whose pets were traumatically killed were saddened by the loss of their pet and, in a few cases, were angry and revengeful towards the person who killed their pet.[61] Abused and disturbed youths were most likely to suffer pet loss, and were more likely to have had their pets killed accidentally or on purpose. Furthermore, abused and disturbed young people experienced more trauma over pet loss because they so rarely had anyone to talk to about it.

Some mental health practitioners indicate that the forms of bereavement from pet loss are similar to those of human loss.[62] Some children might be surprised and embarrassed by the intensity of their grief and feel the need to conceal their grief from the outside world. Parents should be sensitive to the child's grief and not minimize or ridicule its impact. Some young children tend to view the death of a pet as punishment for their misdeeds. If so, children should be assured that they were not to blame for their pet's death. Children should be offered a replacement pet; however, there is some disagreement over whether any such replacement should be immediate or deferred for a little while.[63]

Pet Loss and the Elderly

Death of a pet is a topic that has frequently and spontaneously been observed to occur among residents in nursing homes for the elderly, especially if they are on pet visitation programmes. The circumstances of such losses are often described by them in considerable detail. The richness and emotiveness with which they communicate these sometimes distant events is particularly striking in the case of individuals who commonly exhibit poor short-term memory.

One study found that the association that residents on such programmes made between pet and human loss, however, were often more subtle than simple connections between specific people and animals who had died. Deceased pets were also a subject that engendered thoughtfulness about broader issues of human mortality and morality. Some residents emphasized the longevity of animals that they had owned, showing a special pride in the exceptional life spans these pets achieved.[64] Among elderly people in frail health, surrounded by the death and decline of others, speaking about pets provided an indirect opportunity for addressing some of their own concerns and hopes about life expectancy.

The lives and losses of the animals remembered also had intrinsic meanings of their own. Pets were recalled and mourned not only because they were a connecting thread to memorable experiences and deceased people. Many elderly care residents also spoke of their animals as sources of moral value: they were praised for giving and eliciting love, for demonstrating loyalty and trust, for teaching people how to care and be kind, and for offering opportunities to engage in life in a positive way. The perception of pets as members of the family also allowed people to project onto their deaths a range of personal and domestic meanings. A small number of people told tales of the deaths of cherished animals whom they had never replaced because they could not bear the thought of loving another one like that.

Pet loss even without the death of an animal companion can be very upsetting. The replacement of an ageing guide dog for the blind with a younger successor can be as deeply distressing for guide dog owners as the actual death of the animal and compares, for some individuals, with the loss of a human friend. Often it is better not to completely remove the older companion animal, but, if possible, to leave the animal with its human partner or in a home of the owner's choice.[65]

Pets and Coping with Human Bereavement

Just as pet loss can itself produce emotional distress among pet owners who have formed a strong attachment to an animal companion, pets can also help people cope with the loss of a close human companion. Widowed women have been found to cope more effectively and to display fewer symptoms of physical and psychological distress when they own a pet. Widowed pet owners exhibited less depression after the loss of their husband than did widows without pets, and evidence emerged that the presence of pet animals provided valuable emotional support to these women during a very distressing and unhappy period of their lives.[66]

This evidence was corroborated by other research which indicated that dog owners adjusted better to the loss of a spouse than did non-pet owners. The closer the bond between individual and dog, the stronger this effect became. Though non-pet owners reported numerous physical and psychological symptoms associated with the distress caused by losing their spouse, individuals who had a close bond with a pet dog were much less likely to report any obvious deterioration of their health. Dog owners expressed a greater ability to cope with their loss, especially if their dog had been with them for a long time.[67]

References

1 Rynearson, E.K. Humans and pets and attachment. *British Journal of Psychiatry*, 133, 550–555, 1978.

2 Cain, A.O. A study of pets in the family system. In A.H. Katcher and A.M. Beck (Eds) *New Perspectives on Our Lives with Companion Animals*. Philadelphia: University of Pennsylvania Press, 1983.

3 Nieburg, H.A. and Fischer, A. *Pet Loss: A Thoughtful Guide for Adults and Children*. New York: Harper & Row, 1982.

4 Fogle, B. and Abrahmson, D. Pet loss: A survey of attitudes and feelings of practising veterinarians. *Anthrozoos*, 3(3), 143–150, 1990.

5 Levinson, B.M. *Pet-oriented Child Psychotherapy*. Springfield, IL: Charles C. Thomas, 1969. Levinson, B.M. Pets, child development and mental illness. *Journal of the American Veterinary Association*, 157, 1759–1766, 1970. Macdonald, A. The pet dog in the home: A study of interactions. In B. Fogle (Ed.) *Interrelations between People and Pets*. Springfield, IL: Charles C. Thomas, 1981.

6 McHarg, M. *Pets as a Social Phenomenon: A Study of Man–Pet Interactions in Urban Communities*. Melbourne: Pet Care Information and Advisory Service [117 Collins Street, Melbourne], p.14, 1976.

7 Levinson, B.M. *Pets and Human Development*. Springfield, IL: Charles C. Thomas, 1972.

8 Fogle, B. *Pets and Their People*. Glasgow: Williams, Collins, Sons, 1983.

9 Schneider, R. Pet ownership: Some factors and trends. Paper presented at the second Canadian Symposium on Pets and Society, Vancouver, BC, Canada, 1979.

10 Netting, F.E., Wilson, C.C. and Fruge, C. Pet ownership and non-ownership among elderly in Arizona. *Anthrozoos*, 2, 125–132, 1988.

11 Shirley, V. and Mercier, J. Bereavement of older persons: Death of a pet. *The Gerontologist*, 23, 276, 1983.

12 Keddie, K.M.G. Pathological mourning after the death of a domestic pet. *British Journal of Psychiatry*, 131, 21–25, 1977.

13 Messent, P.R. Animal-facilitated therapy: Overview and future directions. In A.H. Katcher and A.M. Beck (Eds) *New Perspectives on Our Lives with Companion Animals*. Philadelphia: University of Penssylvania Press, 1982.

14 Beck, A.M. and Katcher, A.H. A new look at pet-facilitated therapy. *Journal of the American Veterinary Medical Association*, 184(4), 414–421, 1984.

15 Shirley V. and Mercier, J. 1983, op.cit.

16 Levinson, B.M., 1972, op.cit.

17 Nagy, M. The child's theories concerning death. *Journal of General Psychology*, 73, 3–27, 1948. Swain, H.L. Childhood views of death. *Death Education*, 2(4), 341–358, 1979.

18 Levinson, B.M., 1972, op.cit.

19 Katcher, A. and Friedmann, E. Potential health value of pet ownership. *Compendium on Continuing Education*, 2(2), 117–122, 1980.

20 Quackenbush, J.E. Pet bereavement in older owners. In R.K. Anderson, B.L. Hart and L.A. Hart (Eds) *The Pet Connection*. Minneapolis, MN: University of Minnesota Press, pp. 292–299, 1984

21 Macdonald, A. The role of pets in the mental health of children. In *Proceedings of the Group for the Study of the Human/Companion Animal Bond*. Dundee, Scotland: University of Dundee, pp. 6–9, 1979.

22 Nieburg, H.A., 1982, op.cit.

23 Hopkins, A.F. Pet death: Effects on the client and the veterinarian. In R.K. Anderson, B.L. Hart and L.A. Hart (Eds) *The Pet Connection*. Minneapolis, MN: University of Minnesota Press, pp. 270–282, 1984. Keddie, K.M.G., 1977, op.cit. Levinson, B. M., 1972, op.cit.

24 Lombardo, W.K., Cretser, G.A., Lombardo, B. and Mathies, S.T. Fer cryin' out loud – There is a sex difference. *Sex Roles*, 9, 987–995, 1983. Williams, D.G. and Morris, G.H. Self-reports of crying behaviour by British and Israeli adults. *British Journal of Psychology*, 87, 479–505, 1996.

25 Stewart, M. Loss of a pet – loss of a person: A comparative study of bereavement. In A.H. Katcher and A.M. Beck (Eds) *New Perspectives on Our Lives with Companion Animals*. Philadelphia: University of Pennsylvania Press, pp. 390–404, 1983.

26 Wilbur, R.H. Pets, pet ownership and animal control: Social and psychological attitudes. In *Proceedings of the National Conference on Dog and Cat Control*. Denver: American Humane Association, pp. 1–12, 1976.

27 McCulloch, M. The pet as prosthesis-defining criterion for the adjunctive use of companion animals in the treatment of medically ill, depressed outpatients. In B. Fogle (Ed.) *Interrelations Between People and Their Pets*. Springfield, IL: Charles C. Thomas, 1981

28 Keddie, K.M.G., 1977, op.cit.

29 Carmack, J. The effects on family members and functioning after death of a pet. *Marriage and Family Review*, 8, 149–161, 1985.

30 Brown, B.H., Richards, H.C. and Wilson, C.A. Pet bonding and pet beareavement among adolescents. *Journal of Counselling and Development*, 74(5), 505–509, 1996.

31 Yoxall, A. and Yoxall, D. Proceedings of meeting of Group for the Study of Human Companion Animal Bond, Dundee, Scotland, 23–25 March, 1979.

32 Stewart, C.S., Thrush, J.C., Paulus, G. and Hafner, P. The elderly's adjustment to the loss of a companion animal: People pet dependency. *Death Studies*, 9(5–6), 383–393, 1985.

33 Katcher, A.H. and Rosenberg, M.A. Euthanasia and the management of the client's grief. *Compendium on Continuing Education*, 1, 887–891, 1979.

34 Cowles, K.V. The death of a pet: Human responses to the breaking of a bond. *Marriage and Family Reviews*, 8, 135–149, 1985.

35 Cowles, K.V., 1985, ibid.

36 Weisman, A.S. Bereavement and companion animals. *Omega*, 22, 241–248, 1990.

37 Katcher, A.H. and Rosenberg, M.A., 1979, op.cit. Thomas, C. Client relations: Dealing with grief. *New Methods*, 19–24, 1982.

38 Nieburg, H.A., 1979b, op.cit.

39 Cowles, K.V., 1985, op.cit.

40 Harris, J.M., 1984, op.cit. Katcher, A.H. and Rosenberg, M.A., 1979, op.cit.

41 De Groot, A. Preparing the veterinarian for dealing with the emotions of pet loss. In R.K. Anderson, B.L. Hart and L.A Hart (Eds) *The Pet Connection*. Minnesota, MN: University of Minneapolis Press, pp. 285–290, 1984.

42 Bernbaum, M. The veterinarian's role in grief and bereavement at pet loss. *Cornell Feline Health Centre News*, 7, 1–3, 6–7, 1982. De Groot, A., 1984, op.cit.

43 Harris, J.M., 1984, op.cit. Levinson, B.M., 1972, op.cit.

44 Harris, J.M., 1984, op.cit.

45 Archer, J. and Winchester, G. Bereavement following death of a pet. *British Journal of Psychology*, 85, 259–271, 1994.

46 Quackenbush, J.A. and Glickman, L. Social work services for bereaved pet owners: A retrospective case study in a veterinary teaching hospital. In A.H. Katcher and A.M. Beck (Eds) *New Perspectives on Our Lives with Companion Animals*. Philadelphia: University of Pennsylvania Press, 1984.

47 Carmack, J., 1985, op.cit.

48 Carmack, J., 1985, op.cit.

49 Weisman, A.S., 1990, op.cit.

50 Carmack, J., 1985, op.cit.

51 Parkes, C.M. *Bereavement: Studies of Grief in Adult Life*, 2nd edn. London and New York: Tavistock, 1986

52 Fox, M.W. Relationships between human and non-human animals. In B. Fogle (Ed.) *Interrelations Between People and Pets*. Springfield, IL: Charles C. Thomas, 1981.

53 Levinson, B.M., 1972, op.cit.

54 Levinson, B.M. The pet and the child's bereavement. *Mental Hygiene*, 51, 197–200, 1967.

55 Robin, M., ten Bensel, R., Quigley, J. and Anderson, R. Childhood pets and the psychological development of adolescents. In A.H. Katcher and A.M. Beck (Eds) *New Perspectives on Our Lives with Companion Animals*. Philadelphia: University of Pennsylvania Press, pp. 436–443, 1983.

56 Stewart, R.B. Sibling attachment relations: Child–infant interaction in the strange situation. *Developmental Psychology*, 19, 192–199, 1983.

57 Nieburg, H. and Fischer, A. *Pet Loss: A Thoughtful Guide for Adults and Children.* New York: Harper & Row, 1982.

58 Stewart, C.S., 1985, op.cit.

59 Nieburg, H. and Fischer, A., 1982, op.cit.

60 Nieburg, H. and Fischer, A., 1982, op.cit. Stewart, R.B., 1983, op.cit..

61 Robin, M. et al., 1983, op.cit.

62 Levinson, B.M., 1967, op.cit.

63 Stewart, R.B., 1983, op.cit. Nieburg, H. and Fischer, A., 1982, op.cit.

64 Stallones, L., Marx, M.B., Garrity, T.F. and Johnson, T.P. Attachment to companion animals among older pet owners. *Anthrozoos*, 2, 118–124, 1988.

65 Nicholson, J., Kemp-Wheeler, S. and Griffiths, D. Distress arising from the end of a guide dog partnership. *Anthrozoos*, 8(2), 100–110, 1995.

66 Akiyama, H., Holtzman, J.M. and Britz, W.E. Pet ownership and health status during bereavement. *Omega: Journal of Death and Dying*, 17, 187–193, 1986.

67 Bolin, S.E. The effects of companion animals during conjugal bereavement. *Anthrozoos*, 1(1), 26–35, 1987.

Chapter 10
Why do relationships with pets go wrong?

We have seen that pets serve a variety of functions in their role as animal companions in our homes. Despite the argument by some writers that pets can be classified, in a strict Darwinian sense, as parasites,[1] millions of people around the world nevertheless voluntarily choose to share their homes with domesticated animals (and a few with wild animals). Pets provide ready-made and unquestioning companions, substitutes for human contact among the socially isolated and lonely, alternative parents or siblings for children, and additional members of the family in whom we may confide and with whom we can enjoy affectionate, caring relationships.[2] There is a view also that animals can bring stability to our lives and serve as sources of psychological equilibrium for adults and children.[3]

Pet ownership in adult life is often associated with having lived with animal companions as a child. A survey of pet owners by James Serpell revealed that current adult pet owners were significantly more likely than non-owners to have had a pet as a child. Furthermore, of those individuals who did not currently own pets, those who had lived with a pet as children were significantly more likely to consider getting a pet again if their circumstances allowed.[4] Those of us who have been brought up with pets more readily form bonds with animals when we have grown up and established homes of our own. A survey of Californian animal lovers reported that people identify more closely with the type of pet with which they grew up.[5] Thus, experience of pets in childhood not only means an increased likelihood of pet ownership as an adult, but also a greater likelihood of strong attachment to animal companions in later life.[6]

Despite the many positive social and emotional benefits that have been identified for pets for people of all ages, relationships with companion animals do not always run smoothly. Indeed, there are many occasions when the relationship goes badly wrong. For some pet owners, their companion animal fails to meet the expectations they had when they first acquired it. When pet owners get a new dog or cat, they anticipate a certain relationship with the animal and expect it to fulfil certain wishes with respect to the kind of companion it will be. The success of our relationship with our pets, however, can depend crucially on how committed we are to the animal to begin with. If we are disappointed that the pet has not met our initial expectations, this will sour the entire relationship with the animal. Dog owners who feel that their dog did not meet certain early expectations generally form weaker attachments with it and will grow progressively less satisfied with the animal. Disappointment for dog owners is usually linked to how playful, friendly and confident the animal is. Cat owners, likewise, form weak attachments to their pets and become more and more dissatisfied with it when the animal fails to show expected levels of affection towards the owner.[7]

Parents may acquire pets for their family in part because they may have lived with domesticated animals in their own childhood, but also because they perceive real benefits for their own children in doing so. The main reasons for getting a pet for the child is that it will provide something for the child to play with, take responsibility for and learn from. However, parents' expectations for the benefits pets will have for their children are not always met. Indeed, the pet that was bought for the child with the view that the child would assume responsibility for its well-being frequently ends up being cared for by the mother.[8] When parents expect the pet to teach the child responsibility and care-taking and the child does not learn and display these behaviours, parents may become disappointed and regret adopting the pet and frequently end up rejecting and abandoning the animal.

Men often have higher expectations for the role pets will play in the lives of their children than do women. In particular, men regard pets as providing playmates for children and as teaching them responsibility. Women regard pets as sources of love and affection. Parents who acquire dogs as pets for their children are especially likely to perceive such a pet as a companion, confidant and source of emotional support for their children. The weaker the perceived success rate of pets as regards their companionship and playfulness, the more likely pets are to be rejected. In contrast, the more attached pet adopters become to their animals, the less likely they are to abandon them.

Pet rejectors may be people who did not really know what to expect. Many tend to be first-time owners lacking prior experience in looking after pets. This may mean that they have few realistic ideas about what to expect and what caring for an animal entails. Pets require money, time and nurturance. It is interesting that people who keep and people who reject their pets both describe the same problem behaviours with their animals, but interpret and react to these behaviours in different ways. Owners with weak attachments to their pets will describe cats clawing the furniture and climbing curtains and dogs chewing toys and carpets as sufficient grounds for getting rid of the animal. People who have strong attachments to their pets, on the other hand, recognize these behaviours as normal and as representing a passing phase which the animal may be trained out of or may eventually grow out of on its own.[9]

Cruelty to Pets

Cruelty to pets is one aspect of a broader range of punitive behaviours towards animals in general. Tolerance of animal cruelty can vary between individuals and cultures, and is closely linked to societal norms associated with animals, their control, and their perceived cultural and social roles. What is deemed to be acceptable and unacceptable treatment of animals is often bound up in legislation.

The seriousness with which people in Britain view animals, for instance, became apparent in the 18th century with a marked growth in the extent to which dogs and horses featured in the works of leading artists of that time. Animal icons captured in paintings of this period encapsulated the part that these animals played in certain sections of society. Horses and dogs played key supporting roles to humans who engaged in animal blood sports. These works of art were commissioned, of course, by the social class that indulged in such pursuits. In other lower-class 'sporting' contexts, animals were pitched more directly against animals by their human masters in activities such as bull baiting and cock fighting.

Anti-cruelty Legislation

The first legislation designed to protect animals was debated at the beginning of the 19th century. Initially a Bill was launched that focused on bulls, but within a few years there was an attempt by Parliament to introduce legislation to protect a broader range of animals including cockerels.

In 1822 Martin's Act was passed making it illegal to mistreat farm animals such as horses, cattle and sheep. The same Act also protected some household animals. It is interesting to note that animal cruelty was outlawed several decades earlier than wife or child beating within the family context. By the mid-1820s the Society for the Prevention of Cruelty to Animals had been founded (receiving its 'Royal' prefix in 1840). In 1911 the Protection of Animals Act was passed and in 1966 the Wild Mammals Act made it unlawful to practise cruelty against wild animals in Britain, though even then deer and foxes were exempted.[10]

Another activity that has attracted hostile public reaction from some quarters is the use of animals in scientific experiments. This is regarded by some lobby groups, most notably the National Anti-Vivisection Society, as a form of legalized animal cruelty that is hidden from the public. Even though there is legislation such as the 1986 Animals

Scientific Procedures Act, which is designed to control and set standards for the use of animals in scientific research, a considerable amount of research is carried out in which live animals are surgically altered, poisoned or placed in uncomfortable life-threatening conditions, often without anaesthetic. The use of animals as expendable subjects of scientific studies may, however, be regarded as justified when it leads to cures, treatments or other discoveries that will eventually save human lives, and where there may be no other way of finding out these things. Nevertheless, public acceptance of such practices may prevail only because few people have ever witnessed first hand what happens to animals in these experiments. In other settings, when public attention has been drawn to cruel practices such as seal culling, public opinion can very quickly be activated to produce tighter legislative protection of animals' interests.

Other cases, such as the British public's reaction to a Levi jeans television advertisement that featured a hamster called Kevin that apparently died on screen, provide further illustration of how sensitive we can be to the mistreatment of animals when evidence of it is brought directly to our attention. In this instance, the hamster suffered no real harm. The 'dead' hamster shown in the advertisement was in fact a stuffed version of the real thing. Even so, such was the level of public outcry that the advertisement was quickly discontinued. The main concern of complainants had been that young children may not have realized that 'Kevin' had not really died. It is also likely, however, that the scene showing the deceased animal struck a raw nerve with more television literate adult viewers as well, reflecting how sensitive to any hint of animal cruelty this nation of animal lovers can be.

Origins of Cruelty to Pets

Cruelty to pets represents a more specific form of animal cruelty. Its special status arises from the position a pet frequently occupies in the household. We have seen already that for many pet owners, their animal companion is regarded and treated as a member of the family. Cruelty to pets therefore is analogous to cruelty inflicted upon family members. As with other forms of violence in the home, hostility towards domestic animals often has its roots in childhood.

Interest in childhood cruelty to animals grew out of the notion that cruelty to animals has a disabling effect on human character and leads to cruelty among people.[11] This idea was articulated by Saint Thomas Aquinas (1225–74) who said: 'Holy scriptures seem to forbid us to be cruel to brute animals...that is either...through being cruel to animals one becomes cruel to human beings or because injury to an animal leads to the temporal hurt of man'.[12] Likewise the philosopher Montaigne (1533–92) wrote that 'men of bloodthirsty nature where animals are concerned display a natural propensity toward cruelty'.[13]

Until the 17th and 18th centuries there was relatively little awareness that animals suffered and needed protection because of this suffering. This new sensibility was linked to the growth of towns and industry which left animals increasingly marginal to the production process. Gradually society allowed animals to enter the house as pets, which created the foundation for the view that some animals at least were worthy of moral consideration.[14]

The English artist, William Hogarth (1697–1764) was the first artist to both condemn animal cruelty and theorize on its human consequences. His *Four Stages of Cruelty* (1751) was produced as a means of focusing attention on the high incidence of crime and violence in his day. The four drawings trace the evolution of cruelty to animals by a child, to the beating of a disabled horse when a young man, to the killing of a woman, and finally to the death of the protagonist himself. As Hogarth declared in 1738, 'I am a professional enemy to persecution of all kinds, whether against man or beast'.[15]

The link between animal abuse and human violence has been made by Margaret Mead, who suggested that childhood cruelty to animals may be a precursor to anti-social violence as an adult.[16] Childhood cruelty to animals, along with enuresis and firesetting, have been identified as effective predictors of later violent and criminal behaviours in adulthood. A study of 31 prisoners charged with aggressive crimes against people found that three-quarters had a history of all or part of the triad. The researchers argued that the aggressive behaviours of their subjects were a hostile reaction to parental abuse or neglect.[17]

Elsewhere additional links have been found between animal abuse, child abuse and anti-social behaviour.[18] Of 18 young boys who were identified with histories of cruelty to animals, one-third had also set fires, and parental abuse was the most common aetiological factor. Another study found that the same three variables had predictive value for later criminality. Extreme physical brutality from parents was common in cases of child animal abuse, but also parental deprivation rather than parental aggressiveness may be more specifically related to animal cruelty.[19]

A study of 152 criminals and non-criminals in Kansas and Connecticut found an inordinately high frequency of childhood animal cruelties among the most violent criminals. It was reported here that 25% of the most aggressive criminals had a history of five or more specific incidents of cruelty to animals, compared with less than 6% of moderate and non-aggressive criminals, and no occurrence among non-criminals. Moreover, the family backgrounds of the aggressive criminals were especially violent. Three-quarters of all aggressive criminals reported excessive and repeated abuse as children, compared with only 31% for non-aggressive criminals and 10% among non-criminals. Interestingly, 75% of non-criminals who experienced parental abuse also reported incidents of animal cruelty.[20]

While most children are usually sensitive to the misuse of pets, for some abused or disturbed children pets, represent someone they can gain some power and control over. As one writer remarked: 'No matter how put upon or demeaned one feels, it is still often possible to kick the dog'.[21] Cruelty to animals thus represents a displacement of aggression from humans to animals. Severely abused children, lacking in the ability to empathize with the sufferings of animals, take out their frustrations and hostility on animals with little sense of remorse. Their abuse of animals is an effort to compensate for feelings of powerlessness and inferiority.

The Nature of Dysfunctional Relationships

Reports of the role of the animal in the dysfunctional family fall into two main categories. One group of reports discusses the relationships of children from disturbed families with companion animals present in the home; the other group of reports focuses on the way in which the family pet itself may be drawn into the dysfunctional family system.

A child psychiatrist with experience of such cases observed that family disturbances over children and companion animals fall under three headings. First, the normal formation of attachments can go awry and result in anxious attachments and impulsive care-giving, often involving pathological mourning when the pet dies. Second, fear of a parent may be displaced onto animals resulting in phobias. Third, unresolved fear and rage may be displaced or projected onto animals and result in cruelty towards them.[22]

It does not automatically follow that problems in a family result in maltreatment of pets. A study involving 500 abused and non-abused adolescents showed that most abused children had very positive experiences with their pets.[23] This study found that abused children, with their characteristically low self-esteem, are more likely than non-abused children to experience pets as their sole love-objects and to turn to them for love and support. However, pets of abused children are more likely than those of non-abused children to experience violence or death at the hands of someone other than the abused child, and the abused child is less likely to have someone to talk to regarding the loss of their pet.

Pets have been found to react to the stresses of living with a problem family. They may become ill or experience such distress that they die.[24] Pets may be very sensitive to the emotions of family members.[25] One case was reported of a family in which social phobia was a symptom which pervaded the household to such an extent that even the pets became afraid to go outside.[26]

Children in a dysfunctional family may use the pet as a means of escape. There are times when a child in this situation becomes so attached to a pet that it replaces all human relationships. Such children develop a basic distrust of people which becomes over-generalized. This basic distrust of attachment to humans contributes to an intense displacement of attachment to a pet which is consistently receptive as an object of love and caring. Such children have very low self-esteem and turn to pets for warmth and affection, while their ability to establish emotional relationships with other people is diminished.[27]

Childhood Cruelty to Pets

As noted already in Chapter 7, disturbances in children may also involve cruelty to animals but we must not be too quick to label a child as disturbed at the first sign of rough behaviour with animals. Very young children, for example, will often pull animals about, roll them over and treat them carelessly but, because they are inexperienced with animals, they may not understand what they are doing. However, persistent cruel behaviour which may involve extreme incidents such as setting fire to animals, tying their tails together or killing them are signs of problematic personalities.[28] Another illustration of disturbed behaviour towards animals which reflected wider problems was recounted by one child psychiatrist. In this case, a nine-year-old boy of normal intelligence assaulted other children, including his own brother, together with his pet cat and dog. His psychiatrist discovered that the boy's anger stemmed from the news that he had been diagnosed with a terminal, muscular illness.[29]

Many early studies of childhood cruelty to animals have not considered whether the abused animal belonged to the child or whether the child was cruel to any animal with which he/she came into contact, but had never owned a pet themselves. Michael Robin and Robert ten Bensel reported a study of 81 violent offenders imprisoned in Minnesota, 86% of whom had had a pet at some time in their life that they considered special to them. Overall 95% of the respondents valued pets for companionship, love, affection, protection and pleasure.[30] Violent offenders were more likely to have a dog in their home while growing up. The control group had more animals as pets other than dogs or cats, but the offender group had more 'atypical' pets such as a baby tiger, cougar and wolf pup. When asked what had happened to the special pet, over 60% of both groups had lost their pets through death or theft; however, there were more pets that died of gunshots in the inmate group. In addition, the offender group tended to be more angry at the death of the pet. Strikingly, among the violent offenders, 80% wanted a dog or cat now as compared with 39% of the control group. This suggested something about the deprivation of the prison environment as well as the possibility of therapeutic intervention with pets among prison populations.[31]

Michael Robin and Robert ten Bensel reported another survey of 206 teenagers between the ages of 13 and 18 living in two separate juvenile institutions and 32 youths living in an adolescent psychiatric ward with regard to their experiences with pets. This sample was compared with a group of 269 youths from two urban high schools. Of the 238 abused institutionalized youths surveyed, 91% said that they had had a special pet and of these youths 99% said they either loved or liked their pet very much. Among the comparison group (*n* = 242), 90% had had a special pet and 97% said they either love or liked their pet very much. These results suggested that companion animals do have a prominent place in the emotional lives of abused as well as non-abused children. It is also a corrective to those who suggest that pet ownership in itself will prevent emotional or behavioural disturbances in children.[32]

In considering the issue of abuse of animals, the same authors found that the pets of the institutionalized group suffered more abuse; however, the abuser was usually someone other than the child. In a few instances, youths had to intervene against their parents to protect their pets. One child wrote: 'My dad and sister would hit and kick my cat sometimes because he would get mad when they teased him. I got mad and told them not to hurt him because he's helpless.'[33]

Of those youths who indicated that they mistreated their pets, sadness and remorse were the most common responses. One child said: 'I remember once I was punished for letting the dog out and so I hit him for that. I felt real bad after that and comforted it a lot.' All of those who mistreated their pets, except for one youth, indicated that they loved or liked their pets very much and felt bad about hurting their pets. Only one youth said he did not care that he hurt his pet. There was no self-reported evidence of sadism toward pets.

There have been a number of reported instances of pets being harmed or killed as punishment to a child. Threatening to harm a child's pet is a common technique of child abusers to keep the child quiet about the abuse. In a recent child sexual abuse case discovered in a Los Angeles day care centre, the adults involved allegedly silenced the children by butchering small animals in front of the children and threatening to do the same to their parents if they revealed the abuse.[34]

Problem Owners

Not all responses to pets are positive ones. One American survey reported that one in five dog owners said they did not like their dog.[35] However, problem relationships with pets can go far beyond mere dislike of the animal. Some owners may actually abuse their pets. In some instances the aggression may originally have been targeted at another person in the household. The concept of displaced aggression is conventionally illustrated with references to the frustrated person who rages inwardly and goes home to kick the cat. Pent-up anger can be displaced onto pet animals by their owners. Pets also provide a ready target when the real source of frustration is not immediately to hand. As one writer noted: 'A pet may represent for the child a figure which is lower on the family totem pole, and no matter how put upon or demeaned one feels, it is still often possible to kick the dog' (p.70).[36]

In some households beset by personal problems relationships with pets may break down. In some cases, pets are maltreated by callous owners who care little enough about other people, never mind animals. Pets may come in for abusive treatment in homes where child abuse is also present. A family member who is violent towards other members of the family may also exhibit violence towards the family pet. A number of parallels have been observed between the treatment of pets and the treatment of children within child-abusing families, suggesting that animal abuse may be a potential indicator of other family problems.[37]

Pets may be scapegoated. One study examined the role of pets in 53 child-abusing families. The pattern of pet ownership was similar to that of other families. Of pet-owning child abusers, nearly nine out of 10 of the families in which physical abuse took place also had animals that were abused.[38] The parallels between the treatment of pets and the treatment of children in child-abusing families suggest that animal abuse may be an early warning signal of domestic violence.

Pets may also become direct targets of abuse intended to cause the owner vicarious pain. A dramatic fictional example of this is given in Mario Puzo's story, *The Godfather*, in which an offer that cannot be refused is accompanied by the severed head of a prize horse. In more conventional circumstances the threat to take away a pet may become an important force for social control, or attempted social control. One study has reported that a high proportion of adolescent delinquents were closely attached to pets that were killed by a parent or guardian.[39]

Pet owners with a history of violent crime and psychotic disorders have also been found to hold unusual perceptions of pet animals and to sometimes exhibit violence towards the animal. This fact was underscored by a study of two cases of men accused of violent crimes who displayed psychotic tendencies, who both allegedly killed their wives shortly after killing their pets. Such evidence is insufficient to prove that all individuals with psychotic tendencies will invariably show violence towards animals, or that violence towards pets is indicative of potential violence towards people. Nevertheless, psychotic aggression against animals *per se* suggests serious disturbance with poor control of aggressive impulses.[40]

Cruelty to animals often starts in childhood. It is a behaviour wrapped in a wider syndrome of aggressiveness. Children who are cruel to animals have been found to display other kinds of aggression as well.[41] Indeed, as has been mentioned earlier, cruelty to animals, enuresis and fire-setting have been shown to form a triad of danger signals predicting later violence in adolescent males.[42] Further corroboration of the above findings has emerged from research with male psychiatric patients who were found to have shown cruelty to animals as one among a number of aggressive behaviours as children. The absence of a stable father figure was identified as a major underlying cause. Thus, aggression towards companion animals may be a substitute for aggression against people, but it may also be a kind of 'practice' which later escalates to more serious violence.

The reactions of owners to their pets and the way in which pets are treated by their human companions often boils down to a matter of control. In some cases the pet has the upper hand and learns to control its owner in terms of what and how it is fed, where it is allowed to roam in the house and outside, and the extent to which it obeys the owner's commands. In some situations the owner may be characterized by a personality profile which is authoritarian or even dictatorial in its disciplinary style. Very often disciplinary practices revolve around the use of physical punishment which is deployed against pets, children and anyone else in the household who fails to comply with the head of household's wishes.

References

1 Archer, J. Why do people love their pets? *Evolution and Human Behaviour*, 18, 233–259, 1996.

2 Levinson, B.M. *Pets and Human Development*. Springfield, IL: Charles C. Thomas, 1972.

3 Heiman, M. Man and his pet. In R. Slovenko and J.A. Knight (Eds) *Motivation in Play, Games and Sports*. Springfield, IL: Charles C. Thomas, 1967

4 Serpell, J.A. Childhood pets and their influence on adults' attitudes. *Psychological Reports*, 49, 651–654, 1981.

5 Kidd, A.H. and Kidd, R.M. Personality characteristics and preferences in pet ownership. *Psychological Reports*, 46, 939–949, 1980.

6 Kidd, A.H. and Kidd, R.M. Factors in adults attitudes toward pets. *Psychological Reports*, 65, 903–910, 1989.

7 Serpell, J.A. Evidence for an association between pet behaviour and owner attachment levels. *Applied Animal Behaviour Science*, 47(1–2), 49–60, 1996.

8 Soares, C. and Whalen, T. The canine companion in the family context. Paper presented at the Delta Society Conference, Boston, MA, 1986.

9 Kidd, A.H., Kidd, R.M. and George, C.C. Successful and unsuccessful pet adoptions. *Psychological Reports*, 70, 547–561, 1992.

10 Kean, H. *Animal Rights*. London: Reaktion Books, 1998.

11 ten Bensel, R. Historical perspectives on human values for animals and vulnerable people. In R.K. Anderson, B.L. Hart and L.A. Hart (Eds) *The Pet Connection*. Minneapolis, MN: University of Minnesota Press, 1984.

12 Thomas, K. *Man and the Natural World*. New York: Pantheon Books, 1983.

13 Montaigne, M. de *The Essays of Montaigne*. New York: Oxford University Press, 1952.

14 Thomas, K., 1983, op.cit.

15 Lindsay, J. *Hogarth: His Art and His World*. New York: Taplinger, 1979.

16 Mead, M. Cultural factors in the cause of pathological homicide. *Bulletin of Menninger Clinic*, 28, 11–22, 1064.

17 Hellman, D.S. and Blackman, N. Enuresis, firesetting and cruelty to animals: A triad predictive of adult crime. *American Journal of Psychiatry*, 122, 1431, 1966.

18 Tapia, F. Children who are cruel to animals. *Child Psychiatry and Human Development*, 2, 70–71, 1971.

19 Felthous, A. Aggression against cats, dogs and people. *Child Psychiatry and Human Development*, 10, 169–177, 1980.

20 Kellert, S. and Felthous, A. Childhood cruelty toward animals among criminals and non-criminals. Unpublished paper, 1983.

21 Schowalter, J.E. The use and abuse of pets. *Journal of the American Academy of Child Psychiatry*, 22, 68–72, 1983.

22 Van Leeuwen, S. A child psychiatrist's perspective on children and other companion animals. In B. Fogle (Ed.) *Interrelations Between People and Pets*. Springfield, IL: Charles C. Thomas, 1981.

23 Robin, M., ten Bensel, R., Quigley, J. and Anderson, R. Childhood pets and the psychosocial development of adolescents. In A.H. Katcher and A.M. Beck (Eds) *New Perspectives on Our Lives with Companion Animals*. Philadelphia: University of Pennsylvania Press, pp. 436–443, 1983.

24 Speck, E. The transfer of illness phenomenon in schizophrenic families. In A.S. Friedman (Ed.) *Psychotherapy for the Whole Family in Home and Clinic*. New York: Springer, 1965.

25 Friedman, A.S. Implications of the home setting for family treatment. In A.S. Friedman (Ed.) *Psychotherapy for the Whole family in Home and Clinic*. New York: Springer, 1965a.

26 Friedman, A.S. The 'well' sibling in the 'sick' family: A contradiction. In A.S. Friedman (Ed.) *Psychotherapy for the Whole family in Home and Clinic*. New York: Springer, 1965b

27 Rynearson, E.K. Humans and pets and attachment. *British Journal of Psychiatry*, 133, 550–555, 1978. Levinson, B.M., 1972, op.cit.

28 Hellman, D.S. and Blackman, N., 1966, op.cit. Justice, B., Justice, R. and Kraft, I.A. Early warning signs of violence: is a triad enough? *American Journal of Psychiatry*, 131, 457, 1974.

29 Van Leeuwen, J., 1981, op.cit.

30 Robin, M., and ten Bensel, R. Pets and the socialisation of children. In B. Sussman (Ed.) *Pets and the Family*. New York: Haworth Press, pp. 63–78, 1985.

31 ten Bensel, R, Ward, D.A., Kruttschmidt, C., Quigley, J. and Anderson, R.K. Attitudes of violent criminals towards animals. In R.K. Anderson, B.L. Hart and L.A. Hart (Eds) *The Pet Connection*. Minneapolis, MN: University of Minnesota Press, 1984.

32 Robin, M. and ten Bensel, R., 1985, op.cit.

33 Robin, M., et al., 1983, op.cit. Robin, M. et al., 1984, op.cit.

34 Summit, R. The child sexual abuse accommodation syndrome. *Child Abuse and Neglect*, 7, 181, 1983.

35 Kidd, A.H. and Kidd, R.M. Personality characteristics and preferences in poet ownership. *Psychological Reports*, 46, 939–949, 1980.

36 Schowalter, J.E., 1983, op.cit.

37 De Viney, E., Dickert, J. and Lockwood, R. The care of pets within child abusing families. *International Journal for the Study of Animal Problems*, 4, 321–329, 1983

38 De Viney, E. et al., 1983, op.cit.

39 De Viney, E. et al., 1983, op.cit

40 Felthous, A., Psychotic perceptions of pet animals in defendants accused of violent crime. *Behavioural Sciences and the Law*, 2(3), 331–339, 1984.

41 Tapia, F., 1971, op.cit.

42 Wax, D.E. and Haddox, V.G. Enuresis, fire-setting and animal cruelty: A useful danger signal in predicting vulnerability of adolescent males to assaultive behaviour. *Children Psychiatry and Human Development*, 14, 151–156, 1974. Wax, D.E. and Haddox, V.G. Enuresis, fire-setting, and animal cruelty in male adolescent delinquents: A triad predictive of violent behaviour. *Journal of Psychiatry and the Law*, 2, 45–71, 1974.

Chapter 11
Do pets make us more sociable?

There are different schools of thought on whether pets make us more or less sociable with other people. One view is that owners' affection for their pets can be so strong that it leaves little room for other meaningful relationships.[1] Another viewpoint is that pets actually make people seem friendlier and more approachable. Linked to this observation is the finding that other people are more likely to approach us and speak to us if we are accompanied by a pet. As we will see later in this chapter, this last effect of pet companionship can have very important benefits for individuals who, because of personal handicaps, tend to be ignored or avoided by others.

Pets as People Substitutes

Certainly, we know that for lonely and isolated people, who have little contact with other people or few friends either because of where they live or because they lack self-confidence and social skills, pets provide not just valued companions but substitutes for human relationships. Even among individuals who do have a network of friends and relatives and who enjoy regular human companionship, close bonds can form with pet animals who may be seen as more loyal than humans and unconditional in their giving of affection.[2]

There is mixed evidence to back up the claim that pets reduce the extent to which their owners enjoy relationships with other people. Whilst pets are used by some owners as substitutes for friendships with people, there are many pet owners who are warm, sensitive and gregarious individuals who have a wide network of friends and an active social life. There is some evidence to suggest also that the degree to which pets serve as substitutes for human relationships depends on the kind of pet. There is no doubt that we form closer relationships with certain types of pets than others because of the intelligence and personality of the species. Many dog owners, for example, will readily cite companionship as a primary reason for having a dog. Among cat owners, however, the same level of emotional involvement is likely to be less widespread because the character of dogs and cats differs. Indeed, most cat owners tend to express relatively shallow attachments compared with dog owners.[3] Cats are more independent and require less attention than do dogs. Our expectations of cats and dogs vary and the nature of any relationship formed will differ between these two species. Dog owners often value their animals not only as companions but also as protection against crime and violence.

There is no doubt that, for many owners, pets fulfil a variety of social needs in their own right. They are dependable companions, serve as child substitutes, make their owners feel more secure, and represent status symbols.[4] The idea that pets are invariably substitutes for the lack of human companionship, however, has not been universally supported by studies of pet ownership and the benefits it bestows upon people.

Contradicting the view that pet lovers are people haters, some dog lovers have been found to like the company of people more than dog haters. In contrast, people who have low affection for dogs may also have low regard for other people as well.[5]

Sociability-enhancing Effects of Pets

A positive impact of pet ownership on sociability may occur at two levels: actual and perceived. The presence of animals has been found to render the interpretation of social scenes less threatening and can improve the perceived character of people associated with animals.[6] People associated with animals are often judged by others to be friendlier, happier, more confident and more relaxed than people not associated with animals.

In studies of pet perceptions in artificial surroundings, several investigations have noted that people of all ages, and not only children, use animals to feel safe and create a sense of intimacy. Thus, by pairing an animal with a strange person, the situation surrounding that person can be made to feel less threatening. In another example, in a study in which children were brought into a room with an interviewer alone or by the interviewer accompanied by a dog, the children were found to be more relaxed upon entering a strange room when the animal was present.[7] It is well known that when we talk to other people, our blood pressure goes up, but when animals are present there is a tendency for blood pressure to remain at a lower level.

Not only do pet owners often emerge as more friendly, socially active people, but in the eyes of others they appear more approachable. People accompanied by a dog may be perceived by others as happier and more relaxed as compared with those seen on their own in a similar situation, and as a result easier to approach when in the presence of a dog.[8]

In addition to making scenes appear more friendly, the presence of pet animals may actually impart certain social benefits to their owners. Although not proving any form of causality, at least one study has produced the interesting finding that in families that own pets, the parents are less likely to get divorced than are parents in non-pet-owning family households.[9]

There is a school of thought that believes that pets can have positive social benefits for their owners. Pets can also represent part of a wider social network that includes humans and other animals. It does not automatically follow that people who love their pets are incapable of developing meaningful relationships with other people. On the contrary, people who find it difficult to relate to others may also find it difficult to give affection to animals. People who can show great affection for pet animals are also more able to show affection towards other people.[10]

Though there is no clear evidence that more extrovert and outgoing people are more likely to be pet owners, it does appear that pet owners are less anxious and feel less isolated from the rest of the world compared with people who do not own pets.[11] Evidence has also emerged from research among college undergraduates that pet owners tended, if anything, to report having more active social lives than did non-pet owners.[12]

How Do Pets Improve Sociability?

Pets can lead to increased companionship by facilitating interactions with other people. Observations of people walking their dogs have clearly indicated that dog owners experienced more social contacts and conversations with other people.[13] They also engaged in conversations which lasted longer than did individuals who were walking alone. Pets can also provide important links to friends and relatives in the outside world for hospitalized patients.[14] Over 80% of the 36 hospitalized pet owners interviewed by Erika Friedmann and her colleagues continued to receive information about their pets from relatives or friends, with 60% receiving this information at least once a day. More than one in five 'talked to' their pets on the telephone daily. Thus, the desire to find out how their pets were faring during their absence necessitated communication with the people who were caring for their pets.

Membership in a network of mutual responsibility is an important element of social support. Frequently people who live alone or lose reciprocity in their relationships with others become depressed, feel unneeded, and lose self-esteem. A lack of social support increases responses to stressors. Increased stress responses lead to diminution of the body's ability to fight infections and resist disease. Social support decreases the impact of stress on the body and reduces the likelihood of the development of new diseases or recurrence of old ones.[15] Among the elderly, caring for a pet can improve self-image and boost the extent to which older people will care for themselves. Elderly pet owners feel more self-sufficient, self-confident and optimistic about life than do non-pet owners.[16]

Quite apart from the direct social companionship enjoyed by keeping a pet such as a dog, which exhibits obvious displays of affection, sometimes isolated individuals can benefit socially from pet ownership in other ways. Research among older people (and as we will see in the next section, among the disabled) has found that dog owners enjoy more social attention when out and about with their pets. When walking the dog, pet owners are more likely to strike up a conversation with another person than when they are out on their own. Very often these conversations are initially directed at the animal.[17]

Pets to Help the Disabled

Dogs are used in a number of assistance programmes to help people who suffer from various physical handicaps, such as blindness, deafness and other disabilities that cause their sufferers to be restricted to a wheelchair. A number of studies have shown, however, that there are various spin-off benefits for disabled people from having canine companions.

Although the stated purpose of assistance dogs is to perform tasks related to a disability, they presumably also confer on their owners some of the benefits or changes in lifestyle that are associated with the more typical companionship of a dog. Studies have reported that following the adoption of a dog, new owners have fewer health problems and increase their outdoor walks,[18] and elderly pet owners make fewer medical visits than non-owners.[19]

Among various disabilities, total or nearly total deafness stands out as an invisible and prevalent disability, which has a high likelihood of disrupting communication with hearing individuals. Research has documented that able-bodied people typically evidence discomfort and awkwardness in social interactions with individuals having more evident disabilities, such as those who use wheelchairs. This is shown by less eye contact and increased personal distance.[20] Able-bodied people are often so unclear about how to respond to disabilities that they choose to avoid people with them or remain emotionally distant from them. This contributes to the social limitations experienced by people with disabilities. Thus, the facilitating contribution of a dog, if it exists, could be crucial for more social interaction.

Evidence has begun to emerge which shows that assistance dogs do appear to ameliorate the social awkwardness of able-bodied individuals towards those with disabilities. For example, adults or children using wheelchairs received an enhanced number of social acknowledgements from passers-by when they were accompanied by assistance dogs.[21]

Bonnie Mader and her colleagues at the Human Animal Programme, University of California observed wheelchair-bound teenagers either at school or in a shopping mall. On some occasions they had a dog with them, whereas on other occasions they were alone. The presence of a dog, regardless of location, elicited more friendly glances and smiles from other people and resulted in more people striking up a conversation with them. Very often the social contact was aimed initially at the dog, but inevitably the disabled youngster would be drawn in as well.[22]

Several unpublished studies have explored the psychosocial contributions of assistance and guide dogs to their owners. A prospective study of individuals with severe physical disabilities reported that significant improvements in psychological well-being, self-esteem and community integration were associated with the presence of an assistance dog.[23] But two other studies did not find improvements, either prospectively,[24] or by comparing adults who owned service dogs with others on the waiting list for service dogs.[25]

Interviews of people who were blind, half of whom had guide dogs, suggested that those with guide dogs showed greater independence, mobility, security and sociability.[26] Guide dog owners reported appreciating not having to ask for help or make conversation with human aides.

Social benefits to their owners have also been observed to occur among the hearing impaired who live with dogs trained to assist them. Hearing dogs are used to alert deaf individuals to certain significant sounds such as door bells, ringing telephones, fire alarms, or babies crying. A national survey of hearing dog programmes in the USA estimated that 3000 dogs had been trained, with a rate of about 440 hearing dogs trained per year.[27] Unlike other assistance programmes, the hearing dog programmes are willing to train dogs that are already owned by a recipient or are from shelters. They also use a wide array of different breeds. As with other assistance dogs, hearing dogs are expected to be well trained and should exhibit a low incidence of behaviour problems while also providing the companionship that dog owners find rewarding.

Three retrospective studies investigated the psychosocial role of hearing dogs for their owners. A majority of 14 people with hearing dogs in the only published study reported improvements in seven of 26 psychosocial categories, including feeling safe, independent, content, confident, relaxed, active and healthier.[28]

In unpublished work, ratings by 33 hearing dog owners before and after they acquired a hearing dog differed significantly on eight of 10 items: responding to sounds, feeling safe, dependency, avoiding socializing, inactivity, fearfulness, loneliness and boredom.[29] In a survey of 550 hearing dog owners, most felt they had problems with an array of measures, including depression, physical health, self-confidence, independence, loneliness, companionship and security prior to having a hearing dog, and approximately half of the individuals reporting these problems stated that their dogs had helped reduce them considerably.[30] Preliminary findings from a prospective study of hearing dog owners in England, beginning one year before dog placement, claimed that after three months of ownership there were improvements in depression, tension, social functioning, aggression, fatigue and sleep.[31]

One research group studied the relationships between hearing dog ownership and the owners' levels of loneliness, changes in social interactions with people and life stress, in a sample of 38 hearing dog owners and a control group of 15 prospective owners. The hearing dogs fulfilled the owners' primary expectation of alerting them to sounds. A sense of security, their second highest concern, was also addressed. Owners felt safer when they were alone but with their hearing dog than before obtaining one. Companionship was the third-rated reason for acquiring the dog and owners reported being significantly less lonely after receiving a hearing dog. Most owners and prospective owners described a role of the hearing dog as changing interactions within the family. Owners also felt that the dogs changed their interactions with the hearing community and neighbours, whereas few prospective owners foresaw this effect of the dog. Owners also scored lower on a life stress score than the prospective owners.[32]

Hearing dogs wear capes that clearly identify their special role and ensure that the owner's disability is no longer invisible. The findings of decreased loneliness and the broader socializing within the hearing community suggest an importance of hearing dogs that goes well beyond alerting owners to sounds. Hearing dog owners experience the same socializing benefits that have also been reported with ownership of companion dogs among non-hearing-impaired people. The hearing dogs appeared to fulfil the chief expectations of their owners. Participants with hearing dogs credited their dogs with making it possible to respond to bells and alarms, their greatest concern. They also reported feeling safer since receiving their dogs, and in this respect were similar to individuals from the general population in England who adopted companion dogs and in subsequent months reported a lowered fear of crime.[33]

Pet Assistance Programmes for the Wheelchair Bound

Disabled people restricted to a wheelchair may acquire a service dog to perform a wide range of manual tasks. The advantages of service dogs in physically assisting paralysed people in wheelchairs are well known. Such dogs retrieve objects and pull the wheelchair, for example. However, the primary advantage of such dogs may, in fact, be an unappreciated influence they have in facilitating social interactions with able-bodied people who might otherwise be less likely to approach a person in a wheelchair.

Service dogs generally accompany their wheelchair-bound owners on all of their public outings. Several studies suggest that animals might serve to reduce the social awkwardness many people exhibit in the presence of people with disabilities. The term 'social lubricant' was adopted in one study in which pets frequently were noted to serve as a focal point of conversation for elderly pet owners and family and friends who visited them.[34] The presence of pet animals can have a positive impact on the first impressions of people, similar to the impact of physical attractiveness. Mention has earlier been made of the effect of companion dogs on the reactions of other people to the dog owner. The presence of a dog was associated with a significant increase in both the number of greetings and the length of conversations.[35]

In a retrospective survey of the socializing effects of service dogs for people in wheelchairs, the control group had no dogs and the experimental group had service dogs that assisted them throughout the day.[36] The people with disabilities reported an average of eight friendly approaches from adult strangers during their typical trips downtown when their service dogs were with them, as compared with one friendly approach when their dogs were not with them. The average number of friendly approaches reported by the control group was also one.

Another study examined whether people in wheelchairs with service dogs received more frequent social acknowledgements from able-bodied strangers than did people in wheelchairs without dogs. Behaviours of passers-by were recorded by an observer who followed a person in a wheelchair at a distance of 15 to 30 feet. Observations were made in public areas amid pedestrian traffic, areas such as shopping malls and a college campus. The behaviours of passers-by to the person in a wheelchair, with or without a service dog, were recorded, including smiles, conversation, touch, gaze aversion, path avoidance, or no response.[37]

Results indicated that both smiles and conversations from passers-by increased significantly when the dogs were present. The findings suggested that the benefits of service dogs for their owners extended beyond working tasks to include enhanced opportunities for social exchange. The service dogs substantially reduced the tendency of able-bodied people to ignore or avoid the disabled person.

Most of the conversations of passers-by with the participants who had a service dog centred on the dog. Often a stranger would praise the dog in some way, particularly if the dog was well trained or well behaved. Some people remarked on the dog's characteristics, including colour, size, temperament, cuteness and breed. Some patterns were reported that related to the dog's role as social facilitator. One participant said he thought more people in town knew the name of his dog than knew his name. Another reported that he had to allow extra time when he went out with the dog because of the strangers who stopped to talk.

It has been well documented that people with disabilities are often subjected to social isolation; the presence of a service dog may contribute to overcoming social rejection. Although the presence of a person with physical impairments creates discomfort in able-bodied people, competing response tendencies (i.e. an approachable animal) can override an able-bodied person's tendency to withdraw.

The above findings have been corroborated by research conducted among disabled children in wheelchairs. When accompanied by dogs trained to assist them in different ways, the children found that they got more attention from able-bodied strangers who were walking by them, and that this attention was a direct consequence of being accompanied by a dog.[38] This effect was observed whether the children were with their dog in the playground at school or in a shopping mall.

This increased exposure to the social environment and the greater attention obtained from other people may result in an exchange of good feelings, which can produce increased understanding between disabled children and their able-bodied peers.[39] Increased knowledge about disabilities can itself facilitate closer interactions among children with and without disabilities.[40] Thus, when a service dog is introduced to a school, the children are instructed that the dog's role is to work, rather than to play. This means that much of the social attention is directed at the disabled child rather than the dog, which other children recognize is there to fulfil a working role.

Whether the children were moving among familiar peers at school or among strangers in a shopping mall, the dog's presence was associated with increased social acknowledgement. People were more likely to smile at disabled children, approach and talk to them when the dog was present. Significantly, when the dog was absent these behaviours tended to virtually disappear.

To conclude, pets are very important parts of our lives. They provide companionship, unstinting friendship and a source of affection. They make us feel wanted and worthwhile. They bring benefits to young and old. They make us feel good about ourselves and they can enhance our image among others. This may be especially important for those individuals who, because of disability, age or background may find themselves on the social margins. Although pets do require our attention and place demands on their human owners for free food and shelter, they give much in return. While a cynical, evolutionary view might be that pets represent little more than parasites on their human hosts, most pet owners would probably argue that their animal companions are worth the effort and expense. The benefits experienced by pet owners are physical, emotional and social. Companion animals can reduce stress by inducing relaxation, provide unquestioning affection and loyalty, enhance social contact and may even improve our social image.

References

1 Szasz, K. *Petishism: Pets and Their People in the Western World*. New York: Holt, Rinehart & Winston, 1968. Cameron, P. and Mattson, M. Psychological correlates of pet ownership. *Psychological Reports*, 30, 286, 1972.

2 Levinson, B.M. Pets, child development and mental illness. *Journal of the American Veterinary Association*, 157, 1759–1766, 1970. Levinson, B.M. *Pets and Human Development*. Springfield, IL: Charles C. Thomas, 1972.

3 Wilbur, R.H. Pets, pet ownership and animal control: Social and psychological attitudes. In *Proceedings of the National Conference on Dog and Cat Control*. Denver, CO: American Humane Association, pp. 1–12, 1976.

4 Fox, M.W. The needs of people for pets. In *Proceedings of the First Canadian Symposium on Pets and Society and Emerging Municipal Issues*. Toronto: Canadian Federation of Humane Societies and Canadian Veterinary Medical Association, 1976.

5 Brown, L.T., Shaw, T.G. and Kirkland, K.D. Affection for people as a function of affection for dogs. *Psychological Reports*, 31, 957–958, 1972.

6 Lockwood, R. The influence of animals on social perception. In A.H. Katcher and A.M. Beck (Eds) *New Perspectives on Our Lives with Companion Animals*. Philadelphia: University of Pennsylvania Press, pp. 64–71, 1983.

7 Beck, A.M. and Katcher, A.H. A new look at pet-facilitated therapy. *Journal of the American Veterinary Medical Association*, 184(4), 414–421, 1983.

8 Rossbach, K.A. and Wilson, J.P. Does a dog's presence make a person appear more likeable? Two studies. *Anthrozoos*, 5(1), 40–51, 1992.

9 Paden-Levy, D. Relationship of extraversion, neuroticism, alienation and divorce incidence with pet ownership. *Psychological Reports*, 57, 868–870, 1985.

10 Brown, L.T. et al.,1972, op.cit.

11 Paden-Levy, D., 1985, op.cit.

12 Joubert, C.E. Pet ownership, social interest and sociability. *Psychological Reports*, 61, 401–402, 1987.

13 Messent, P.A. Social facilitation of contact with other people by pet dogs. In A.H. Katcher and A.M. Beck (Eds) *New Perspectives on Our Lives with Companion Animals*. Philadelphia: University of Pennsylvania Press, 1983.

14 Friedmann, E., Katcher, A.H., Lynch, J.J. and Messent, P.R. Social interaction and blood pressure. *Journal of Nervous and Mental Diseases*, 171, 461–465, 1983.

15 Cobb, S. Social support as a moderator of life stress. *Psychosomatic Medicine*, 38, 300–314, 1976. Dubos, R.J. Second thoughts on the germ theory. *Scientific American*, 192, 31–35, 1955.

16 Feldman, B.M. Why people own pets. *Animal Regulation Studies*, 1, 87–94, 1977.

17 Rogers, C., Hart, L. and Holtz, R. The role of pet dogs in casual conversations of elderly adults. *Journal of Social Psychology*, 133(3), 265–277, 1992.

18 Serpell, J.A. Beneficial effect of pet ownership on some aspects of human health and behaviour. *Journal of the Royal Society of Medicine*, 84, 717–720, 1991.

19 Siegel, J.M. Stressful life events and use of physician services among the elderly: The moderating role of pet ownership. *Journal of Personality and Social Psychology*, 58, 1081–1086, 1990

20 Thompson, T.L. Gaze toward and avoidance of the handicapped: A field experiment. *Journal of Nonverbal Behaviour*, 6, 188–196, 1982. Worthington, M.E. Personal space as a function of the Stigma Effect. *Environment and Behaviour*, 6(3), 289–294, 1974.

21 Eddy, J., Hart, L.A. and Holtz, R.P. The effects of service dogs on social acknowledgements of people in wheelchairs. *Journal of Psychology*, 122, 39–45, 1988.

22 Mader, B., Hart, L.A. and Bergin, B. Social acknowledgements for children with disabilities: Effects of service dogs. *Child Development*, 60, 1529–1534, 1989.

23 Allen, K. Physical disability and assistance dogs: Quality of life issues. In G. Hines (Ed.) *Pets, People and the Natural World*. Renton, WA: Delta Society, p.59, 1994.

24 Donovan, W.P. The psychosocial impact of service dogs on their physically disabled owners. PhD dissertation, California School of Professional Psychology, Los Angeles, 1994.

25 Rushing, C. The effect of service dogs on the self-concept of spinal injured adults. PhD dissertation, Wright Institute Graduate School of Psychology, Berkeley, CA, 1995.

26 Bergler, R. People who are blind and their dogs. *Alert: Service Dog Resource Centre Newsletter*, 5(4), 2, 1994.91.

27 Hines, L. National Hearing Dog Centre survey results. *Alert: Hearing Dog Resource Centre Newsletter*, 2(2), 4, 1991.

28 Valentine, D.P., Kiddoo, M. and La Fleur, B. Psychosocial implications of service dog ownership for people who have mobility or hearing impairments. *Social Work Health Care*, 19, 109–125, 1993.

29 Marcoux, J. Do hearing dogs make a difference? Paper presented at the annual Delta Society Conference, Boston, MA, August 1986.

30 Mowry, R.C., Carnaham, S. and Watson, D. *Contributions of Hearing Assistance Dogs to Improving the Independent Living and Rehabilitation of Persons who are Hearing Impaired*. Project Final Technical Report No. H133310001. Little Rock, AS: National Institute for Disability and Rehabilitation Research.

31 Guest, C. *The Social, Psychological and Physiological Effects of the Supply of Hearing Dogs on the Deaf and Hard of Hearing*. Issues in Research in Companion Animal Studies, Study No.2. San Francisco, CA: Society for Companion Animal Studies.

32 Hart, L.A., Zasloff, R.L. and Benfatto, A.M. The socialising role of hearing dogs. *Applied Animal Behaviour Science*, 47, 7–15, 1966.

33 Serpell, J.A., 1991, op.cit.

34 Mugford, R.A. and M'Comisky, J. Some recent work on the psychotherapeutic value of cage birds with old people. In R.S. Anderson (Ed.) *Pet Animals and Society*. London: Bailliere Tindall, pp. 54–65, 1974.

35 Messent, P. Correlates and effects of pet ownership. In R.K. Anderson, B.L. Hart and L.A. Hart (Eds) *The Pet Connection*. Minneapolis, MN: University of Minnesota Press, pp. 331–341, 1984.

36 Hart, L.A., Hart, B.L. and Bergin, B. Socialising effects of service dogs for people with disabilities. *Anthrozoos*, 1, 41–44, 1987.

37 Eddy, J. et al., 1988, op.cit.

38 Mader, B. et al., 1989, op.cit.

39 Rapier, J., Adelson, R., Carey, R. and Croke, K. Changes in children's attitudes towards the physically handicapped. *Exceptional Children*, 39, 219–223, 1972.

40 Perkins, M.A. The effect of increased knowledge of body systems and functions on attitudes toward the disabled. *Rehabilitation Counselling Bulletin*, 22, 16–20, 1978.

Index

pets as surrogates for 10–11
treated as pets 11, 97
cockateels 18
Comfort from Companion Animals Scale
41
companionship (pet) 6–12
children's attachment 99
social competence and 24–5
see also attachment to pets
Corson, Elizabeth 79, 111
cost of pet ownership 2, 21–2
over-indulgence 5
cruelty to animals/pets 101, 138–45
cultural aspects 35–6

dangerous animals 45
death of pet 35, 120–35
among children 95, 100, 102, 122–3,
129–31
intense grief reactions 44, 120, 124–6,
129
death of spouse/partner/friend 9–10, 68,
108, 132
depression in the elderly 34, 112
disabled people 83–4, 151–5
'doggerel' (pet talk) 8, 55
dogs
attachment studies 37–8, 41, 148–9
behaviour problems 50–8
children and pet dogs 91–2, 100
dominance in 56–7
eating dog meat 7, 16–17
fear of 35, 59–61
female owners 28
global statistics 18
health benefits 68, 69, 71–2
historical aspects 2–4
male owners 27, 28
medical costs 22
obedience training 51–4, 57
pet care responsibility 92–3
as service animals 80, 152
therapeutic roles 81, 84–5, 151–5
dolphins 83
dominance behaviour 56–7
dysfunctional families 141–2

economics *see* cost of pet ownership
elderly
pet-assisted therapy 81–2, 111–15
pets in retirement homes 34

elderly pet owners 12, 26–7, 106–11
death of pet 123, 131–2
health benefits 78
elephants 4
'empty-nesters' 19, 20, 39
equine programmes 83, 85
erotic aspects 10
euthanasia (of pet) 123–4, 127
exotic pets 4–5

fairy tales 1, 95
family life-cycles 19–20
fear of animals 35, 59–61, 100–1
feeding/timing of meals 52
female pet owners 22–3, 27, 28, 29
affection to pets 36
attachment to pets 45, 126
first-time owners 52, 137
fish 18, 27, 69, 112
folklore 1, 95
Friedmann, Erica 78, 79, 123
frogs 18

gender of owner *see* female pet owners;
male pet owners
guide dogs 80, 152

hamsters 139
health benefits 66–76
mental well-being 77–88
hearing dogs 80, 152–3
historical aspects 2–4
Hogarth, William 140
homeless pet owners 9
homes/houses 20–1
clean and tidy 24
horses
eating horse meat 7
male/female owners 22, 23, 28, 29
in therapeutic roles 83, 85
hospices 82
hospital programmes 80–1
hypertension 70

illness
recuperation from 70–1, 82
terminal illness 82
income *see* cost of pet ownership
inherited problems 52
institutional settings 80–1